God, Desire, and a Theology
of Human Sexuality

Also by David H. Jensen from Westminster John Knox Press

Living Hope: The Future and Christian Faith
The Lord and Giver of Life: Perspectives on Constructive Pneumatology
Responsive Labor: A Theology of Work

GOD, DESIRE, AND A THEOLOGY OF HUMAN SEXUALITY

David H. Jensen

WESTMINSTER
JOHN KNOX PRESS
LOUISVILLE · KENTUCKY

First edition
Published by Westminster John Knox Press
Louisville, Kentucky

13 14 15 16 17 18 19 20 21 22—10 9 8 7 6 5 4 3 2 1

Scripture quotations from the New Revised Standard Version of the Bible are copyright © 1989 by the Division of Christian Education of the National Council of the Churches of Christ in the U.S.A. and are used by permission.

Scripture quotations marked RSV are from the Revised Standard Version of the Bible, copyright © 1946, 1952, 1971, and 1973 by the Division of Christian Education of the National Council of the Churches of Christ in the U.S.A., and are used by permission.

Chapter 1 is an updated version of "The Bible and Sex," in *The Embrace of Eros: Bodies, Desires, and Sexuality in Christianity*, ed. Margaret D. Kamitsuka (Minneapolis: Fortress Press, 2010), 15-32.

Portions of chapter 6 first appeared in *Christian Marriage, Gay Marriage: A Reformed Theological Perspective*, audio CD, produced by Janet Maykus (Austin: Austin Presbyterian Theological Seminary, 2009).

Book design by Sharon Adams
Cover design by Dilu Nicholas
Cover illustration: Bird of Paradise © eROMAZe/istockphoto.com

Library of Congress Cataloging-in-Publication Data
Jensen, David Hadley, 1968–
  God, desire, and a theology of human sexuality / David H. Jensen. — 1st ed.
    p. cm.
  Includes index.
  ISBN 978-0-664-23368-6 (alk. paper)
  1. Sex—Religious aspects—Christianity. I. Title.
  BT708.J46 2013
  233'.5—dc23

                                              2012033433

Most Westminster John Knox Press books are available at special quantity discounts when purchased in bulk by corporations, organizations, and special-interest groups. For more information, please e-mail SpecialSales@wjkbooks.com.

For Molly

Contents

Introduction ix

1 Scripture and Sex: Narratives of Desire 1
2 God and Sex: Holy Desire 17
3 Christ and Sex: The Resurrection of the Body 39
4 Eschatology and Sex: Making All Things New 55
5 The Lord's Supper and Sex: A Sumptuous Banquet 73
6 Vocation and Sex: Living in Light of Desire 99
7 Ethics and Sex: Flourishing Desire 119
Conclusion 139

Notes 141
Index 155

Introduction

Sex is an expression of Christian faith. Some may find this assertion puzzling, especially considering how many voices in the history of Christianity have viewed sex with suspicion. Sexual desire, according to much inherited wisdom, runs counter to Christian faith, especially when desire burns too hot. Christian disciples are those who constrain and channel desire so that they might love God more fully and follow Christ more nearly. This book, though it draws on much of this inherited wisdom, offers another interpretation of sexual desire, grounded in the beauty of God's desire revealed in Christ's incarnation. At the heart of Christian faith is a wondrous claim that Word becomes flesh and dwells among us. This divine embrace of human flesh entails the blessing of sexual life: not as something to escape in order to attain salvation, but to nurture as we grow in faith. Sex matters for Christians.

Amid its historical suspicion of sex, the church has sometimes behaved as if sex were the *most* important dimension of Christian life. Gender and sexual practice often determined who could preach and preside at the Lord's Table, who was forgiven, and even who could become a member of a particular church. Current debates over ordination standards in many Christian denominations reflect our culture's obsession with sex. This book, by contrast, situates sexual life within the broad tapestry of Christian life. Our deepest faith commitments are connected intimately to our bodily loves. Word becomes flesh and dwells among us, affecting and embracing all of life and all our loves.

Most Christian denominations these days are endlessly debating human sexuality. In national meetings and local congregations, persons recite supposedly self-evident biblical texts and theological beliefs that exclude queer persons from Christian ministry and prohibit their marriages. Arguments from those supportive of gay marriage and expansion of ordination rites often mimic the movements of the opponents: biblical texts get cited and critiqued, traditions are summoned as proof for various stances, and sexual behaviors are dubbed right or wrong. Often in these disputes, theology—reflection on God's presence in the body's life—gets relegated to the sideline. This book, by contrast, offers a *theology* of human sexuality. Though the church's various theologies have often resulted in an overly suspicious view of sex, I remain hopeful that some of its most deeply held beliefs can generate a more holistic understanding of intimacy that integrates sexuality and spirituality. The commitments that we stake our lives on bear fruit in our most intimate, fleshiest expressions of life. Any theology of sexuality, however, needs to examine some of the ambiguous heritage of the church's teachings on sexuality. This book, therefore, is both *deconstructive* in its critique of dominant modes of sexual discourse in the church and *reconstructive* in its attention to past traditions and how they might be reclaimed today, especially in light of the wounds the church's dominant discourse has often inflicted upon queer persons. Wounds remain, but healing is also possible in our various traditions.

Ten years ago, I never would have considered writing a book on theology and sexuality. But as the decade passed, I became increasingly frustrated about the way conversations about sex often proceeded in the churches. I write with that current context of debate in mind, especially among Protestants. I also write out of a particular location: I am a middle-aged, middle-class, married, Anglo male who is a parent to two children. I am particularly conscious of some of the conflicted and confusing messages about human sexuality that American children and teenagers are bombarded with on a daily basis. I would have written a different book fifteen years ago, before Molly and I had children. This book also reflects the observations and limitations of my own experience of sex as a man, but I hope that it can also say something to others who inhabit different contexts. Sexual desire is cross-cultural; though our desires are invariably shaped by culture and gender, they strike some of the fundamental notes of human experience, regardless of where we live. Christian faith, in my read, does not smother or sublimate desire, but nourishes desire in hope. A theology of sexuality speaks first of the importance of desire for faith and how desire might flourish in relationship to God and our beloved.

Some sections of the book contain graphic language. Though these sections are short, the words in them will strike most readers as shocking and offensive. There is a brief discussion of pornography and the economic distortions of human sexuality that often accompany it. I also consider the dangerous blurring of sex and violence in contemporary society. I have chosen to employ graphic language because it illustrates the extent of some of the problems surrounding sexuality in our time. Ignoring sexual violence and pornography is hardly an effective way of promoting alternative interpretations of human sexuality. My hope is that in exposing some of this damaging language, the churches might be better equipped to heal wounds caused by sexual violence and develop understandings of sexuality grounded in God's desire for us to live in fullness.

This book contains seven chapters that focus on particular theological themes. The first chapter examines Scripture and sex. The oft-heard question, "What does the Bible say about sex?" is related to the equally important question, "How do we read the Bible?" In this chapter I survey three approaches to Scripture: a rule-based approach that understands the guidelines for sexual behavior in the Bible to be self-evident, a hermeneutic of suspicion that claims the sexual rules no longer apply, and an approach that situates our understanding of sexuality along a long arc of divine desire. Chapter 2 explores connections between Christian claims of a triune, covenantal God and human sexuality. The God of Christian faith is a God who desires us and creates us as creatures who yearn. Yet God's desire contrasts with some common notions of desire that saturate media portrayals of sex. Whereas many visions of sexual desire in the modern world are perennially restless and roaming, the shape of desire in Christian faith finds a home in covenant.

Chapter 3 turns to Christ's incarnation and resurrection, both of which affirm the beauty of flesh and counter the violence that surrounds contemporary portrayals of sex. If modern society sometimes fuses sex and violence, Christian faith sees flesh and embodiment as a witness for life abundant. Chapter 4 focuses on eschatology, particularly as it relates to sexual identity. Whereas many modern notions of the sexual person isolate a stable sexual self (straight or gay) that determines one's position in the church, Christian eschatology suggests something different: an instability of all sexual, gendered categories in light of baptism. Baptism fits persons for freedom and elicits a playfulness in life that extends to sexuality.

Chapter 5 explores the ramifications of the Lord's Supper for human sexuality. This central sacrament is sensual and intimate, inviting believers to taste and see that God is good. Sex, likewise, involves taste, touch, and intimacy. The Table gestures take root in sexual life and invite believers to partake in an economy of abundance, counter to the rampant commercialization of sex in modern society that views sex as yet another object sold on the marketplace. I then turn to questions of vocation in chapter 6 by charting three callings in Christian life, each of which is blessed, holy, and central to the church's life: marriage, celibacy, and singleness. Finally, I turn to sexual ethics in chapter 7. Here I offer suggestions for a Christian vision of good sex that resonates with the theology explored in the previous chapters.

This book has been years in the making and has been patched together in small pieces over time. Several congregations have hosted me in workshops and Sunday morning lessons, and I have learned from each of them: Faith Presbyterian Church, Austin, Texas; Westminster Presbyterian Church, Austin, Texas; First United Methodist Church, Austin, Texas; University Baptist Church, Austin, Texas; First Baptist Church, Austin, Texas; Metropolitan Community Church of Austin, Texas; and First Presbyterian Church, Bella Vista, Arkansas. Thanks also go to wonderful colleagues at Austin Seminary who have encouraged me to pursue this research and present some of it on campus in rudimentary form. Annual gatherings of the Workgroup on Constructive Christian Theology continue to stimulate my teaching and writing. Don McKim and the editorial staff at Westminster John Knox routinely support my efforts at writing accessible theology. I write this book with an eye to my children Grace and Finn's future, in the hopes that the churches might provide one place where their own questions are taken seriously. Most of all, I owe thanks to Molly, who makes life new each morning. She has shown me the shape of desire and how desire finds a home in a shared life. I dedicate this book to her.

Chapter 1

Scripture and Sex

Narratives of Desire

For centuries Christians have argued about sex. The Bible figures prominently in the history of this argument, perhaps more prominently than anything else in Christian tradition. Across the generations, Christians have cited biblical texts for endorsing or prohibiting various sexual behaviors, argued with those same texts, and attempted to place them within broader theological frameworks. In the history of Christian theology, biblical texts are summoned as truth, dismissed as irrelevant, cited in isolation, and woven together in broad tapestries. What does the Bible say about sex? How do we read its varied texts and trajectories in ways that reflect salvation in Jesus Christ and the freedom given in the Spirit?

Questions about sex and the Bible invariably revert to the question of how Christians *read* biblical texts, a question that accompanied the ministry of Jesus. In the Gospels, scribes often argue with Jesus about texts. Jesus, in their eyes, seemed to ignore the plain sense of texts and the traditions that had accumulated around texts. They questioned whether he read texts carefully enough and whether he took the Sabbath seriously enough. Yet Jesus knew biblical texts intimately, probed them for meaning and resonance, and claimed that texts and traditions were made for humanity, not the other way around (Mark 2:27). Contrary to the scribes' suspicions, Jesus did not ignore texts, but radicalized them, pointing to how they take root in people's lives: "'Do not think that I have come to abolish the law or the prophets; I have come not to abolish but to fulfill'" (Matt. 5:17).

What does the Bible say about sex? This seemingly simple question yields anything but a simple answer. Indeed, the Bible says and has said many, often conflicting, things about sex. "What does the Bible say about sex?" is in some regards the wrong question. We ought to first ask ourselves *how* we read and what is the character of the book we call Scripture. Attention to that question helps us address the often thorny subject of the Bible and sex. Becoming better readers equips us to better engage questions of human sexuality. In that light, this chapter surveys three approaches to the Bible and sex, which broadly frame current debates: (1) an approach that focuses on the explicitly "sexual texts" of the Bible and determines rules for sexual behavior from them; (2) an approach that deems the codes and rules from these texts as outmoded in the contemporary age; and (3) an approach that views Scripture as a narrative of desire, situating sexuality as one moment within that life. In this last approach, which I advocate, the "nonsexual" texts of Scripture often affect our reading of the sexual.

THE TEXT AS A GUIDEBOOK FOR SEXUAL BEHAVIOR

Perhaps the most common way of reading Scripture with regard to sex is to view it as a guide for sexual behavior. The Bible, in this view, offers clear prohibitions of specific sexual behaviors and might be described as a "how not to" manual, though Scripture also provides some general principles for conceiving "godly" sex. An assumption in this approach is that sex is a gift in the proper context but dangerous in the wrong context. One of the fundamental guides for godly sex occurs near the beginning of the biblical canon in the creation stories. "Therefore a man leaves his father and his mother and clings to his wife, and they become one flesh. And the man and his wife were both naked, and were not ashamed" (Gen. 2:24–25). Here "one flesh" is taken both as a metaphor for the nuptial covenant and for the intertwining of bodies in sex as the seal of that covenant. The evangelical theologian Stanley Grenz offers one interpretation of this text, with an eye to sex in marriage: "Whenever the couple engages in sexual intercourse they are reaffirming the pledge made on their wedding day and are giving visual representation of the content of that vow."[1] Adam and Eve become the pattern for rightly ordered sex: without shame, with restraint, shared with one other person (of the opposite sex) in marriage. Whatever departs from this pattern, ipso facto, is questionable. What is cause for the cry of elation, "'This at last is bone of my bones and flesh of my flesh'" (v. 23), within marriage is cause for lamentation anywhere else.

Once this norm—marriage between a man and a woman—has been established for godly sex, the sexual prohibitions within Scripture appear to make sense. Sex that occurs outside of marriage must be viewed under a hermeneutic of suspicion, not merely because it undermines the marital covenant, but also because it also does injury to the body of Christ. Paul's vice lists enumerate activities that inflict such injury. In 1 Corinthians, for example, Paul admonishes his readers for abusing the Lord's Supper in ways that marginalize the poor (11:17–34) and in power struggles (1:10–17), but also in a specific instance of a man living with his father's wife (5:1). This specific instance of illicit sex Paul names *porneia*, generally translated as "fornication" or "sexual immorality" in the NRSV, but a term that he never clearly defines (cf. 6:12–18, where Paul uses the term in relation to prostitution). Paul often constructs vice lists related to *porneia*. For readers who assume that Paul offers specific rules for sex in this passage and in other passages, *porneia* has come to mean nearly *any* sexual behavior other than penile-vaginal intercourse within marriage: masturbation, oral sex, anal sex, sex practiced with inordinate passion or desire.[2] One problem with the understanding of these vice lists as a guide is that it is difficult discerning what Paul is actually condemning. In 1 Corinthians, Paul mentions *porneia* in reference to prostitution and illicit marriages; in Galatians he seems to use it more generally, without connection to specific sexual behaviors. The term, in short, has come to mean whatever each generation assumes it means, whatever departs from the supposedly self-evident mores of each era. Today's fornication, in short, often becomes tomorrow's sexual norm.

The chief prohibition that often comes to the fore in the guidebook approach to sex is a condemnation of homosexuality, supposedly another instance of *porneia* that violates the conditions of godly sex. The holiness codes of the Old Testament, in this view, can be applied to contemporary society. Leviticus 18, for example, is devoted exclusively to sexual holiness, prohibiting various degrees of incest, sex with women during menstruation, adultery, bestiality, and the oft-cited: "You shall not lie with a male as with a woman; it is an abomination" (Lev. 18:22). In chapter 20, this command is reiterated, this time with the stipulation that those who commit such acts shall be put to death (Lev. 20:13). These two verses are the only times the phrase, translated more literally as "the lying down of a woman," occurs in the entire Hebrew Bible. They occur within long lists of prohibitions meant to distinguish Israel's religious practice from other Near Eastern tribes. Certain behaviors, and the avoidance of certain behaviors, distinguish the people of the covenant from all others: from clothing to diet to rules for appropriate sacrifice. Prohibition of specific sexual behaviors occurs in the midst of these other prohibitions. But for the guidebook approach to reading Scripture, this historical context does not negate the force of the prohibition, as the behaviors prohibited for Israel are valid for our time as well. Hence Robert Gagnon can write that anal intercourse constitutes a conscious denial of the complementarity of male and female found not least in the fittedness (anatomical, physiological, and procreative) of the male penis and the female vaginal receptacle by attempting anal intercourse (or other forms of sexual intercourse) with another man. Anal sex not only confuses gender, it confuses the function of the anus as a cavity for expelling excrement, not receiving sperm. . . . For one man to "lie with" another man in the manner that men normally "lie with" a woman was to defile the latter's masculine stamp, impressed by God and evident in both the visible sexual complementarity of male and female and in the sacred lore of creation.[3]

The "lying down of a woman," for Gagnon, means *any* male-male sexual intercourse, whether in the context of a committed partnership or in the midst of an orgy. Gagnon's approach, moreover, assumes to know what "the lying down of a woman" means: it means gay sex, which constitutes a violation of the created order. But such extrapolation avoids the specificity of the text. Strictly speaking, even if one were to accept the correlation between the Levitical prohibition and gay sex, the prohibition would only extend to the partner who penetrates the other in instances of male-male anal intercourse.[4]

Contemporary rule-based understandings of sex, however, do not simply appeal to Levitical holiness codes. They often claim a broader framework for condemning homosexuality in Romans 1–3. Embedded in a sweeping indictment of Jew and Gentile are these phrases: "For this reason God gave them up to degrading passions. Their women exchanged natural intercourse for unnatural, and in the same way also the men, giving up natural intercourse with women, were consumed with passion for one another. Men committed shameless acts with men and received in their own persons the due penalty for their error" (Rom. 1:26–27). Among all scriptural references to same-sex acts, this is the only one that includes women. Again, determining what sexual behaviors Paul condemns here is difficult: temple prostitution? ritual sex? pederasty? While scholars have argued incessantly about what kinds of behavior are implied, Paul seemed to be rather unconcerned with the specifics. His chief concern is idolatry, exchanging the glory of God for other images, serving "the creature rather than the Creator" (v. 25), which causes God to give them up "to degrading passions" (v. 26). Paul focuses first on idolatry, which subsequently gives birth to all kinds of disorder—including sexual disorder—in the body.

A rule-based approach to sex and Scripture offers clear prohibitions based on select biblical texts. In the rightly ordered sexual universe, one simply says no to prostitution and homosexuality; extramarital sex and premarital sex; fornication and too much passion within marriage; bestiality and masturbation. One says no because the Bible tells us so. Though most rule-based approaches distinguish between many sexual behaviors, with some practices being more serious violations of rules than others, the norm against which all behaviors are measured is a marriage between one man and one woman.

THE RULES DON'T APPLY ANY MORE:
BIBLICAL TEXTS AND REVISIONIST THEOLOGY

Can we comb Scripture for self-evident rules about sex? Other contemporary theologians would deny that we can. I have already noted one problem with the rule-based approach: passages that seem to talk about sex or have come to mean sexual subjects are primarily devoted to other matters. Romans 1–2, which routinely gets cited in condemnations of homosexuality, is instead concerned with demonstrating the need for the gospel; Sodom and Gomorrah, another oft-cited text (Gen. 19:1–29), is chiefly about hospitality and the denial of hospitality, not sex. Leviticus is concerned with idolatry first, and only derivatively with sexual behaviors that are evidence of idolatry. Only recently have the so-called sexual meanings of these texts come to the fore. All these factors have led some to throw up their hands when it comes to the Bible and sex. Mark Jordan, for example, states this frustration baldly: "There are, in short, no self-evident lists of biblical passages about sexual matters."[5]

Compounding this frustration are the patriarchal assumptions of Scripture itself, which suggest that Scripture alone is an insufficient guide to sexual matters and must be read with a hermeneutic of suspicion. Take the paradigm of marriage as an example: The commandment against coveting a neighbor's wife (note the gender)—and by implication, the commandment against adultery—is couched in the language of property. Adultery becomes in this context less an affront to marriage than it is to the property rights of the possessor: "You shall not covet your neighbor's house; you shall not covet your neighbor's wife, or male or female slave, or ox, or donkey, or anything that belongs to your neighbor" (Exod. 20:17). Scriptural rules of sexual behavior tend to implicate women more than men. Some of the Pastoral Epistles especially evince this tendency, singling out younger widows as particularly prone to sins of the flesh. Take 1 Timothy as an example: "But refuse to put younger widows on the list; for when their sensual desires alienate them from Christ, they want to marry, and so they incur condemnation for having violated their first pledge" (5:11–12). Though the author here is urging his audience not to have younger widows make vows of perpetual chastity and urges that they remarry instead of taking such vows, it is interesting that women are singled out in this list, as if they were more prone to sexual vice than men. Given this perspective, it is not surprising that the Pastoral Epistles also suggest that women are more likely to be swayed by false teaching: "silly women, overwhelmed by their sins and swayed by all kinds of desires, who are always being instructed and can never arrive at a knowledge of the truth" (2 Tim. 3:6b–7). This correlation of women as more susceptible to sin is by no means restricted to deuteropauline literature. As we read in 1 Peter, husbands are to "show consideration for your wives in your life together, paying honor to the woman as the weaker sex, since they too are also heirs of the gracious gift of life" (3:7). Texts like these pepper the New Testament and have affected many modern approaches to gender, sexuality, and marriage. In the eyes of some who would use these texts to frame an understanding of theology and sex, the approach is straightforward: be wary of sex, and be particularly wary of women who display their sexuality openly. Texts that assume these characteristics of women and sex, however sacred we name them, cannot be taken at face value as guides for godly sex. The rules they appear to offer may no longer apply.

The majority of voices in Scripture, in other words, assume male privilege and the secondary status of women. Within the broad swath of biblical narrative, women are blamed for sin (Gen. 3:12; 1 Tim. 2:12–15), enjoined to remain silent in assembly (1 Cor. 14:34), and assumed to belong to their husbands in a manner analogous to property (Exod. 20:17). More glaringly, the trope of the loose woman or harlot is used throughout Scripture to epitomize unfaithfulness, whether the whore of Hosea (Hos. 2–4), who is stripped naked and exposed, or the whore of Babylon who is burned and devoured (Rev. 17:16).

Even the more benignly sexual texts of Scripture—such as the paeans for marriage—are soaked in patriarchy. In the deuteropauline Epistles, patriarchy is assumed and celebrated. Ephesians, for example, enjoins wives to be subject to their husbands, comparing a husband's "headship" to Christ as "head of the church" (Eph. 5:22–23). Husbands, by contrast, are enjoined to love their wives, "just as Christ loved the church" (v. 25). Subjection, in this view, is a decidedly one-way street (cf. Col. 3:18–19). Where mutual submission to one another is encouraged, as in Paul's first letter to the Corinthians, marriage is connected to slavery and the problematic assumptions of "owning" another person: "For the wife does not have authority over her own body, but the husband does; likewise the husband does not have authority over his own body, but the wife does" (1 Cor. 7:4). It is no coincidence that the exhortations to husbands and wives in deuteropauline literature occur near injunctions toward slaves and masters. Paul simply makes this connection even more explicit—marriage itself is a kind of mutual slavery, by which one's bodyright is given over to another. For Adrian Thatcher, these connections between male headship, slavery, and even mutual submission, make the biblical framework for marriage nearly irredeemable:

> The institution of slavery with its attendant violence and injustice is accepted as part of the general world-view of the New Testament. The point to carry forward is that the theology of marriage is so integrated into the institution of slavery and the hierarchical order of social relations which slavery services that, once slavery has been repudiated by Christianity (after nineteen centuries), the theology of marriage based upon it must also be repudiated.[6]

From a revisionist perspective, use of the Bible alone in constructing a view of sex and marriage is naive and anachronistic at best, and dangerous at worst. It leads either to ignoring the patriarchal context in which these texts arise or to perpetuating patriarchal patterns without end. In Thatcher's words, such a literal approach to the words of Scripture and applying them for today "oppresses its victims and it undermines the gospel."[7]

In light of these difficulties, William Countryman has proposed a reframing of sexual ethics that eschews the concerns of purity and property so prevalent in Scripture. For Countryman, the freedom of God's reign offers the fundamental criterion for construing godly sex, a reign that relativizes our attempts to establish purity. The Bible, in his view, "takes sex more or less for granted and does not explicitly lay out a theological or philosophical understanding of it."[8] One's participation in that reign is not incumbent upon maintaining the purity codes expressed in Scripture, because to do so would elevate sexual life over the reign of God. The experience of grace always relativizes the attempt to establish sexual purity. Individual Christians may subscribe to "the purity codes of their culture, but they may not demand that other Christians do so. If one wishes to assert that any given proscription is a part of Christian sexual ethics, one must justify that claim by showing that the act in question infringes some principle other than purity."[9] The typical restrictions against "masturbation, nonvaginal heterosexual intercourse, bestiality, polygamy, homosexual acts, or erotic art and literature"[10] are no longer valid for their own sake. For revisionists such as Countryman, the standard rules no longer apply and must be improvised as we go along.

Some feminist theologians add to this chorus by arguing that one needs to read against Scripture in the name of a more liberating understanding of sex. Anne Bathurst Gilson claims that the Christian tendency to prize disinterested agape at the expense of eros infects the history of the church and the canon itself. It is better in the tradition's eyes to love another selflessly than to affirm the self (and others) through eros. It is better to love without too much passion than to desire. Gilson claims that this preference for agape over eros reaps rotten fruit that we must cast aside. For example, biblical prohibitions of specific sexual behaviors create a culture of compulsory heterosexuality among Christians: "the belief that the one-man, one-woman, one-flesh relationship in the context of lifelong marriage is not only God-given but God-*demanded*."[11] So entrenched is this belief within Christianity that the church generally abhors other expressions of sexual relationships. In the face of Scriptures that demean women and even foster violence against nonheterosexual persons, Gilson argues for the development of an erotic faith, a faith articulated less in scriptural narratives than it is in the power of an immanent God: "God is the power of eros, affirming bodyselves, yearning with us away from eroticized violence and into embodied justice and erotic mutuality. . . . God as the power of eros is She who is with us, who is moved and changed and touched by and with us."[12] In this vision, the Bible appears only on the margins, often as a foil to erotic justice.

SCRIPTURE AS A NARRATIVE OF DESIRE

But what if we construed Scripture not as rules of sexuality that ought to be upheld or relativized? What, instead, if we recovered the more ancient practice of reading it as a narrative of desire? From start to finish, the Bible expresses relationships: of creation's relationship with God, of human persons' relationship with one another, of God's election of a nation for particular relationship with God in covenant, and of the extension of that covenant to the world in Jesus Christ. As the Bible narrates these relationships, which are intimations of grace and incidents of sin, the reader glimpses divine desire that makes us participants in desire. The breath of God that stirs all to life in creation breathes through our being and upon our necks at every turn. Like a lover who longs for consummation, God desires our fulfillment in communion with God and one another. Read as a narrative of desire, the Bible's supposedly nonsexual texts have much to say about sex.

The first glimpse of God's desire occurs in the Genesis creation stories. The desire to create in the first narrative stems from God's delight, illustrated in the frequent recurrence of the phrase, "God saw that it was good," and the final word, "God saw everything that he had made, and indeed, it was very good" (Gen. 1:12, 18, 21, 25, 31). Everything in creation is contingent, made for relationship with God and the rest of creation. God creates not out of lack, but out of the desire for others *to be*, a desire that is fulfilled by word and breath. The opening word of desire in the Bible, then, causes us to reframe some contemporary understandings of desire. Whereas most accounts of desire, especially sexual desire, conceive it as stemming from an internal hunger or emptiness, an absence that can only be filled by clinging to another to make one whole, this opening biblical account of desire proceeds from fullness to fullness. In Grace Jantzen's words, "Creativity bespeaks fullness that overflows, that wants to give of its resources to express itself. The paradigm case is once again the creation of the world. As God is portrayed in the Hebrew Bible and Christian theology, God does not lack. The divine is in need of nothing. Yet God desires to create the world and desires to make it beautiful."[13] God desires out of abundance and creates in order to share that abundance with all that is.

The second creation story further specifies the shape of desire. Here God's desire becomes intimately physical, as God forms the man from the dust of the ground and breathes into his nostrils the breath of life (Gen. 2:7). As human beings speak for the first time, they become partakers of God's desire, a desire expressed in the longing for companionship with another. After the creation of a partner, the man's exclamation in the garden rings with the satisfaction of desire and desire's intensification in sex, the sharing and mingling of flesh: "'This at last is bone of my bones and flesh of my flesh'" (v. 23). The approach of a companion does not extinguish desire, but makes it flourish in togetherness.

Yet Genesis also narrates the distortion of desire. Desire becomes a hollow shell of itself when it proceeds out of perceived lack, when one seeks to possess someone or something for oneself alone, apart from God. Divine desire proceeds from abundance and wanting to share in abundance so that others might flourish. Human persons distort desire when they crave for possession. The first instance of this distortion is the multifaceted story of the tree, the serpent, and the first humans. Adam and Eve's failure is not the desire for knowledge, not the breaking of a divinely given rule, but their perception that the tree has something that they lack, that they simply *must* have for themselves: knowledge of good and evil apart from God. Their culpability is believing the serpent's lie that God wants to withhold something good from them. The "fall," read thusly, is not about disobedience or the seeking of knowledge, but about Adam and Eve's refusal to partake in the abundance of the garden that allows desire to flourish, falsely believing that they can obtain a scarce resource outside God's provision by holding it and keeping it for themselves. Thus, the fruit of the tree becomes all the more desirable, a "delight to the eyes" (3:6), that can only be satisfied by hoarding it. Almost as soon as human beings become participants in God's desire, they begin to think that it is meant for possession, not sharing. In its twisted form, desire turns in upon itself and becomes insatiable: for the fruit, in the end, does not satisfy, but only leaves the two ashamed, seeking satisfaction elsewhere, in work that degenerates into toil, in unjust relations between man and woman (3:16–17). Begun in fullness, desire soon devolves into scarcity in human hands.

God's response to this twisting of desire is to seek relationship more intensely, to pledge fidelity to a particular people even amid misdirected desire. God's expression of relationship takes the shape of a concrete pledge made to an otherwise insignificant people, and through this pledge to this people, to show the world the fullness of God's desire. The covenant with Abraham is an extension of the creation story: for fruitful land, for offspring that flourish, for everlasting relationship with the Creator. As the narration of covenant unfolds, God displays the shape of desire: expressed in love and faithfulness to a covenant people and grief and anger when covenant is broken (Exod. 34:6–7; Num. 11:33; 32:13). Covenant becomes the shape of God's desire, the way God sinks an anchor of flesh into the world by making concrete promises to a particular people. Desire does not become diffuse, but gathers intensity as it pledges fidelity and fruitfulness to a particular people. The divine desire shows us that love for the world emerges in particular promises to a beloved.

Covenant, in other words, is for the sake of life, that all might partake in life in fullness. In Deuteronomy, Moses speaks these words to Israel as they are on the verge of the promised land: "See, I have set before you today life and prosperity, death and adversity. . . . Choose life so that you and your descendants may live, loving the LORD your God, obeying him, and holding fast to him; for that means life to you and length of days, so that you may live in the land that the LORD swore to give to your ancestors, to Abraham, to Isaac, and to Jacob" (Deut. 30:15, 19b–20). Covenant reveals a biophilic God, who desires that all might live into the fullness of relationship. Covenant teaches us that we need not choose between a generalized love for the world and love for a particular beloved; rather, the two are inextricably intertwined. God is the God of creation, who loves and breathes the world into being and the God who makes concrete pledges to particular people. Israel pledges fidelity to God and thereby becomes a light unto the nations, that God's "salvation may reach to the end of the earth" (Isa.

49:6). Covenant teaches us that we can love God and the world at the same time, as long as we love the world as *God's world*.

The New Testament continues these trajectories of desire, personified in Jesus of Nazareth, the one in whom we meet desire face-to-face. Jesus is both the object of desire, the focus of those who seek him, and also the Desiring One, who will not cease desiring until all partake in life's fullness. First, Jesus is the focus of desire, the One in whom the human desire for God finds its incarnational home. When he calls the disciples, Jesus awakens in them a desire for him: "And Jesus said to them, 'Follow me and I will make you fish for people.' And immediately they left their nets and followed him" (Mark 1:17–18). By his very presence and his word, Jesus kindles Simon and Andrew's desire, so much that they drop their nets at the call. As Jesus finds them, their desire finds a home.

Jesus' touch also focuses desire: in most of the stories of healing, Jesus touches indiscriminately, without regard to a person's status in life. But at times those who long for healing also reach out to touch him, as in the case of the unnamed hemorrhaging woman. She appears on the heels of another healing, amid another crowd, approaches Jesus from behind, and touches the fringe of his cloak, saying "'If I only touch his cloak, I will be made well'" (Matt. 9:20–21). The language here is delicate, as the fringe of a garment can also serve as a euphemism of sexual touch. The woman's bleeding is related to her sexuality, of flow that will not cease and thus prevents her from sexual intimacy according to purity codes of the time (Lev. 18:19). Her touch intimates sex and the desire to be healed. Jesus' touch imparts sexual healing and the gift of life. To touch him is to desire him.

This focus of desire does not evaporate in the resurrection. Indeed, as the appearance narratives in John indicate, desire for Jesus' touch intensifies rather than abates. Mary, having first mistaken the risen Christ for a gardener, upon having her eyes opened by hearing her name, also desires to touch Jesus' body. She reaches out in desire, longing to hold the risen rabbi, only to be told by him, "'Do not hold on to me, because I have not yet ascended to the Father'" (John 20:17). Mary longs for the consummation of her heart's desire, communion with the Lord, a communion that expresses the life and touch of the body, the longing to embrace and be embraced. Yet this embrace will not occur until others have been told the news and invited to embrace him. Even in this intimate resurrection appearance, others are invited to touch.

For Thomas, who sees the risen Christ after Mary does, the desire to touch achieves consummation. Thomas, aggrieved with desire, despondent over the loss of his beloved,[14] not only touches his beloved, but enters his body through the wound in Jesus' side. Jesus invites Thomas in, and Thomas reaches out and enters Jesus, quite literally, quite physically. Thomas now "knows" Jesus in the knowledge of flesh touching flesh. In this penetration of flesh, which carries a hint of sex, we too are invited into communion with Jesus. Desire seeks communion with the body and blood of the Risen One. What Jesus offers Thomas— "'Reach out your hand and put it in my side'" (v. 27)—he also offers to all who believe: to receive his body at Table. Thomas desires to touch Jesus, and at Jesus' invitation, he penetrates Jesus' resurrected body. At Table, all Christians are invited to take Jesus into their bodies, to be penetrated and permeated by him.

Seen in this way, the institution of the Lord's Supper is itself a narrative of desire. As Jesus takes, blesses, breaks, and gives the bread, the disciples (and we, by invitation) recall how Jesus takes, blesses, breaks, and gives his life to us borne by desire. What Jesus establishes in this meal is also what he has established in his ministry and promises in God's coming reign. In this meal, Jesus both embodies and gives voice to desire: "I have eagerly desired to eat this Passover with you before I suffer; for I tell you, I will not eat it until it is fulfilled in the kingdom of God" (Luke 22:15–16). The meal is the fulfillment of Jesus' desire for communion, and the continual offer for communion with him in the taste of bread and wine. As Leanne van Dyck reminds us, taste is the intimate form of human touch.[15] In the sacrament of Holy Communion, we taste and see that the Lord is good by taking him into our mouths, as lovers taste one another. The meal expresses his desire for us, our desire for him, and the desire for the whole earth to taste and see. So long as any grow hungry, so long as any do not partake in the fullness of life, so long as bread is hoarded and wine guarded, the economy of this table kindles the desire to share and give, a desire that will not be quenched until all partake of the heavenly banquet. If this heavenly banquet is the fulfillment of desire, the earthly celebration of it intensifies our longing for Jesus and his for us.

In the book of Revelation, desire displays a tortuous path. The book documents the distortion of desire: what happens when the nations twist desire into greed, violence, and lust that make martyrs out of believers. Revelation depicts the nations' lust for power in the well-worn image of the whore of Babylon, the woman who personifies the Roman state and captures the gaze of the nations. As the whore becomes "drunk with the blood of the saints and the blood of the witnesses to Jesus" (Rev. 17:6), the kings of the earth who have grown rich in her empire commit "fornication with her and the merchants of the earth [grow] rich from the power of her luxury" (18:3). Yet this luxury is short-lived, as the whore's body is laid in waste. The imagery here is horrifying and inherently problematic: vice is symbolized in a woman, who is ultimately consumed in the fire of God's judgment (vv. 8–9). These texts of terror locate vice upon a woman's body, products of a male gaze that glimpses greed, treachery, unfaithfulness, and lust in the "other." As a trope, this age-old pattern has unleashed its share of disaster, from blaming rape on victims, to the commercial sexualization of girls at increasingly younger ages, to domestic and sexual abuse that makes the home the most dangerous place in society for women. Much of Revelation locates the distortion of desire upon the female body. The whore image, in short, may be irredeemable, suggesting that the idolatry that the author sought to shake is evident in his own interpretation of the female figure. Desire in Revelation displays a distorted and tortuous course.

The tortured weave of the Bible's closing pages hardly presents a template for desire's flourishing. The text's concern with purity yields anything but a pure description of desire, tainted as it is with misogyny and violence. Revelation is not an easy text to read, understand, or stomach. Readers should struggle with it, just as the early church struggled with whether to include it in the biblical canon and as feminist theology struggles with its meaning and legacy.[16] Yet a struggle with the text can yield surprising riches, for embedded amid its problematic imagery is another shape of desire and its flourishing, depicted in images of the renewal of heaven and earth and the re-creation of Jerusalem, the heavenly city. In this narrative, Christ comes to be our bridegroom, and we are to prepare for that marriage (Rev. 21). When Babylon falls, the Lamb emerges to take the church as his bride, a new covenant where death and tears no longer reign, where the home of God appears among mortals (21:3–4, 9). Traditional as the image is for expressing desire, it also accomplishes queer things for the saints of the church since it makes all people, women *and* men, brides of Christ. In anticipation of this marriage, moreover, the erotic permeates the text.[17] In a tradition that supposedly bears the seeds of the condemnation of homosexuality, the marriage outlined in Revelation betrays more than a hint of homoeroticism, nuptials in which Christ takes John and his brothers as his bride. In Revelation, if desire finds a home in marriage, that home is distinctly queer, for the male saints who populate the book become, in the end, the brides of Christ.

Thus far, I have suggested biblical texts read as narratives of desire when the sexual desire implied in those texts was at best oblique and at worst problematic. There is, however, one book of the Bible, the Song of Songs, that is redolent of sex. Even here, however, we need an interpretive lens. Throughout the ages the Song has been the subject of varying attention. Some rabbinic traditions deem it the "holy of holies" within the canon. In medieval Christendom, the Song generated more commentaries than any other book among monastics. Bernard of Clairvaux, for example, preached eighty-six homilies on the Song and never finished his sermon series. Yet today in most churches—particularly Protestant congregations—the text is rarely proclaimed in the context of worship. A sensual poem that lingers on the body, conveying touch and desire, the Song contains the voices of two unnamed lovers. The woman's voice occupies significantly more space than the man's (a comparative rarity in patriarchal traditions) and speaks without reservation or restraint concerning sex. "O that his left arm were under my head and his right embraced [made love to] me" (Song 2:6); "My beloved thrust his hand into the opening, and my inmost being yearned for him. I arose to open to my beloved, and my hands dripped with myrrh, my fingers with liquid myrrh, upon the handles of the bolt" (5:4–5); "My beloved is mine and I am his; he pastures his flock among the lilies" (2:16). In this text, bodies are relished and desired for their taste, compared with pomegranates and nectar, milk and spices. These are bodies meant for lingering and touching, tasting and feeding. Given the relative explicitness of its cadences, it is no surprise that most Christian traditions have tended toward allegory: the primary theme is not the earthly love between lovers, their longing for one another, but the love between God and Israel (or God and the church). Otherwise the pomegranates appear too juicy.

Though much of Christian tradition has interpreted the Song allegorically, and much contemporary biblical interpretation focuses on the Song as a poem of sexual love, it represents a false dichotomy to choose one interpretation over the other. The Song expresses desire in its earthy and divine fullness, "*rightly* [taking] human sexual love as an analogue of the love between the Lord and Israel."[18] The Song neither impels us to gloss over the sex that is dripping from the pages nor encourages us to understand sex only as an end in itself. The point here is comparison: God's desire for us is *like* a lover's desire for the beloved, body and soul: a desire to touch, commune, be close, enter into, to make room for, to taste. Christian traditions have had a notoriously difficult time considering the sexual alongside the divine. Earthly love for a beloved, in most cases, is construed as in some way inhibiting the soul's communion with God: hence Paul's lukewarm defense of marriage—"For it is better to marry than to be aflame with passion" (1 Cor. 7:9)—and the church's fourth-century condemnation of Jovinian, who taught the spiritual equality of marriage and celibacy.[19] Throughout much of the tradition, the implicit message is that desire for our earthly lover obstructs our desire for God. But the Song suggests another way. Without mentioning God at all, the imagery encourages us to linger: to linger over our beloved, to touch and to taste, to linger in God's presence and grace. We follow the voices, touches, and desires of the lovers in the Song, witnessing them tasting one another. This is imagery of sex in its earthiness: the lovers on the pages of the Song are focused on one another, attend to one another, and delight in each other simply because they are present to each other. They know each other's skin as much as their own. This narration of knowing and being known, without the mention of God's name, is an invitation to compare the love of God for us with the beauty, pleasure, and taste of sex. Such is the desire of God for us; no wonder this song, for many, constituted a holy of holies.

Here, in the most sexual text of the Bible, is an absence of the rules that have come to characterize much subsequent Christian discussion of sex. Instead, we find desire, its intensification, and even its intoxication when focused on the beloved. The Song invites the reader to see and taste that desire. The desire of the Song, which flourishes in its focus, is not an either-or—either my earthly beloved or God—but an exuberant both-and to the lover and to God as lover. The desire of the Song thus "spills out beyond the limits of the Song itself,"[20] finding expression in sex but not restricted to sex.

READING SCRIPTURE AGAIN

Controversy over sex has been a part of Christian traditions since the calling of the disciples. Amid this controversy, the church has turned routinely to Scripture for guidance. The New Testament records some of these controversies: Paul's letters, for example, document arguments over sexual behaviors that were subjects of Christian disagreement. Though the particulars of these New Testament controversies have receded from light, the rhetoric that Paul

employed to address them abides. So, too, do Jesus' disruptive sayings on marriage and families. Though the terms of controversy about sex have changed
over the centuries (with marriage ultimately gaining a status as legitimate as
celibacy), the controversy remains. Even though the amount of space devoted
in Scripture to sexual behavior is comparatively small—especially in comparison to economic behavior—Christians still turn to Scripture for clarity about
sex in tumultuous times.

The default position for reading sex in Scripture is to discern in the biblical
text rules that we apply to govern behavior. Though explicit rules about sex are
generally absent even in Paul's enumeration of vices and *porneia*, the church
has had no difficulty extrapolating rules from disparate texts: sex is made for
the marital bond and procreation; all other sex is inherently sinful; sexual desire
must be bridled even in marriage; homosexuality is wrong, period. Even today
when arguments over sex surface in the churches—typically concerning homosexuality—the same texts surface: Paul's vice lists, Levitical purity codes, perhaps
an allusion to Sodom and Gomorrah. Rules, rules, and more rules: sex must fit
within these rules and it is one task of the church to clarify and police them. Yet,
as I have attempted in this chapter to show, the rule-based approach to Scripture
is fraught with problems. First, it reads Scripture in a strikingly nonnarrative
manner. Scripture becomes a handbook for behavior rather than a story of God
and God's beloved. The biblical story, however, shapes us not by particular
codes, but by the tenor and trajectories of the characters within it: God's establishment of covenant with Israel, Israel's stumbling in maintaining covenant, the
extension of covenant to the world in Jesus Christ, and his rejection by those he
loved. The Bible, simply put, encourages us not merely to apply its varied lit-
eratures in the form of rules, but to become a part of the narrative itself. George
Lindbeck has claimed that the biblical world absorbs the universe,[21] that it shapes
us as a people not by its codes but by the story that unfolds on Scripture's pages.
If we comb the text merely for rules about sex, we not only miss the Bible as narrative but also close our eyes to the narrative of sex, a narrative among beloveds,
who reflect in some small manner God's desire for the world.

A second problem with combing the text for sexual rules is its invariable
selectivity and refusal to acknowledge the problematic contexts within which
one finds the rules. For example, the lukewarm endorsements of marriage in the
New Testament assume a patriarchal view of male headship in the household.
Adultery, as prohibited in the Old Testament, is connected to property rights.
Even when rules seem specific in the Bible, the circumstances surrounding them
are morally abhorrent for contemporary readers: whether in regard to slavery or
the status of women. How, then, can one blithely apply what few rules there are
in Scripture regarding sex?

No wonder that the contemporary period has witnessed many voices who
claim that the rules regarding sex no longer apply. In diagnosing the patriarchal
baggage of the circumstances surrounding sexual rules in Scripture, these critics
hit the mark. Yet their reading of Scripture, surprisingly, also reflects readings of

advocates of rule-based approaches: namely, that the Bible supplies rules about sex, however inappropriate and anti-gospel they are for us today.

The alternative that I have illustrated in this chapter is to read Scripture as a narrative of desire: of God's desire for us, of our desire for communion with God, and of our desire for relationship with others. Sex is one dimension of the desire for communion and relationship. It is integral to who we are as an expression of longing for connection and intimacy. As Scripture invites us into the cadences of its narrative, it shows us how desire intensifies in its focus: God's desire for relationship with a people expresses itself in covenant; God's love for the world is expressed in particular relationship in the incarnation; God's revelation of God's very self in one human being. In each case, desire for the world gets expressed in *particularity*, in a focused intensification of God's love.

The church has often claimed that sexual desire has to be contained and restricted, lest it become dangerous. Hence, the only place to channel sexual desire is in marriage—never outside marriage, never with the same sex. But the narrative of desire as it unfolds in Scripture suggests something different: not the bottling up of desire, but its growth and increase, where "flashes are flashes of fire, a raging flame" (Song 8:6). God's desire for communion does not dissipate with the establishment of covenant with Israel or the incarnation of Jesus; rather, it continues to kindle desire until all creation finds a home in the new creation. God's desire is not quenched until the end of days; neither will ours.

Contemporary culture often claims that desire wanes over time. Stay in any sexual relationship long enough—whether marriage, partnership, or otherwise—and the flames eventually fade. The jaded view of sexual relationships in contemporary culture is that intimacy quickly becomes banal; as time goes by with the beloved, mystery evaporates as people take each other increasingly for granted. Irritation rather than surprise characterizes the relationship as the years pass. The more I know about my beloved, the less there seems left to know, and thus familiarity breeds laziness and dissipation. Sex becomes, as it were, old hat, unless desire finds a new home with someone else while the old love is left behind.

The covenant that Christ establishes with his beloved is different. In Christ, intimacy leads to deeper mystery: the more I know my beloved, the more there is yet to know. Covenant does not extinguish desire so much as it intensifies desire. In this context, the beloved becomes all the more enticing and desirous along the way, as we come to know each other. Such is the journey of sex when conceived in light of covenant and incarnation, God's desire for us. Sex, in this context, does not become banal, but becomes a passage to deeper knowing of our beloved, surprise, and the yearning of desire. The passage of time results in neither the smothering nor containment of desire, but in a growth stronger than death: "Set me as a seal upon your heart, as a seal upon your arm; for love is strong as death, passion fierce as the grave" (8:6).

When we read Scripture as a narrative of desire, we are encouraged to linger: to linger over the body of Christ, to linger over the history of God's desire for the world, to linger over Holy Communion, to linger in the presence of our beloved.

In Western consumer economies, sex is meant for consumption—rather rapid consumption—as desire roams from place to place in search of new loves. One problem with sex in this context is that it has lost the capacity to linger. Lingering is present in the pages of Scripture, just as the lovers linger over one another in Solomon's Song, drinking each other's nectar, attending to the folds and features of each other's bodies. If the commercialization of sex in culture encourages the rapid movement of getting what we can, the lingering narrative of desire in the Song encourages us to pay attention. Sex offers one form of paying attention, of attending to another's person and pleasure so intently that their pleasure and person mingles with one's own. In sex, perhaps as much as any other dimension of human experience, pleasure and desire become intermingled, so that in the midst of sex it becomes difficult—and often pointless—to separate one person's pleasure from the other's: her pleasure is also mine and my pleasure is also hers. But this mingling is only possible when we linger and pay attention. Then sex becomes lovemaking. When we make love, we also respond to the communion that God establishes with us in a person who is a mingling of the human and the divine, the incarnation of God's love for the world.

Chapter 2

God and Sex

Holy Desire

Does Christian faith, in the end, suppress or unleash desire? Sigmund Freud suggested that religion sublimates desire and channels the libido, directing our sexual yearnings for a lover toward an elusive heavenly Father. As we live in Freud's wake, it is no surprise that modern movie and television portrayals of clergy and religious persons often emphasize repression. How many times has the prudishness of Ned Flanders of *The Simpsons* fame or Father Mulcahy of *M*A*S*H* been contrasted with the conviviality and earthiness of those around them? We laugh at Ned and Mulcahy because desire seems eviscerated from their bodies. Both of them flee desire and find refuge in faith, however precarious that refuge may be. In the post-Freudian mindset, people of faith attempt to harness desire; saints are those who eliminate desire completely.

The previous chapter offered an argument for how we might read the broad trajectory of Scripture as a narrative of God's desire for us. In this narrative, God does not disinterestedly rule over creation but seeks others for covenant, for intimacy and passion, simply for the sake of God's gracious love. This is a narrative of attraction, of God desiring us so that we might partake in the life of God. Of course the narrative involves our rejection of that desire: The paradox of

Christian life is that we are attracted by God's desire so that we might desire God more fully *and* that we spurn God's offer of Godself, turn from life, thwart the intent of desire, and twist it into an idol. In our lives, desire is often misdirected, but the good news is that God intensifies our desire by coming in the flesh so that we might be suffused with a love of God that animates and sustains our love of neighbor and our neighbor's love of us. The Christian story, as I read it, is consumed by desire. Freud, Flanders, and Mulcahy simply do not get that part of the story. This chapter offers a continuation of the themes developed in the first chapter. God creates us as subjects of God's holy desire who desire communion with others and with God. Human sexuality is one reflection of God's intent to create beings for desire. The holiness of sexual desire, then, is best glimpsed within the larger narrative of God's desire for us, the promised end God has in store for us, an end that summons our own imperfect response.

In order to clarify "holy desire," in this chapter I will first identify some secular and ecclesial distortions of desire prevalent in history and our day. Next, with the help of select Christian mystics, I will explore some of the dynamics of desire oriented toward God and neighbor, showing how the mystical trajectory of desire differs from some contemporary theologies that claim to celebrate the erotic. Finally, the chapter will suggest covenant as the intensification of desire rather than its suppression. In the end, Christian faith finds a home for desire, not in suppressing it, or even in its transformation, but in allowing desire to flourish as it leads to God and neighbor.

SECULAR MYTHS ABOUT SEX: ROAMING DESIRE SAVES US

Throughout this chapter I use both terms "desire" and "eros," though the former appears more frequently. Both words capture the longing for another, whether in relation to God or to another person. Relationships, in this read, cultivate desire rather than suppress it. The long history of Christian spirituality bears witness to this truth. As a spiritual practice that expresses the relationship between believers and God, prayer increases our desire for God, so that we long to behold God face-to-face. Friendships, likewise, can increase feelings of attachment and yearning. If a friend moves across country, most of us will experience yearning to be reunited. The more that friendship is cultivated, despite physical distance, the more intensely our desires grow to see each other face-to-face. Vast physical distances are not necessary for desire to flourish, however, as desire may also grow particularly intensely in relationships (such as marriage) where persons share the same living and sleeping space. Yet desire requires some degree of separation: the sheer physical otherness of a partner, friend, or lover, or the infinite Otherness of our Divine Lover. Desire, simply stated, is our longing to be with that other (Other), to know that other more deeply and fully. It seeks not acquisition of another but passionate involvement with another. *Desire seeks communion* and becomes distorted when it seeks possession.

In the popular mindset, however, desire must roam; it is never content with one thing or relationship, but must invariably seek the new, the thrilling and titillating for possession. When desire finds expression in sex, it quickly becomes restless. This popular understanding is an *assumption* about how desire works, but it often takes the air of a scientific truism, especially as it regards male sexual desire. Some popularized versions of sociobiology claim that men, by nature, are prone to seek a wide variety of sexual partners. Call it what one will—sowing wild oats, playing the field, diversifying the species—the assumption is that males roam for sex because of the nature of desire. Beneath an endless parade of barhopping and pleasure seeking is a deeply engrained reproductive strategy: to ensure the propagation of one's own genetic material, one best sows one's seed as widely as possible. Women, because of ovulation cycles and limited periods of fertility, have a different strategy: in order to reproduce successfully, they need to secure the attachment of one dependable male, who will provide and protect. Their strategy is to make a "dad" out of a "cad." These two strategies run at cross-purposes but ultimately reach a kind of compromise: domesticating the cad, yet tolerating the man's need to range from time to time. Deep down inside, the roamer is not really a lothario, he's just being himself. Thus, men's conformity to the sexual mores that have taken root in Christian societies only comes at the high price of working against biology. Men, we are told, by nature have more difficulty being monogamous. Desire, after all, must roam unless it is harnessed by an alluring mate.

The problem with this theory is it both claims and ignores too much, shrouding its assumptions in the mantle of scientific objectivity. It errs by ignoring the socially constructed nature of human sexuality, setting aside the numerous ways—among widely different cultures—that sexual behaviors are endorsed or prohibited. To claim that men are restless "by nature" in desire is simply to claim too much about nature. From the beginning of our lives we are introduced, through culture, through family, to what it means to be a sexual person. Behaviors aren't fixed in genetic stone; they are molded and shaped by culture. And, as Lisa Cahill argues, "Human beings are not *only* interested in genetic self-perpetuation, or in maximizing their sexual and reproductive opportunities. They care about the establishment of long-term interpersonal relationships, especially to mate, children, and family members."[1] Many arguments about how men and women behave sexually amount to quasi-genetic reductionism. It makes us accept certain sexual behaviors as "inevitable" that we would never stomach in other realms of human behavior. Once we accept the idea that men are by nature "cads," are we then to assume that certain others are by nature violent and are justified in expressing that violence to be true to themselves?

Nonetheless, the assumptions of roaming desire seem to be accepted unequivocally by wider publications devoted to men's interests. The assumptions of *Playboy* and *Penthouse* are rather obvious: all men are gripped by sexual desire for any woman who fits a limited (and surgically-enhanced) image of beauty, even—or perhaps especially—if they don't know her name. As issue after issue unfolds in glossy detail, desire never gets to know the object of one's desire; instead, month after month new women with no names or made-up names are paraded before the man. He has voice; she does not. Never do the two meet. By the end of the month he wants something new.

These assumptions about roaming desire are evident in more innocuous publications as well. *Men's Health*, a magazine devoted exclusively to the physical and mental well-being of men, always contains columns and articles on male sexuality. Month after month, the writing invariably sounds the same. An article in a recent issue begins, "The way to a woman's bedroom is through her ears," and subsequently relates talking strategies for moving toward the "next level of intimacy,"[2] in other words, landing a babe in bed. Other columns in the same issue offer tips on how a "stepped up PDA [public displays of affection] will deepen her connection to you, so she'll be more willing to give herself to you in the bedroom,"[3] how "touching a woman's forearm will lower her guard"[4] in the club, and how bonding with a dog "might just make her smile and drop her defenses."[5] In the end, the man always gets what he wants, whether in bed, the park, or the club. Variety is the only thing that will satisfy roaming desire.[6] Whether one is on the prowl for a new sexual partner or practicing endless variation with the same partner, the message is effectively the same: Desire can only be sustained through novelty. Whatever is familiar is shunned or disposed so that the man can have what his desire demands.

One of the effects of the sexual revolution is to extend these "benefits" to women as well. As the enormously popular television series, *Sex in the City* attests, women, too, are now assumed to have roaming desires. Samantha, the personification of this understanding of desire, elicits excitement and sympathy from her viewers. Amid her innumerable spicy trysts, we are left commenting "maybe I should try that" at the same time that we may sigh "she'd be happier if she just settled down." As Samantha's character unfolds, the message is clear: to live in the city is to be exposed to the widest possible array of sexual partners; to be a woman is to try many on for size until one settles down (if ever). Without a bit of roaming, however, desire quickly grows cold.

Another related myth that American popular culture sells is that sex saves. Interestingly, this slogan finds a home along a wide spectrum of sexual behaviors. At one extreme are those who urge single persons to "save themselves" sexually for marriage. The message here is that sexuality is uniquely sacred in human experience: so intense that it can only be shared with one person for the full course of one's life. Listening to NPR one afternoon, I heard an "abstinence only" advocate exhorting a group of teenagers, comparing sex to kissing a frozen steel pipe: every time you "do" it, he said, you lose a piece of yourself. You should only kiss (i.e., have sex with) the person you marry and kissing is to be reserved for the wedding night. Once one has sex in marriage, though, it is the warmest, most intoxicating, most exhilarating thing imaginable. Sex within marriage, from the abstinence perspective, is salvific. All other sex is damaging and dehumanizing.

The chief problem with this illustration is not with its ethics. In some senses I also argue for a pattern of monogamy that this "abstinence expert" urges, though with significant modifications as it relates to premarital sex. The problem, rather, is with his fantastic assumptions about sex: that within a marriage it is a uniquely holy experience. One senses that sex can never be ordinary or seen within the larger trajectory of a couple's togetherness. Sex must be so mind-blowing and awesome that it cannot be everyday, reflecting the ebb and flow of desire over time. The same practices that are bed-shaking and orgasmic in marriage are flat-out hurtful prior to marriage. Such understandings of sex and marriage verge on the magical, transforming pain into pleasure. Our abstinence friend renders sex within marriage uniquely holy while considering it blasphemous anywhere else. Just as earlier generations of Christians may have panicked over eating and drinking at the Lord's Table unworthily, advocates of abstinence suggest that sex outside marriage defiles the holy and demeans the person. The problem with this view is that it attributes far too much to sex. Fraught with the holy, it becomes a means of salvation, transforming a kiss of frozen steel into ecstatic bliss. The good news of Christian faith, however, is not that sex saves, or that we save ourselves for another through (or by abstaining from) sex. The good news is that in Jesus Christ, God redeems us, body, soul, spirit, flesh. Sex is part of what God redeems, but is neither the chief object nor the fullest analogue of redemption. As Denise Carmody writes, "Nothing makes sex either uniquely holy or uniquely dirty."[7] Sex becomes holy not because in coitus (or in abstinence) are we uniquely connected to the *mysterium tremendum*, however much sexual manuals (Christian and otherwise) would suggest. Rather, sex becomes holy because in the flesh of Jesus Christ, God has redeemed us, body and soul. Seen in light of creation, sex is a means of procreation, pleasure, and communication, all of which God declares as good. Glimpsed incarnationally, sex becomes a part (one part, to be sure) of the grand story of redemption, how in our brokenness we are carried by grace back to where we belong, in the embrace of God. As we respond to that embrace in the embrace of another person, grace arrives upon grace.

Advocates of abstinence are not the only bearers of the myth of sexual holiness. The myth has even greater staying power in the parlance of many sexual liberationists who advocate the overturning of traditional sexual mores, such as monogamy. In the pursuit of the transcendent and the ecstatic, sex works best when it shakes free of any restraints that would channel desire. For too long, the holiness of sex has been wrapped in rigid confines; part of the spiritual quest is to unleash its holiness to be shared more widely. Ronald Long, a scholar of religion who has contributed much to a reevaluation of sexual ethics, has written an essay, "Toward a Phenomenology of Gay Sex," in which the language is both explicit and saturated with the holy. Unvarnished descriptions of sexual penetration occur side-by-side with liturgical language. Long describes the phenomenon of "tricking," or casual, noncommittal sex, as a way of gaining closeness to God. The first time one embarks on this path is a rite of initiation: "'The first time you suck dick, it really is like Holy Communion.'"[8] Tricking is, for him, interpersonal veneration, an act of worship. The holiness of sex is uncovered not in an intimacy that increases over time, but in a continual search for the new. Sex, for him, does not at its best settle into a pattern; were it to do so, holiness would be domesticated. Holiness, rather, is wild and reveals itself in an ever-widening array of sexual partners. He writes, "Good sex between intimates is difficult. . . . Sex between intimates must chart its course between the Scylla of a familiarity . . . and the Charybdis of trivialization. . . . Sex with a stranger is just plain 'hotter sex.' And gay couples will experiment with a variety of forms of open marriage— so much do they value hot sex and so rarely do they find relational sex hot."[9] Long's understanding of sexuality contains an imperative toward promiscuity, which he claims enriches far more lives than it desensitizes.[10]

The sexual pilgrim, in Long's world, is continually restless. As soon as a partner is found, one is already thinking about the next. In this version of the story, covenant and the unfolding of meaning over time are antithetical to sexual holiness. Hot sex with a stranger saves us, but it never ceases from roaming. In the end, this pilgrim is a rather lonely person, constantly on the road, ceaselessly on the prowl. Here is the "cad" of sociobiology or the liberated male of *Men's Health* writ large over society: a guy ultimately left on his own. Fulfillment can only be found in the new, but then again, fulfillment is never found, since desire, ipso facto, is restless. Despite its radical intentions, Long's understanding of sex, in the end, reverts to a rather hackneyed pattern that has proved as tiresome as it has unfulfilling. Though the language of Communion is invoked, this reference is merely a parody of Communion that God offers us in covenant. The ephemeral "communion-like" bliss of sex is exchanged for the gift of true communion that emerges over time with a beloved in the embrace of the Divine Lover. In the end, Long's vision of sexual pilgrimage attributes an awful lot to sex: Though few could be further from advocates of abstinence in terms of sexual ethics, Long shares with those advocates a rather plain assumption: sex is *sui generis* the holiest life gets on earth. Whereas the advocates of abstinence suggest that this uniqueness constitutes the reason why sex should be reserved, Long claims that this holiness needs to be disseminated as widely as possible. Both, however, freight sex with more holiness than it can carry by itself.

PIOUS MYTHS ABOUT SEX:
THE UNDER- AND OVER-ESTIMATION OF EROS

Throughout most of its history, the church has rarely been accused of harboring desire. That charge has typically been reserved for heretics and dissenters. One of the most effective ways to disparage an opponent has been to label him or her as one possessed of excessive desire, a libertine. Already in the New Testament we witness this tendency. Paul often wrote to combat those who stirred up desire, or turned desire in inappropriate directions. In the first chapter of his Letter to the Romans, a sweeping description of sin that winds up indicting all humanity (and not merely persons who partake in same-sex sexual practices, as some interpreters would claim), Paul singles out the disorientation of desire as it relates to sex: "For this reason God gave them up to degrading passions. Their women exchanged natural intercourse for unnatural, and in the same way also the men, giving up natural intercourse with women, were consumed with passion for one another" (Rom. 1:26–27). Living in Paul's wake, the church has typically suggested that desire must be channeled appropriately. We have been skeptical about desire, since it can be too easily twisted.

Our love for others, accordingly, must be glimpsed within appropriate bounds, lest it become contaminated by excessive desire. One of the reigning assumptions of modern Protestant theology is that disinterested love is superior to passionately interested love. Anyone can love a person in the particular; anyone can bind oneself in love to a beloved other; it is a more difficult and more excellent way to love humanity in general. The problem with love that seeks attachment, according to this perspective, is that it conceals the real motive beneath it: desire for the self and its fulfillment. In this vein, attachment to a partner is inferior to generalized love for humanity because the former seeks the gratification of the self while the other does not. The *locus classicus* for this sentiment, in modern theology at least, is Anders Nygren's *Agape and Eros*, which contrasts a selfless vision of Christian love with the eros of desire. The point of this work is to disentangle agape from its corruption in eros. In Nygren's words, "In Eros and Agape we have two conceptions which have originally nothing to do with one another; and . . . in the course of history they have none the less become so thoroughly bound up and interwoven with one another that it is hardly possible for us to speak of either without our thoughts being drawn to the other."[11] The Christian is called to love as God loves. Christian agape prohibits self-regard, but as William Madges notes in his assessment of Nygren, "since only God can love in a wholly other-regarding way, people love others without seeking personal benefit only to the extent that they are passive channels through whom God works."[12] We are called to love as God loves, but only fulfill that call as God acts through us. Nonetheless, this is a portrait of God devoid of desire. One wonders, in this portrayal, how to account for God's longing and lament, passionate involvement rather than disinterested sovereignty, as portrayed in the narratives of covenant that we explored in the previous chapter.

Even our love of God, when glimpsed through this lens, seems constrained by an attempt to control desire. Karl Barth, who was critical of Nygren at certain junctures, follows him in the main, particularly in his rejection of human love as an analogue to divine love or as a ladder by which we ascend to God. Eros, according to Barth, "will always be a grasping, taking, possessive love—self-love—and at some point it will always betray itself as such."[13] Glimpsed through this lens, the mystic who longs for union with God is also one who desires the fulfillment of the self; indeed, the latter desire invariably takes over, frequently leading the mystic to mistake momentary ecstasy for genuine communion with God. Throughout the *Dogmatics,* Barth is skeptical of mysticism and pietism, since they, in his view, tend to stress the experience of love over the divine beloved. In the end, this stress on experience leads in disastrous directions: "*Eros* is love which is wholly claim, wholly the desire to control, wholly the actual attempt to control, in relation to God. This is inevitable, seeing it is the love in which the one who loves and the object of love are one and the same, so that from first to last it is self-love."[14] Both Barth and Nygren are concerned with accounts of love that accentuate the human lover at the expense of the divine beloved. Their alternative accounts are to be applauded for how deeply they ground any instance of authentically human love in the God who first loves us (1 John 4:10–11). Yet at the same time these accounts compartmentalize eros in such a way that it has little bearing on the Christian life. Indeed, their work seems to suggest, somewhat oddly, that restlessness and longing are strangers to the journey of discipleship.

There is a much older motif in the Christian church, where the experience of desire for God (which can both nurture and afflict the self) is an indication not of selfishness, but of proper orientation to God. The Christian journey, in this motif, is marked by a constant desire to know God more clearly, love God more fully, and follow God more closely. Augustine falls in this tradition as he begins his *Confessions* with a note of desire: "The thought of you stirs him so deeply that he cannot be content unless he praises you, because you made us for yourself and our hearts find no peace until they rest in you."[15] Christian desire, thus construed, is instilled by God and always on the way toward God, for the rest that Augustine refers to is only reached at the end of our days. Nygren and Barth err in suggesting that eros is invariably selfish; glimpsed in the context of a desiring God, we are creatures made to desire God and find ultimate fulfillment and rest in God. One lie that modern piety has told us is that desire inevitably elevates the self; viewed rightly, desire intensifies our relationship with the divine because it comes from God. In this process of cultivating desire, our desire for one another is transformed from possession toward freedom.

The first pious myth to dethrone is that eros has no place in Christian life or is merely a way station on the road to sainthood to be superseded with a more disinterested kind of love. Christian love, according to the biographies of saints and mystics, is passionately interested. Indeed, their biographies reveal the opposite of the modern assumption: it is not more difficult, but easier, to love humanity (or God) in the abstract; the real test of love is to promise to stay with another for better or worse, richer or poorer, and, as the psalms of lament attest, the real test of our love of God is to keep loving an intensely personal God in spite of and in the midst of affliction that comes from God. Love is easy, in other words, until it takes a uniquely human face or the long history of covenant with God. The Christian life, thus viewed, is a life of eros as well as agape, of longing that fulfills self and other. As Karen Baker-Fletcher writes, "*eros* is the desire for union with the sacred."[16] Or, in the words of Wendy Farley, "Eros is the power of love in the form of desire."[17] Seen in this light, eros is no stranger to discipleship, but an intimate along the way, "the great seal on our souls, marking where we have been 'oned' with God in the instant of our creation."[18]

In response to the historical maligning of eros (at least in Christianity's modern period), several theologians have labored to recover the desire that frames the path of the Christian journey. They have rightly noted that neglect of eros—and at worst the blaming of eros for a host of ills—has led to further oppression of women. In the eyes of much of the theological tradition, eros is a peculiarly female predisposition, though all are capable of falling under its sway. This identification of women with eros, earth, and flesh (as opposed to agape, heaven, and spirit) simply re-inscribes the codes of patriarchy. Women become a source of (male) temptation toward what is inferior and are somehow, despite all claims to the contrary, to be blamed for distortions of Christian love.

Yet in resurrecting the erotic as a marker of Christian life, some of these attempts at reframing our understanding of love and desire have resulted in an overvaluation of eros that mimics the promises of our commercial age. The problem with some theologies of eros is that they are unattuned to its ambiguities—how eros on its own is not merely a force for good in the universe but can also be twisted by the commercial forces of our age. As much as these theologies should be applauded for their recovery of eros, they might also be critiqued for an uncritical celebration of eros. This section will only look at two such attempts by Rita Nakashima Brock and Christine Gudorf, though there are other studies that offer surveys of the relevant literature.[19] Again, this examination is not exhaustive; rather, it merely suggests some complications that have arisen in recent rediscoveries of eros for Christian life.

Rita Nakashima Brock's *Journeys by Heart* is a watershed book. A striking indictment of Christologies and theories of atonement that perpetuate violence, abusive family relationships, and the maintenance of patriarchy, Brock's work offers a constructive alternative to the sad tale of violence that infects the body of theological reflection. Instead of focusing on atonement as the payment for sin or as the selfless act that satisfies the claims of divine justice, Brock develops a thoroughly relational Christology that reframes power and love. Jesus' activity of exorcism and healing become paradigmatic instances of erotic power in action, building community and life in the face of suffering and death. The power of Jesus, witnessed in his earthly ministry, is the power that sustains life and relationship from his infancy to his resurrection. Brock dubs this power on behalf of life and relationship "erotic." For her, eros is primarily relational and only derivatively sexual: "Erotic power is the power of our primal interrelatedness. Erotic power, as it creates and connects hearts, involves the whole person in relationships of self-awareness, vulnerability, openness, and caring."[20] In her vision, in the beginning is relationship, and we participate in life as we are drawn in relationship to one another and the divine.

In contrast to Nygren and Barth, Brock celebrates the power of eros as it promotes attachment and engagement: "Unlike agape, which is often defined as a disinterested, or objective form of love, most exemplified in the dispassionate divine love, Eros connotes intimacy through the subjective engagement of the whole self in a relationship."[21] The Christian journey neither shuns passionate engagement nor mistakes such engagement for selfishness. The full development of the self occurs in relationship; we desire relationship for the sake of the other and for ourselves as we are drawn into God's fullness. Indeed, Barth misinterprets eros as that which seeks to control. Eros, in Brock's eyes, is that which resists the imposition of self upon others: "Erotic power, unlike control, domination, or authority (which we believe, self-deceptively, we can possess), cannot be fixed or clung to because it cannot be controlled, won, possessed, or created."[22] In eros, one neither controls others nor is given over to them as the object of control; rather, as God seeks us for relationship, we are made for relationship with one another. To be in relationship with another is to be fully human, to live from and for God.

Some have faulted Brock for lapsing into unacknowledged assumptions about gender, rendering women "more" relational than men.[23] I would add to this concern her relatively monolithic portrayal of relatedness. Relatedness, in her view, is conflated with eros, and is, as such, an unambiguous good. The problem with this view is that relatedness also amplifies our distortedness and sin. Eros is both a source of celebration and grounds for despair. In our age, eros takes on many divergent connotations, suggesting bonds of fidelity as well as pornographic film. Simply naming "good relatedness" as erotic, in my opinion, doesn't do justice to the ways in which eros becomes distorted and flawed. Brock would no doubt consider pornography and sexual abuse to be examples of the denial of the erotic, and so would I. But the scars caused by these distortions of sex and eros remain. Abuse and dehumanizing relationships often parade under the banner of eros. In the end, Brock's theology offers a much-needed celebration of eros, but it is not sufficiently attentive to how erotic relationships are twisted. A theology of eros must attend not only to the flourishing of relationships, but how relationships also give birth to violence and rupture, especially when one of the prime distortions of sexuality and eros in our time is the fusion of sex with violence. Just as agape can lead to acts of self-annihilation as well as human flourishing, eros can lead to violent self-assertion as well as the intensification of desire for others.

Brock's account of eros also suffers because it renders eros diffuse. Indeed, eros eludes definition throughout her book. It is the sheer fact of relatedness in some places, the promise of right relation in others, and a force on behalf of life in others. Surprisingly, what is missing from this account of eros is *desire*. More explicit attention to desire would address the concerns just mentioned, for desire, too, is ambiguous. The nub of the issue lies in the direction of desire: when oriented toward God and the other for her sake, desire promotes flourishing and stirs desire so that all might flourish, as desire intensifies without succumbing to sheer greed and possessiveness; when turned in upon itself, however, desire becomes insatiable because it is directed only at the self and its "fulfillment." Were Brock's account to attend to the dynamics of desire and how desire gets twisted, her reading of eros would also outline the peril of eros and not just the promise of its relatedness, which she so magnificently illustrates.

Another approach toward rehabilitating eros is offered in Christine Gudorf's

Body, Sex, and Pleasure. This creative and path-breaking volume focuses on pleasure rather than procreation as a touchstone for sexual ethics. Pleasure, in Gudorf's read, is a pre-moral good for the sake of human flourishing. Sex provides one expression of pleasure. In some ways, her approach to sexual ethics is utilitarian: "We need to limit as much as possible the pain to which we are prey, and to maximize our experience of body pleasure. While no one kind of body pleasure is necessary, we need to create so far as is possible a life and a lifestyle which satisfies human needs for pleasure."[24] Pleasure, in the end, is about nourishing the body: the body in whom the Son becomes incarnate, the body through which we relate to others. In this account, pleasure is not simply about gratifying the self, as the theological tradition has often suspected, but about the flourishing of the body of Christ. The Christian sacraments celebrate basic acts that care for the body—eating, drinking, touching, bathing—while they also celebrate God's presence and gift to us through the body. Sexual pleasure thus becomes an echo of the sacraments, one way in which we rise from the eucharistic table and respond to the gifts of God in the life of our bodies.

Though Gudorf does not dwell at length on eros and magnify the chords of desire that animate human sexuality, it is clear that her work holds a central place for sexuality in the human encounter with God. Erotic touch is not where we escape from God and lose ourselves in another, but where we meet God. "For many, the primary *experience* of divinity itself, as well as of God's intention for the reign of God, is sexual. There is in sex, as in the Eucharist, the potential for participating in divinity."[25] This is a lot to claim, that sex is the *primary* experience of divinity for many humans. My question here is not whether sex mediates the presence of God; any incarnational theology has to embrace the affirmation that God in Christ comes to us in and through the body. My question is, rather, whether one need elevate sex as the primary conduit of God's grace. In doing so, I fear we repeat the apotheosis of sex in U.S. culture that I surveyed earlier in this chapter. Whether we claim sex as salvific or as the primary point of encounter with God doesn't seem to matter much: in the end, both views demand more and more from sex.

Perhaps not surprisingly, this is part of Gudorf's argument. "The general direction in which humanity needs to move is toward more pleasurable, spiritually fulfilling, frequent sex, coupled with a reduction in world population."[26] Again, the only quibble I have is with the adjective "frequent." Who determines what is frequent or not? Does frequency help define what kind of sex is "good" or not? Gudorf's assumption tends toward "more is better," an attitude that already permeates popular culture, especially with regard to sex. According to this mindset, those who are not sexually active cannot be fulfilled, are "frigid," or incapable of relationship in the first place. The only difference here is that frequency is coupled with spiritual fulfillment, loading even more baggage onto a host of already high expectations about sex. Gudorf is right to find a prominent place for pleasure in our discussions of sexuality. Sex is not merely an instrumental means for propagating the species but is also about the experience of touching and being touched. Indeed, the latter experience gives meaning to the former, as we formed by God's touch and breath (Gen. 2:7). But her recovery of pleasure and eros mimics the sex saturation of contemporary society when it claims sex as a primary point of contact with the divine and urges frequency as a criterion of good sex.

Christian mystics, as we shall soon see, suggest something different: the pleasure of the body involves both immersion in pleasure and restraint from pleasure. Some of the enduring satisfaction in sexual life, in fact, emerges after long periods of abstinence. The long, slow journey of a couple together, when measured over time, entails intense and frequent physical pleasure as well as the discipline of restraint, whether because of illness, physical absence, or emotional misunderstanding. The intensity of physical and emotional bonding that can occur through sex is often not the result of frequency, but because of long periods of abstinence. Good sex, in the end, is not merely determined by how often a couple "does it." Indeed, sexuality can take its primary analogue not from a sex-saturated context that demands frequency, but from the journey of Christian discipleship—a path marked by the intense experience of communion as well as the dark night of the soul. Presence and absence mark the Christian journey; so, too, do they mark our sexual lives. Only as one glimpses the long story does the meaning of sex and eros come into full view: not in isolated acts, not in pious-sounding words about eros.

Pious words about sex that claim it as the pinnacle of human experience merely replicate the sex salvation of the contemporary age. As much as current work toward a theology of eros rehabilitates eros from its historical maligning, this work can also claim too much about eros: that it can save us. One caution against this temptation is issued by Stanley Grenz, who worries about equating sex with sacrament, whether in Catholic or Protestant circles. Sex, in his eyes, "is not a means of grace. Sexual intercourse is not a sacred act, understood in terms of being linked with the worship of God or with the reception of grace in some magical way. . . ."[27] One of the features that distinguished the religion of the Israelites from that of their Near Eastern neighbors was how the Israelites viewed sex as rather everyday and ordinary. Unlike the fertility cults and their celebrations of sacred sex, the place for sex for the people of Israel was not in the temple but in the home. As Christians grow out of this heritage, we celebrate sex not simply as a meeting place for God, but as a response to the God who loves us and encounters us in the flesh. Sexuality is sacred in its ordinariness, in its everyday-ness, as it is shared over the long haul with a beloved. In other words, Christian sexual pilgrims hie not to the sanctuary to celebrate sex, but seek the warmth of hearth and home, where a life together is built.[28] Sex responds to grace. Eros longs for another. As the path of Christian mysticism amply demonstrates, the journey toward God, sustained by desire, encounters the divine in the midst of the ordinary. Here we glimpse not the divinization of sex, but God's claim of sex and desire as God's own.

MYSTICAL STRAINS: CONSUMED BY DESIRE

What do Christian mystics teach us about sex? For much of the theological tradition, it was assumed rather little. Mystical experience and theology detail the extraordinary, the outer-body, the coming of the celestial as it replaces the terrestrial. Mystics, in much of the Christian imagination, are those who master carnal desires so that their desire for God may become more consuming. Glimpsed in this light, the mystics turn their attention from the mundane in order that God may be all in all. Only by leaving behind the ordinary, the fleshy, the earthy, are we able to participate in beatific communion. The mystics show us what a life beyond the flesh, beyond sex, might look like . . . or so we have thought.

But is another reading of the mystics plausible? I want to suggest that what makes mystical theology extraordinary is its attention to the ordinary. Mysticism doesn't flee the terrestrial; it embraces it because this earth, this flesh, these bodies, are named and claimed by God. Indeed, we encounter God through the terrestrial. Mysticism doesn't merely claim flesh and earth as the means of encounter, valuing them because they pave the way toward God; rather, mysticism blesses the ordinary in and of themselves, as objects of the divine love. In directing us toward the good, the beautiful, the beloved, the mystics teach us to celebrate the ordinary, and thus find the extraordinary in the midst of earthly life as it is oriented to the fulfillment of all things in Christ. The mystics also instruct us in the pathways of desire, to cultivate desire that it might intensify by becoming through grace part of God's desire. Our desire is derivative; we desire as a response to the God who desires us. God's desire begets more desire in us, not in becoming diffuse, spread in all directions, but in becoming more concentrated, focused on the beloved. Yet this desire does not turn upon itself, but frees us to love others. One paradox of mysticism is this: the more intensely we are drawn toward our Beloved, the more fully we love the world. All true desire, according to the mystics, finds its home in God who loves the world. This homecoming in God, moreover, does not neglect our earthly loves; since our desire is always on the way to God, nothing is "left behind" as God cultivates desire in us.

Pseudo-Dionysius, a fifth-century mystic, offers a vision of goodness attending to the ordinary as it is sustained by God. Goodness is synonymous with the life of God, radiating outward to envelop all that is. God, the fount of goodness, gives life to all things wherever they are. As objects of divine benevolence, all things seek fulfillment in God as God draws them toward Godself. "The Good returns all things to itself and gathers together whatever may be scattered, for it is the divine Source and unifier of the sum total of all things."[29] Some interpretations have compared this depiction of divine life with a bubbling fountain, that God's extension of goodness to all things is inevitable. As water in a fountain flows outward, the divine goodness seeks others automatically. The Pseudo-Dionysian God, thus read, is preeminently impersonal, enveloping all without the establishment of personal relationships born of desire. But such readings fail to hear the notes of desire in the text, the divine "longing," which is "Good seeking good for the sake of the Good."[30] God does not extend Godself automatically, but out of a longing that all might be recipients of divine goodness and thus participants in the Good.

For Pseudo-Dionysius, goodness is synonymous with beauty. Indeed, the reach of divine desire is so pervasive that all things participate in beauty: "Everything looks to the Beautiful and the Good as the cause of being, and there is nothing in the world without a share of the Beautiful and the Good."[31] A Pseudo-Dionysian account of beauty thus pays explicit attention to the ordinary. All things are beautiful as they are grounded in God. This aesthetic bent runs in direct opposition to contemporary U.S. attitudes about beauty and sex. Our age is saturated with persons who do not recognize their own beauty and are drawn to endless commercial promises of how they can make themselves more alluring. From cosmetics to undergarments that accentuate targeted body parts while minimizing others; from plastic surgery that tears and distorts the body in pursuit of elusive ideals to endless diet and exercise regimens, we are a people that refuses to see the beauty in ourselves, yet believes that the secret to beauty is within our reach, according to this regimen, this product, this procedure. Beauty, thus construed, is enticement to a more exciting (sexual) life where we become wanted by another based upon what he or she sees in conformity with someone else's ideal. Pseudo-Dionysius strikes another chord: all that is participates in beauty and reflects a glimmer of the divine Beauty. The path toward true beauty is not through regimen, but in the grounding of ordinary life, by God's grace, in divine life. God glimpses beauty where we do not and is making us more beautiful all the time as we journey toward the Beautiful. The end of beauty is not allurement, but relationship: you and me, all of creation, in God's very life. As we are drawn toward this life, our eyes are opened to the beauty of others—and ourselves—that was present all the while.

For Pseudo-Dionysius, beauty encompasses all in its reach: "All things must desire, must yearn for, must love, the Beautiful and the Good."[32] Divine beauty begets desire, and desire leads to beauty. For Pseudo-Dionysius we do not desire something that we will never possess or something that another creature possesses, but something that God graces us with from the very beginning. We are creatures who are beautiful and find that beauty here and now, wherever we may be. Unlike narratives of desire and beauty current in our time, Pseudo-Dionysius does not couch his aesthetic desire in narrow terms: you must not weigh too much; your face must be alluring and seductive; your partner must be of an opposite gender; your desire must conform to what others think is beautiful. Rather, the desire that Pseudo-Dionysius uncovers allows all to flourish in their God-given beauty: whatever promotes the flourishing of life is beautiful, and there may we find pleasure and delight.

For the mystics, goodness and beauty find their home in God. Desire is misdirected if it lodges somewhere else, apart from God. But here the words "apart from" hold special significance. Mystical theology, as I read it, does not foster the detachment of so-called earthy desires from God (the separation of the secular from the sacred), but gathers up the earthy within the desire for God, so that God becomes all in all. Desire is eschatological, but it also participates in its own fulfillment here and now as it is drawn by grace into God's very life. The sheerest delight occurs not when the mystic detaches him- or herself from all other things and finds God in isolation; delight happens when God subsumes all things in the midst of all things. The mystics thus encourage not an austere asceticism, the closing down of the sensual, but the enjoyment of the senses— even in supposed excess—as we are drawn toward God. Mysticism, in the end, is a spirituality of excess, but an excess born of restraint. Teresa of Avila, in *The Interior Castle*, offers a stirring portrait of delight in restrained excess: "It moves the soul to a delightful desire of enjoying Him, and thereby the soul is prepared to make intense acts of love and praise of our Lord."[33] Here the language is self-consciously sensual. As Teresa depicts the pilgrimage of the Christian toward fuller relationship with God in Christ, this desire for union finds an analogue in the act of making intense love. Teresa's language provides an alternative to quasi-religious suppression of the sensual and its unrestrained dissemination. She shows us that desire flourishes as it becomes focused, through the discipline of restraint, on the Beloved. Desire for God encompasses the sensual and sexual, so that they, too, might find their continual source of delight.

For Teresa, desire finds its resolution in love. "The important thing is not to think much but to love much."[34] We are made to love, to desire love, and to be loved. Yet this longing for love often emerges as pain. *The Interior Castle* also reads like an account of affliction for the Beloved's sake: the closer one journeys toward communion, the more one aches. As Teresa begins her account of the sixth dwelling place, the penultimate stage of the spiritual journey, she remarks "the soul is now wounded with love for its Spouse and strives for more opportunities to be alone and, in conformity with its state, to rid itself of everything that can be an obstacle to this solitude."[35] Here Teresa compares the longing for communion with Christ to the experience of aching for one's partner. Sexual intimacy, on this read, does not breed lazy familiarity and eventual boredom or neglect, but the intensity of a bodily ache, which can be experienced both at a distance and in physical proximity. The miracle of the Christian sexual journey is not that it constantly seeks the new once the familiar has "become known," but that the intimate is experienced even more achingly the more one comes to know him or her. Desire intensifies rather than subsides in this story. This does not mean that sexual desire is experienced in the same way after thirty years with a partner as it was in the beginning. Rather, it means that desire becomes more all-encompassing, less genitally focused so that lovers' entire bodies ache for each other. We desire to be known and desire to know our beloved more fully. The adventure of pilgrimage, and the adventure of sex, is that in both we are always on the way to fuller knowledge.

For Teresa the path of desire is urgent: "He makes [the soul] desire Him vehemently by certain delicate means the soul itself does not understand."[36]

But the urgency of the mystical path, flamed by desire, is not content with any means or any person. The mystics teach us to focus desire so that it burns more intensely. The flames of longing can only be fueled by the divine Lover, not by running off in multiple directions in an attempt to extinguish desire. God will not tolerate idols; neither will idols satisfy desire for very long. Desire is only satisfied—and intensified—the more we come to know God. This is why the mystics can speak of desire and discipline in the same breath: we think desire can be satisfied by multiple objects of desire, but in the end only God can sustain it. This disciplined focus on the Divine Beloved and Lover, moreover, leads not to the vanquishing of desire, but its growth and variegation. Human love, as it participates in the trajectory of desire borne by a God who desires us, follows this dynamic, albeit in an imperfect way. Sex, as one dimension of human love, also intensifies desire through discipline. The mistake of *Sex in the City* is that it claims to celebrate desire through rather indiscriminate bedroom (or boardroom or bathroom) encounters. Desire runs rampant, seeking satisfaction by anyone attractive enough. The long history of partnership and marriage, however, demonstrates something else: desire intensifies as a life is shared, as long as discipline and attention are also sustained. Without discipline, desire becomes diffuse and a parody of itself; without attention to one's partner, desire dissipates by taking the subject of desire for granted.

Some attempts to focus desire, however, lead to a suffocating enclosure of the couple against the world. The danger, in this sense, is to make one's partner, the covenant relationship, or the celebration of sex within that partnership, an end to the exclusion of other ends. The beloved person thus becomes "my world," as one places love for one's partner in opposition to the world. "You are my everything," claims song after song on the radio. Such heady sentiments and romanticism about love and marriage are not restricted to popular music and culture. They have perhaps their greatest staying power in conservative churches, where the rigid specification of marriage along "appropriate" gender lines fuels rhetoric about family values. Even marriage ceremonies themselves reflect this sentiment, and not only in conservative churches. Rather than proclaiming Christ as the center of marriage, most ceremonies offer a cloying celebration of the couple, complete with a unity candle, orchestrated by a competent wedding planner.[37] The mystics, however, teach us an alternative direction. The intensified focus of love on God does not leave the pilgrim (or a couple) alone with God against the world, but enables the pilgrim to love the world all the more. The caricature of mysticism is that it serves the self and its spiritual gratification; the reality is that most mystics are moved to greater empathy for the world because of their focused love of God. For Francis of Assisi, Bonaventure, and countless others, ecstatic vision of God resulted in aid to the oppressed, care for the earth, and the growth of love for all sisters and brothers. Likewise, marriage and partnerships flourish not when they enclose upon themselves, but when they are opened to the world. The miracle of the disciplined, singular focus of desire is that it also releases us for a fuller world of love. As we love one another in a partnership and intensify

desire in sex, we are also freed to love the world more fully. The entry of children
into a partnership is one physical reminder of how desire, focused intensely, can
draw one into greater love for others.

The climax of Teresa's vision of the Interior Castle is the union of the soul
with Christ the bridegroom in a wedding chamber. Here desire finds its frui-
tion, not because we have made it into the chamber on our own, but because
Christ invites us inside. In an earlier version of her masterpiece, she compares
this invitation to the consummation of marriage: "Between spiritual betrothal
and the spiritual marriage the difference is as great as that which exists between
two who are betrothed and between two who have consummated marriage."[38]
The goal of pilgrimage, the ecstasy of vision, the union of the pilgrim and Christ
are drenched with the imagery of sex. Bonaventure, in *The Tree of Life*, offers a
similar vision, though with a more cosmic emphasis: "When the face of the earth
has been renewed, . . . that holy city of Jerusalem . . . will be led into the palace
of the heavenly court and introduced into that sacred and secret bridal chamber
and will be united to that heavenly Lamb in so intense a covenant that bride and
groom will become one spirit."[39] Spiritual ecstasy and the renewal of heaven and
earth here go hand-in-hand. Eschatology, the end of all things, shapes a mystical
understanding of sex: the coming of the new city for its bridegroom begets an
intensity of desire, a sexual covenant that renews the face of the earth.

In the mystical journey, desire intensifies as it transforms the one who desires,
so that she or he becomes wholly occupied with love for the Divine. Pseudo-
Dionysius describes this transformation succinctly: "This divine yearning brings
ecstasy so that the lover belongs not to the self but to the beloved."[40] As God
yearns for us and we become participants in that yearning, desire finds its home
in God. In his claim that lovers belong not to themselves, Pseudo-Dionysius
rearticulates the gospel injunction that whoever finds their life must lose it
(Matt. 10:39). Typically, this saying is interpreted as a Christian command,
often undertaken begrudgingly: one must relinquish, give up the self and its pleasures—and in extreme cases obliterate the self—to find one's true life. In the sor-
did history of interpreting this text some persons have been enjoined into acts of
self-abnegation—women, slaves, and the economically disenfranchised—while
others have not. But the mystics expand the interpretation of this text, moving
from duty toward delight: losing the self is not experienced as self-flagellation,
but as becoming consumed by love and its pleasures. Ecstasy, not abnegation,
is the result of finding the true self, or rather being found in love by God. Sex,
too, is an analogue for this journey, for in sex one becomes quite physically and
pleasurably a part of the beloved, losing and finding oneself in the beloved as he
or she, too, is lost and is found.

Because desire finds a home in God, the effects of intense physical desire are
experienced not primarily in agitation and distraction, but in the calm and bliss
of God's embrace. Desire intensifies in discipline and focus, but this does not
mean that the pilgrim becomes drunk with desire. In this vision, God "produces
this delight with the greatest peace and quiet and sweetness in the very interior

part of ourselves."[41] Afterglow accompanies ecstasy, the peace that foreshadows the eschatological union of the person with God. The adventure of the Christian sexual pilgrim, likewise, is not endless restlessness or voraciousness. Instead, in desiring, we know that however intense the focus of desire, peace is offered as desire is fulfilled in the rest of our lover's arms. As we stoke the flames of desire, we also find rest in one another. Whereas the consumer narrative of sex fosters an indefatigable quest of doing it all night long, all the time (more, longer, and bigger are always better), Christian narratives juxtapose the pursuit of pleasure with its accompanying rest. Making love, in this regard, is not synonymous with physical acts that lead to orgasm, but in the broad scope of coming to know, coming to touch, coming to pleasure, coming into each other's arms, and falling asleep side-by-side. The intensification of desire also leads to the peace that passes all understanding, given by God. Augustine's restlessness, after all, finds its promised rest.

The mystics teach us that eros and agape are closer than Christians have often suspected. They instruct us not only that agape is the fulfillment of eros, as our longing for the beloved finds its promised rest in the love of God, but they also show us that eros, in some instances, is the fulfillment of agape. Contra Nygren and Barth, who seem to think that eros is primarily self-centered, eros can express the intensity of agape for another, for the beloved's sake. Paraphrasing Gregory of Nyssa, Sarah Coakley writes, "Eros is agape . . . 'stretched out in longing' toward the divine goal."[42] The most significant teaching, however, may be that eros and agape are dimensions of the same love, grounded in God's life, given to us that we might live more abundantly. Without agape, eros becomes obsessive; but without eros, agape risks a disinterested attempt at love altogether foreign to scriptural passion. Eros intensifies and personalizes agape, while agape leads eros to its promised rest.[43]

What, then, do the mystics teach us of desire? They teach us (1) that there is a home for all desire, and that home is found in a God who desires us; (2) that our desire for another is grounded in God's desire; (3) that earthy, sexual desire is not sublimated into a quest for the divine, but that sex is best understood and celebrated from the perspective of heaven or communion with God; and (4) that desire intensified is not diffuse and disseminate, but singular, focused on a beloved, and that this intensified desire also gives birth to a wider world of love. In this narrative, sex finds its place in God's embrace of the persons who covenant with one another, who, in turn, might love the world more fully.

DESIRE, GOD'S FULLNESS, AND THE AMBIGUITY OF EROS

Sebastian Moore has claimed that desire stems not from emptiness or neediness, but out of the fullness of being. "Desire is not an emptiness needing to be filled but a fullness needing to be in relation. Desire is love trying to happen."[44] The origin and home of this desire, accordingly, is the triune life: a communion of persons who desire one another in love. God's life and self-expression are the original desire in which there is no emptiness, no lack. But, as classical teaching on the Trinity has maintained, each person of the Trinity is revealed in and through the others. The persons are what they are *in relation* to one another; hence, the abstraction or separation of one person apart from the others eclipses the fullness of God's desire. Each person seeks relations and it is in and through their mutual relation that God's life is given for the world. This fullness of each person finds its expression in the desire of relationship, and we, as persons molded by this desire, are in the process of becoming desiring persons as we participate in God's desire. When Moore claims that desire stems not from lack, but from fullness, he indicates fullness expressed eschatologically in God's life for the world.

This understanding of fullness, however, runs counter to the economic assumptions of our time. When God gives out of desiring fullness, that fullness is not depleted. God's pleroma is not a finite reservoir that is further diminished as we gain life from it; rather, fullness leads to abundance and fulfillment, inexhaustibly, irresistibly. Desire grows as fullness grows in relationship, since we "can always become more trustful, more connected, which means more desirous."[45] Moore simply restates what the mystics have said all along: desire begets more desire, not because we are insatiable, but because there is always more room for growth in God's fullness. The desire for another person, in body and soul, is not a fallen departure from spiritual pilgrimage, but a covenantal response to the One who makes us full. How different these assumptions ring to consumer attitudes toward sex—witness any supermarket magazine rack—that claim that we must lure another into desiring us, because she or he is the very thing that we lack. The pathway of desire shown by Christian faith has little to do with dressing up for one's partner, or enticing another for ourselves, and more to do with a fullness found precisely because one is bound, body and soul, to another. Binding can increase desire and does not diminish it, because desire seeks relation, not possession.

But how are these assumptions connected to sex? Eugene Rogers offers a clear exposition:

> Human beings want to be wanted. It is the purpose of Christianity to teach human beings that God loves them. Then a Christian is first in a position to understand what sex is for. Sexual desire is a bodily manifestation of my desire to be wanted, which is finally satisfied only by God's desire for me. God does not leave my body out of God's desire for me. That would be Gnostic.[46]

Rogers goes on to say that sex does not provide a kind of knowledge of God only accessible to those in the throes of passion. The marital bed does not provide access to secrets only available to those who have sex. Instead, God makes use of the body either directly—in celibacy—or indirectly, when bodily desire causes "me to understand God's love through the human mediation of one affectional focus . . . in marriage."[47] Both are callings; both are responses to God's desire for us to serve the community; both employ the body's desires. What is more, we are not the ones who master desires or give them their proper focus. The mistake of the early church was to view celibacy as theologically superior to marriage, because the former indicated a vanquishing of desire; the mistake of the contemporary church—Protestant as well as Catholic—is to see marriage as functionally superior to celibacy, because the former ensures procreation and is the most "natural" channel of bodily desire. Instead, God is both the progenitor and the goal of desire, claiming, blessing, and expressing desire for us through the body. Glimpsed thusly, sex—as well as abstinence—are expressions of God's desire for us. But just as much can they be faulty expressions of our attempt to master, channel, or celebrate desire. The answer to what constitutes "good sex" or "good celibacy" in the end is not whether the former is a celebration of body and pleasure while the latter represents their control. Rather, it is whether each is directed to the fullness of God. Thanks be to God that there are many ways to communicate God's fullness: sex and celibacy are only two of them. But these two paths are in some ways indelible since they are imprinted upon the body. As Rowan Williams has written, "The whole story of creation, incarnation, and our incorporation into the fellowship of Christ's body tells us that God desires us, *as if we were God*, as if we were that unconditional response to God's giving that God's self makes in the life of the Trinity."[48] Sex, in the end, is fulfilling for the Christian body because God is the source of all fullness.

A problem with eros, however, is that we often attempt to make it the source of human fulfillment. This occurs particularly when we reduce eros to sex. One of the lies that our culture of consumer sexuality tells us is that more sex will make us happier. We have often fallen captive to the idea that sex generates happiness rather than expressing happiness. Whatever is experienced as empty or loss, thus read, can be filled by sex. Sexual dysfunction and even the ordinary process of aging, accordingly, are sure to bring unhappiness. Male sexuality seems particularly prone to this distortion in the social construction of sex. A cursory glance at mass media suggests that sex equals happiness for men. Hence, blurbs for Viagra and Cialis saturate ESPN, and the sports pages of most national newspapers urge men to "have the best sex of your life today," if they will only buy this product. Women's magazines are catching up to speed in this frantic race, as their covers promise the most fulfilling sex imaginable, with superlatives galore. Everything related to sex is over-the-top and the best ever. But the more we read and the more we buy in the name of sex that promises happiness, the more things stay the same. Buying into these products and these promises, in the end, does little to nurture and intensify desire and happiness, and more to dissipate it into an endless array of junk. Indeed, these promises and these products do little to sustain attentiveness on our beloved and more to turn our attention to the newest product or technique until the next one comes tomorrow.

Sex is not the cause of happiness or fulfillment; it is an expression of happiness and attention. We cannot make sex ultimately fulfilling by ourselves, no matter how many techniques we develop or drugs we take. God is the one who makes sex fulfilling, using and blessing it as an instrument of God's love, expressed through the body. The very thing that we make an idol, however, can become an expression of grace, by grace. How ultimately more fulfilling and liberating sex is once we stop heaping endless exaggerated expectations on it (sex will make me happy; tonight will be the best night ever; this technique will really get her or him going), and when we instead welcome sex as an expression of the happiness and peace found in grace, in the embrace of God mediated through one's lover. Sex makes one's own happiness turn its attention on another, body and soul. Its focus is not on the latest gizmo, but the beloved and touching the beloved.

The miracle of sex, in other words, is not that in sex we find God, but that God finds us in sex, just as God finds us wherever we are: "If I ascend to heaven, you are there; if I make my bed in Sheol, you are there" (Ps. 139:8). As Rogers writes, "It is entirely beyond the power of human beings to render sex *spiritually* significant; that expectation would be idolatrous. It is entirely in character for *God*, however, to do just that; to deny it would be to despair of God's ability to make good on the creation of the human being as body and spirit."[49] Here is the great lifting of all inordinate expectations of sex that are doomed to fail, no matter how often we read *Cosmopolitan* or *Maxim*. Sex alone will not make us free, but God's life and grace will. The freedom found in God then leads to a response of freedom in the sexual body. We do not divinize ourselves through sex, but God takes sex as a sign of our eschatological participation in the body of God's life. And for that, we have only God to thank.

The good news is that God redeems eros in its ambiguity. Along the pathways of grace, in the body of Christ, God claims eros for what it was meant to be all along: the love that longs and binds persons in community, intensely personal so that it gives life to the body. "Christian life stretches ahead (*epektasis*) into ever-greater love of God, because God expands desire for God as God fulfills it. . . . Desire does not press ahead into more of the same, but into what is better to desire."[50] If the pious myth about eros claims that it alone offers a privileged pathway to God, an incarnational theology says that eros, as experienced by human beings here and now, is continually tainted by its own embarrassment over embodiment or its own hubris that sex is the source of all fulfillment. But God redeems eros and makes it God's own, as God—through the body of Christ and by the power of the Spirit—makes us the recipients of God's longing, so that we might long, with one another, for God. We bear witness to that longing in our work and play, in sexual union and in celibacy, in activity and at rest. The good news is that our longing—however inadequate it is now—is transformed in the life of God, by the resurrection of Christ, so that our bodies become the vehicles of grace for which they were intended all along. To that risen body we now turn.

Chapter 3

Christ and Sex

The Resurrection of the Body

What does the resurrection have to do with sex? In many Christian traditions, resurrection is the quintessentially *sexless* affirmation: the resurrected body is a body beyond sex and the attractions of the flesh. According to this line of thought, the resurrection transforms our earthly desires so that sex is left behind. In the risen body, sexual difference remains, but sexual attraction disappears. "'For in the resurrection they neither marry nor are given in marriage, but are like angels in heaven,'" Jesus says (Matt. 22:30), leading many of his historical disciples to conclude that the resurrected body conquers the passions of our mortal coils. Sexual passion runs counter to God's passion for us, and it is in resurrection that we experience the disappearance of sexual desire. Thomas Aquinas represents one strand of this tradition when he considers sexual intercourse an expression of "the animal life" in humanity that vanishes in heaven: "Though there be difference of sex there will be no shame in seeing one another, since there will no lust to invite them to shameful deeds which are the cause of shame."[1] Most theologians across the ages have claimed an end of sex in the resurrection. But various heterodox groups have asserted the opposite. Contemporary Mormons, for example, offer a vision of the resurrection where marriage continues in

39

heaven. The marital couple experiences the fructification of their union in eternity and become deities of their own cosmos, procreating and endowing others with life. This other end of the theological spectrum suggests not the abolition of sex, but its ongoing intensification, where sex becomes a prime analogy for the life of the resurrected body.

Attention to scriptural narratives on the resurrection of the body reveal that the resurrection implies much about sex, but neither in its dismissal as something left behind at the end of time nor in its celebration as the chief representation of life eternal. As the resurrection directs all flesh toward God, it points not to the apotheosis of our own bodies, but God's claim upon the body as a means of God's self-communication. In the resurrected body, divine communion overcomes the violence that infects the body, thus creating healing amid sexual relationships: in holding fast and letting go, in fidelity and hospitality, in joy that conquers despair. Sex, as practiced by Christians shaped by the risen body, becomes an occasion for the creation of community and the extension of hospitality to the world. Yet, there is no such thing as "good sex" that accomplishes these aims by itself. Short of the eschaton, human sexuality remains ambiguous: where hospitality can degenerate into possessiveness and abuse, where the blessing of the body can become a curse. The church offers no haven for pure practices of good sex, but a community where God claims broken bodies for healing and transformation. Sex, in its ambiguity, is neither left behind in the resurrection nor consummated as the chief activity of heaven; rather, it is redeemed in the risen body of Christ who gives us new life.

SEX AND VIOLENCE

Sex in modernity is enveloped by violence. In the United States, one in six women will be sexually assaulted in her lifetime.[2] Media depictions of sex often dwell on the interconnections between sex and violence, whether in newspaper or Web stories that chronicle sex crimes, or cinematic portrayals of violent sexual acts. For many in the United States, the first experience of sex is also an experience of violence. Men's sexual initiation in U.S. society often fosters violence, from locker-room conversations that focus on "getting her" to a popular song that describes sex as "beating pussy up." Slang for sex also reveals violence in terms that connote pain rather than intimacy: drill, screw, nail, and other terms that communicate men's force imposed upon women. This language of violence does not disappear with adolescence. As women make homes with men, they also experience violence in the household. Statistically speaking, the home is the most dangerous place for women in this country, the place where they are most likely to experience sexual violence and even death at the hands of their partners. One-third of all women murdered each year are killed by their husbands or boyfriends.[3]

We live in violent times. More people worldwide lost their lives to war during the twentieth century than any other previous century: more than 127 million human beings, or at least 3,500 every day.[4] Children under the age of 18, moreover, often experience the brunt of the world's violence. In the United States, between 3.3 and 10 million children witness domestic violence in their homes, and often experience abuse at the hands of caregivers. Approximately ten children per day are killed in American streets and homes by gun violence, and 71 percent of sex crime victims in the United States are children.[5] Violence is in the air we breathe, on the TV and computer screens we gaze at, and in the language we speak.

Does sexual life simply replicate the patterns of violence in society at large? Perhaps it is no surprise that many cinematic portrayals of sex fuse violence and sexuality, with pornography being the most obvious example. The more hard-core films become, the more violence seems to be tolerated. Consider these words by a cameraman filming a recent "adult" movie, starring Justin Slayer (note the violence inherent in the stage name) and Melanie Crush (again, note the violence), having sex in multiple positions, many of which communicate her intense pain. He is active, she is passive. He moans in pleasure; she winces in pain. "I've learned that if you can get the chick into it, she'll do just about any damn thing. . . . Because they're made to get fucked like that. . . . Who can say they ain't made for that."[6] Here the sexual stage purveys violence as entertainment. The consequences of this fusion can be high: objectification of women (and men), acceptance of violence as inherent to any sexual relationship, and the disappearance of mutuality in sex. Consumer society, at times, seems unable to distinguish between pleasure and pain. When sadistic acts are purveyed for others' consumption—whether in print or on film—we can become increasingly inured to the violence that infects human life. Though some would say that *all* expressions of human sexuality convey violence, I remain unconvinced. Indeed, when we consider sex in light of resurrection, it intimates healing and communion rather than violence and pain.

RESURRECTION AND VIOLENCE

Jesus of Nazareth also lived in violent times, as a colonized person in one corner of an empire that expanded through military and economic conquest. If Jesus lived during a time of the heralded Pax Romana, behind that "peace" lurked the threat of military violence that Rome could unleash against troublemakers and agitators. Some of Jesus' fellow colonized persons advocated armed rebellion against the empire; others acquiesced to its power as collaborators. Jesus, however, embodies a different way. He bears on his body the marks of imperial power—a crown of thorns that wounds his head, a lance that pierces his side, a cross that breaks his body. The powers of a military machine put Jesus to death. In Jesus' day, crucifixion was the mark of imperial power, striking fear in the populace through this "ultimate" penalty. Those who resisted empire were put to death naked upon a cross, humiliating the resister, terrorizing those who observed the resister's death. Dogs would nibble the feet of those who hung dying, while carcasses were left for the dogs to devour.[7] As Jesus hangs on the cross, violence appears to have the final word, snuffing the life out of the Savior.

Christ's resurrection, however, points to a different way and a different power. God's response to imperial violence, like the response of Jesus' own life, does not perpetuate vengeance. Jesus submits to the world's violence in the crucifixion, expressing solidarity with all who experience violence, but reveals violence as ultimately empty in light of God's life-giving and renewing grace. The powers of the world kill Jesus, but God raises him to new life. Resurrection thus expresses the refusal to conform to the world's violence, by meeting the sword not with another sword, but with the power of a life-giving word that brings life out of death. Resurrection shows that the real power of the cosmos is not violence tooth and nail, but a God who gives life ever anew and offers possibilities for life's renewal in the midst of agony and suffering. Because Christ undergoes death on a cross, God is in solidarity with us, revealing that there is no place, no experience, where God is not with us. Because God raises Jesus from the dead, life—not violence—has the final word.

The book of Revelation depicts the cosmic dimension of a struggle between death and the life given in resurrection. Many have read Revelation as a preeminent justification of righteous violence. The familiar interpretation is this: countless martyrs die at the hands of the violent empire, Babylon (Rome). God conquers filthy Babylon in a holy war, where battles, blood, and the vindication of the righteous pepper each movement of the story. A more careful reading of Revelation, however, glimpses not battles at the center, but a slain lamb who bears the violence of empire upon his body. This lamb proves victorious not because of a more ruthless extension of violence, but through the power and truth of his word (Rev. 19:21). The culminating battle scenes do not take place on earth, but on the stage of heaven. Indeed, they are "not really battles at all" but symbolic depictions "of the cosmic significance of the resurrection of Jesus."[8]

Christ, the slain Lamb, does not assemble a righteous band to battle against threats posed by different others, but summons all creatures and saints from every people and tribe on earth to worship (Rev. 5:13, 21:22–26). The resurrected Christ has dipped his robe in blood and summons followers cloaked in linen, white and pure (19:13–14). Here, dipping one's robe in blood—a reference to the crucifixion and the forgiveness of sin—yields cleanness rather than bloodthirstiness. The slaughter of this innocent One does not result in cries of revenge against the perpetrators, but in the stopping of blood's flow, symbolized in white. Through the resurrection, those cleansed by the blood of the Lamb are not led out into battle against the wicked, but to worship, guided to the water of life, where every tear will be wiped from their eyes (21:3–6).

The book of Revelation, as it offers an extended reflection on the cosmic power of resurrection in the face of violence, also contains implicit and explicit sexual imagery. Though the book grants special status to men who have refrained from sexual relations (Rev. 14:4), it also is saturated with sex. Some of its imagery is horrific, as we have already seen in chapter 1. The text fixates on imagery of the whore of Babylon, locating all that is blasphemous and idolatrous upon the female body. This woman drinks the blood of the martyrs (17:6), commits fornication with the kings of the earth (v. 2), and gets burned and eaten (v. 16). She seduces and tempts, and ultimately pays for that with her own life. In movements akin to the most degrading pornography, men have their way with a woman and kill her in the end. Though the point of the text is to condemn those who persecute the church, the imagery fuses violence and sex in a toxic mix, all visited upon a female body. Here not only is a woman blamed for sin, she is killed for it.

This text of terror, however, is not the final sexual text of Revelation, for the book concludes with a marriage between Christ the bridegroom and the saints who are his bride. The last chapters of the book read like an anticipation of a wedding night: those who participate in resurrection life are promised intimate communion with their Lover, who is Christ. Yet this wedding, as we have already seen, makes all of the saints—male and female—brides. This is hardly a defense of "traditional marriage." It points to new communion—more intimate than sex, yet expressed in sexual imagery—made possible in the body of Christ. The Lamb who is slain comes to takes us as his lovers. In the end, sex is redeemed.

This tortuous weave of sex in Revelation displays the ambiguity of human life short of the eschaton. In its distorted form, sex gets fused with violence in a nightmare bacchanal; as God redeems the world, however, sex is incorporated into the divine life. The resurrection does not leave sex behind, but gives sex new life as it leaves violence behind.

RESURRECTION AND THE BODY

As Christ's risen body transforms the violence of the world, it recapitulates God's affirmation that all of creation—in its embodiment—is good (Gen. 1:31). But Christ's resurrection does more than restate this unambiguous affirmation by suggesting that human flesh is the eternal habitation of God's Holy One, the divine life given for the world. The preponderance of bodily imagery in Paul's letters suggests as much: together we make up the body of Christ and encounter the risen body in others as Christ meets us in them. Rarely in the theological tradition, however, has the church glimpsed this claim in its fullness. Perhaps some members of the body—our hands, our feet, our head—might be described as the hands, feet, and mind of Christ for the world. But all members of the body? Surely not. Medieval theologian St. Symeon is one of the few to include the *entire* body as God's path in Christ to humankind:

> We become members of Christ—and Christ becomes our members,
> Christ becomes my hand, Christ, my miserable foot,
> and I, unhappy one, am Christ's hand, Christ's foot!

> I move my hand, and my hand is the whole Christ
> since, do not forget it, God is indivisible in His divinity. . . .
> Now, well you recognized Christ in my finger,
> and in this organ . . . did you not shudder, or blush?
> But God was not ashamed to become like you
> and you, you are ashamed to be like Him?
> No, I am not ashamed to be like Him,
> but, when you said, like a shameful member,
> I feared that you were uttering a blasphemy.
> Well, you were wrong to fear, for there is nothing shameful,
> but they are the hidden members of Christ. . . .
> It is truly a marriage which takes place, ineffable and divine:
> God unites Himself with each one—yes, I repeat it,
> it is my delight—and each becomes one with the Master.
> If therefore, in your body, you have put on the total Christ,
> you will understand without blushing all that I am saying.[9]

Yet the blushing has continued unabated in the millennium since Symeon penned this hymn. The loins, the sexual body, are the place where we have not admitted Christ's presence. Surely, there is an area of our bodies that is "private," something that belongs to us rather than to God. But in the resurrection the body is a public matter, because in it we are given to God and to one another. As Christ claims our bodies as his own, no part of us remains forever hidden under loincloths.

Symeon remarks, however, that to affirm such statements is also to court the edges of blasphemy. Whereas some contemporary theologians claim the body, in itself, as revelatory,[10] Symeon specifies that the body is revelatory as Christ claims it as his own and as the human body points beyond itself to Christ. What reveals the presence of God in daily life is not the bare fact of our bodily needs and expressions—eating, drinking, breathing, touching—but the way in which these basic acts of the body point to the Risen Christ: in eating and drinking the Lord's Supper so that the bounty of creation is shared with all, in baths that symbolize our rebirth in Christ, in anointing that recalls Christ's healing touch, in lovemaking that expresses the grace of hospitality and trust.

The resurrection reminds us that our bodies are not husks to be discarded, obstacles along the path toward communion with God, but heralds of the renewal of all God-given flesh. As the Larger Catechism of the Westminster Confession puts it, "the selfsame bodies of the dead which are laid in the grave . . . shall be raised up by the power of Christ."[11] Faced with the glory and presence of God, we are whole human creatures. It is not as if some portions of us are made for communion and others not. Resurrection means, in Karl Rahner's language, "the termination and perfection of the *whole* man before God, which gives him 'eternal life.'"[12] Flesh does not simply groan for redemption, it is made for redemption.

Many of the church fathers that revisionist theology often views with suspicion have also claimed as much. For Origen, the vision of the eschaton includes not the erasure of bodily existence, but a state where "bodily nature will obtain that highest condition to which nothing more can be added."[13] The end of the body is its communion with God, from everlasting to everlasting. Communion occurs not because of any intrinsic property of the body—its capacity for self-reflection, its sexuality, its ability to touch and be touched—but because God assumes the body to communicate God's self to us nearly and intimately. If God's self-communication were dependent upon a particular quality of the body, then we fall invariably into the theological trap that some persons are capable of greater nearness to God than others. The church has stepped down this perilous path before, as if those who were most self-reflective, least (or most) expressive of sexual desire, or most free from physical deformity were somehow closer to God or more accurate bearers of the divine image. The good news, however, is that God draws near to all bodies in resurrection, redeeming the ways in which we communicate nearness to and with one another: with our words, with our touch, with our gestures, with our lovemaking. These ways of communicating, in themselves, are ambiguous. Touch that conveys intimacy, connection, care, and hospitality can be twisted to foster abuse, manipulation, and distance. When left to ourselves, longing for communion often degenerates into violence and separation. Yet in Christ's risen body, we are all invited to the home God makes for us in that body, in our bodies. Here humanity finds its fulfillment: in a risen body that seeks other bodies to participate in new life.

Sex is one way that human persons respond to this gift and promise of communion. The God who desires communion with all things creates persons who also desire communion with one another and God. Sexuality, at a basic level, is about communicative touch. Persons often express the desire to draw near to one another through touch. Whether in the handshake of a colleague, the touch of a friend's shoulder, or the embrace of a loved one, human persons touch and are touched. Each of these ordinary gestures strives to extend communion. They don't create communion *de novo*, but respond to the communion God is already creating among us. Sex extends the act of touching toward its intensification. Physically at least, there is no way to draw nearer to another human person than in sex, because in sex one makes room for another—quite physically, quite literally—within him- or herself. In sex, we accommodate a beloved and are accommodated by our beloved: in tongues, mouths, breasts, and loins. These ordinary members of the body—used also for speaking, nursing, eliminating waste—become gestures of a hospitality that God is continually creating among us in the risen body.

Sex communicates nearness. It cannot be reduced to nearness alone, for its dimensions are far wider. Sex also communicates desire, pleasure, happiness, and longing for future generations. But some degree of nearness is always communicated in sex, even when nearness is not intended. Nearness, after all, can also be an expression of betrayal as much as intimacy and care. Those nearest to us often give birth to the greatest joys in our lives, but are also capable of inflicting the most lasting wounds. If nearness is a prerequisite of communion, it does not guarantee communion, as the gospels remind us, for it is one of those nearest to Jesus who hands him over to the Roman authorities.

Sex can also represent a betrayal of nearness. In its most distorted forms, rape and sexual abuse, the same physical acts that communicate intimacy and fidelity degenerate into brutality. When the same physical acts can communicate such different meanings in different circumstances, Christian sexual ethics needs to account for criteria broader than what-body-part-belongs-where, to include personhood, power dynamics, and the well-being of the couple and the larger community. In the risen body, Christians take these broader considerations into account. As Christ's resurrection brings life out of death, his body (and ours) are not fundamentally ours, but God's own. Living in light of resurrection does not guarantee that our sexual lives will be absent of violence and possessiveness, but it will point to the healing that is present in the risen Christ, and the hope that "joy [may] conquer despair."[14]

THE AMBIGUITY OF SEX IN THE RISEN BODY

Scripture is keenly aware of sex's ambiguity. In the Hebrew Scriptures, the Israelites distinguish themselves from their neighbors by rejecting fertility cults and their rites that see sex and reproduction as uniquely holy and representative of divine life. Sex, in the Hebrew Bible, is rather ordinary, given to humanity, claimed and blessed by God. Thus sex can represent the bonds of covenant (in Song of Songs) as well as the betrayal of faithfulness (in Hosea). In the New Testament, sex's ordinariness occurs in the midst of eschatological expectation. Nearly every place where the New Testament refers to sexual behavior occurs in relation to the expectation of God's renewal of heaven and earth. The risen body, apparently, has a lot to do with sex.

In Romans, Paul argues, "if we have been united with him in a death like his, we will certainly be united with him in a resurrection like his" (Rom. 6:5). Participation in Christ's risen body does not merely await us at the end of days, but is a present reality as we consider ourselves dead to sin and alive to God in Christ (v. 11). We live out of resurrection in our bodies by grace. On one level, Paul is exhortative: "Do not let sin exercise dominion in your mortal bodies . . . but present yourselves to God as those who have been brought from death to life, and present your members as instruments of righteousness" (vv. 12–13). At another level, he is descriptive, because those alive in Christ are "not under law but under grace" (v. 14). For Paul, all members of the body partake of this new life, even when they don't display it fully. Herein lies sex's ambiguity: our bodies live out of the new reality of resurrection, but often do not express it. Here sex is no more uniquely privileged or disparaged than anything else in human life. Sex is neither the chief impediment to participation in the resurrection nor is it our chief hope for communion. Sex, like all else, longs for redemption, where the nearness communicated in sex is no longer twisted into an instrument that ruptures communion. This is part of what Paul means by describing creation's groans: "not only the creation, but we ourselves, who have the first fruits of the Spirit, groan inwardly while we wait for adoption, the redemption of our bodies" (8:23). Bodies long for the communion that only God can establish. When Paul exhorts the Romans to "present your bodies as a living sacrifice, holy and acceptable to God, which is your spiritual worship" (12:1), he does not simply appeal to ritual or sexual purity. Plenty of other religious traditions do that, reserving special places in the pantheon for those who abstain from sex or who engage in temple prostitution for the deity's sake.[15] He recognizes, rather, that our spiritual worship of God occurs in the body broken by sin, but graced by God. Short of the eschaton, there is no gesture of the body that is exempt from sin, yet the body communicates our worship of God and is even a sacrifice, indicating that our bodies are not simply our own.

In 1 Corinthians, Paul reiterates where our bodies belong. On the heels of the passage that is probably cited more than any other biblical text on debates over sexuality—his list of those who will not inherit the kingdom of God (1 Cor. 6:9–10)—Paul claims that "'the body is meant not for fornication but for the Lord, and the Lord for the body'" (v.13b). It is disappointing that the vice list—and the contested interpretations of that list—have summoned most of the church's attention over the past decades, since Paul's listing of vices—not only here, but elsewhere—gathers up all people, since all fall short of God's glory. His point in listing vices here is to show how they give the body over to something other than God: alcohol, greed, theft, as well as sexual licentiousness. In resurrection-life, which is the life of the church, our bodies do not belong to ourselves or to anything else that would possess them: "'Do you not know that your body is a temple of the Holy Spirit within you, which you have from God, and that you are not your own? For you were bought with a price; therefore glorify God in your body'" (v. 19). Here the doctrine of the resurrection shatters some myths about sexuality, both pious and secular. Whereas the modern secular myth of sex claims that because the body is my private property, I can do with it whatever I want, so long as it does not harm others; whereas the pious myth says that my body is so precious that I should not "give it away" in sex until I find the "one" person who will rightly possess it; Paul claims that our bodies belong *to God*. As we glorify God in our bodies we look to the well-being of others, not simply ourselves or the supposed well-being of a match made in heaven.

The resurrection gathers up all the ambiguities of bodily existence, all the ways we sin and fall short of God's glory, granting them new life as we participate in Christ's life for the world. The conclusion to 1 Corinthians echoes this theme again. As he describes eschatological hope of the resurrection of the dead, Paul emphasizes renewal and transformation: "What is sown is perishable, what is raised is imperishable. It is sown in dishonor, it is raised in glory. It is sown in weakness, it is raised in power" (15:42–43). The body is made for God and for participation in God's very life, not because of the purity codes we maintain, but because, in Christ, God makes our bodies temples of the Spirit.

New life in the risen body, as we participate in it now, is not characterized chiefly by ritual or sexual purity, whatever that would mean. Hope lies not in our ability to ascribe to designated codes of sexual behavior, but in Christ who redeems the long, joyous and painful, beautiful and ugly story of creation's longing for fulfillment. This is what Irenaeus meant by *recapitulation*, that salvation in Jesus Christ isn't merely a fix-it job, God's perfect balm for the scar of sin. Rather, in Jesus Christ, God takes, blesses, and transforms all the ambiguities of creaturely existence. In Christ nothing is left behind or forgotten, but all is transformed in God's own time. Eschatology, for Irenaeus, is not annihilation of the old or making something new out of nothing; rather, it is re-creation of all in and through Christ: "The Lord, therefore, recapitulating in Himself this day, underwent His sufferings upon the day preceding the Sabbath, that is, the sixth day of the creation, on which day man was created; thus granting him a second creation by means of his passion, which is that [creation] out of death."[16] What, then, does this have to do with sex? It means, despite our near obsessive quests to find perfect sexual fulfillment (witness a near-infinite amount of Internet spam and magazine advertisements), sex remains forever incomplete—and, in a sense, unfulfilled—this side of the eschaton. This becomes clear in any marriage or long-term partnership. The story of sex among couples reaches climactic highs of connection as well as lows of miscommunication. Sexual activity, too, ebbs and flows, with periods of abstinence and distance as well as rollicking passion. Only over the long, slow course of the relationship can patterns be discerned, and how sex is part of the wider circle of responses in light of God's gift of life. But, whatever the partnership, there is no such thing as "perfect" sex. Even—and perhaps especially—in marriage, the communicative nearness of sex can be twisted. But God in Christ redeems the ambiguity of sex, recapitulating the joyous and painful story of human life in response to God. Sex, by itself, is not redemptive; but by God's grace it becomes a celebration of grace.

SEXUAL ATTRACTION AND THE RISEN BODY

Many Christian understandings of the resurrection exclude sexual attraction: the new life of the body is a life beyond sex. In this line of thought, the Risen Christ, like the earthly Jesus, is devoid of sexual desire. Jesus and sex just do not seem to mix in most Christologies. Perhaps this is why literary depictions of Jesus' sexuality—whether the robustly straight Jesus of Nikos Kazantzakis's *The Last Temptation of Christ* or the gay Jesus of playwright Terrence McNally's *Corpus Christi*—attract immediate charges of heresy.[17] A closer reading of the Gospel narratives, however, yields surprising results. Particularly in the Gospel of John, but also in Mark's account of Jesus' arrest and resurrection, readers encounter a Jesus who arouses physical attraction among his disciples. Physical—and even sexual—attraction becomes a component of Christian discipleship in the passionate following of the one by whose passion we live.

I am leery here of a tendency among some schools of textual interpretation to find sex wherever one looks for it. In an era where mass media saturate the air-waves and web pages with sex, American consumer culture finds sex everywhere. The mere whisper of skin in a particular context can turn quickly to intercourse. In such an environment we can sometimes find sex in texts, or understand texts to be mainly about sex, to the exclusion of other themes. When Roland Boer, for example, discovers homoerotic themes in Moses' glimpse of God's backside, the inferences appear far-fetched: "I'm sure he's got a great, pert, upright butt, [Moses] asserts. But Yahweh remains seated, for now. . . ."[18] Even if we derive sexual meanings *from* particular biblical texts, I am not convinced that every text that invokes the back, or skin, is about sex. Sometimes a cigar is just a cigar. We may, in fact, grant sex inordinate importance—as if it were the chief determinant of our engagement with texts and the world—if we see it *everywhere*.

I am cautious, then, of over-sexualizing the Gospel stories, when sex seems somewhat remote from the texts themselves. Nevertheless, some vignettes in the Gospels speak of physical intimacy among Jesus and the disciples and have sustained innumerable communities of faith over the centuries, including medieval monastics and contemporary LGBT Christians. The disciples *are* attracted to Jesus, both in his earthly ministry and resurrection. One example of particularly intense attraction is the Fourth Gospel's Beloved Disciple, who dines next to Jesus during the Last Supper, outruns Peter on the way to the empty tomb, and recognizes the risen Christ while Peter is busy with fishing nets. His prominence also suggests physical closeness to Jesus, as he "was reclining next" to Jesus at the final meal (John 13:23). Lucas Cranach depicts this scene vividly in his altar piece in the Church of St. Marien, Wittenberg. Here the Beloved Disciple rests his head on Jesus' breast, almost burying his head in Jesus, while the teacher holds him close, in intimate terms typically reserved for a spouse. This physical intimacy abides in the crucifixion, as the disciple witnesses Jesus' death along with Jesus' mother and three other women. In some of Jesus' final words, he tells the disciple and his mother that they are now mother and son to one another (John 19:25–27). Here imagery of discipleship, marriage, family, and parenthood become fluid, so that the disciple who functions as a spouse to Jesus becomes the son of Mary, Jesus' mother, while Jesus is revealed in his humiliation as the Father of all. None of this, of course, is overtly sexual. I am not arguing for a sexual relationship between Jesus and the Beloved Disciple. But I am arguing for a nearness that intensifies as the Gospel of John unfolds: he alone among the disciples reclines next to Jesus, he alone of the disciples witnesses the crucifixion. This physicality between Jesus and this disciple is not incidental to the life of discipleship, but signifies a passion for nearness and erotic attraction that leads one to follow Jesus and is promised in the new life granted through him.

In Mark's Gospel, physical intimacy occurs with the appearance of an unnamed bystander who appears perplexingly at Jesus' arrest. After the disciples flee, a young man, "wearing nothing but a linen cloth" follows. Readers never learn his name or why he appears, but his near-nakedness is striking. Then, as soldiers grab hold of him, he leaves "the linen cloth and ran off naked" (Mark 14:51–52). After disappearing as suddenly as he appears, the reader encounters him again in Mark's brief narration of the empty tomb, where he is "dressed in a white robe," announcing that the risen Christ has gone on ahead of the two Marys and Salome to Galilee (16:5–7). Many interpretations of this young man's identity have surfaced across the generations: Is he an angel? A symbol for mystery cult initiation? Mark himself? But perhaps more important than his identity (which Mark chooses not to name) is his physical nearness to Jesus in Gethsemane and at the place where Jesus rose from the dead. Between the dark night of his first naked appearance and the early morning of his new clothes, readers glimpse a physical closeness between Jesus and this follower that suggests some degree of erotic attraction. The longing to stay near the risen Christ, as mystics from across the ages would attest, is akin to eros. Is this what we see in Mark's narration of Jesus and this young man? Perhaps. At the very least, the one who is naked is given new clothes, as he points to the One who desires us all.

In these Gospel narratives we glimpse what sex is for in the risen body. One of the time-honored understandings of sex, ecclesially and cross-culturally, is that sex is for procreation, the establishment of the next generation. But nowhere do the Gospels enjoin readers to procreate. In contrast to a focus on biological kin and preserving family bloodlines, the Gospels depict Jesus creating a new family ("'For whoever does the will of my Father in heaven is my brother and sister and mother'" [Matt. 12:50].) Physical nearness in the Gospels does not primarily serve to bolster ties of kin, but to glorify God. Eugene Rogers writes, "Sex before God is for sanctification, for God's catching us up into God's triune life. Sex is for procreation just as procreation promotes that end. The chief end of sex is not to make children of human beings, but to make children of God."[19] God is at work, in Christ, making a family out of all races of the earth, in a messianic banquet where Jew and Gentile, slave and free, male and female, clean and unclean, dine together. In the risen body, the procreative meaning of sex occurs within its sacramental meaning—the drawing together of women and men to be children of God, focused on a new family that constantly expands the old. In this new family, sex is not forgotten, but intensified as it participates in the life of the Risen Christ for the world. But in our attraction and desire for the risen Christ, he is also continually eluding our possessive grasp.

HOLDING FAST AND LETTING GO

One of the primary distortions of sex in the modern era—though by no means unique to it—is that sexual activity is a form of possession. In sex, we are told, we can possess another. The seemingly innocuous ways in which we talk about our partners—"my" spouse, "my" lover—can belie this attitude of possession. We are likely, moreover, to see infidelity as an affront to ourselves. The biblical commandment against coveting a neighbor's wife occur side-by-side with injunctions against coveting a neighbor's house, slave, ox, donkey, or "anything that belongs to your neighbor" (Exod. 20:17), leading readers to consider even adultery as an affront to male property rights. Though we are only recently emerging from patriarchal attitudes that treat women as the possession of a man (and in many instances, we haven't really emerged from them), similar attitudes of possessiveness are apparent in media portrayals of sex and courtship: "I've got to have her/him." "Take me away, I'm yours." Whether presented under the scourge of patriarchy, the syrupy sentimentality of Harlequin romance novels, or the supposed frankness of *Sex and the City*, the desire to "have" another to hold and keep is hard to shake loose. But it is, I would argue, antithetical to the ways in which sex appears in light of the resurrection. In the risen body, sex does not connote possession, but holding fast and letting go.

In the resurrection, we do not possess one another, but belong to Christ. In the new life, Christ possesses us, even as we attempt to hold fast to Christ. When the Risen Christ appears to his followers in the Gospels, he appears in a mix of holding and release, where disciples embrace and are warned not to embrace. In Matthew, after Jesus greets the two Marys who have just left the empty tomb, "they came to him, took hold of his feet, and worshiped him" (Matt. 28:9). Here, followers' first response to the surprising good news is to hold fast to the One by whose passion they live. In Luke, Jesus encourages his disciples to touch and hold him: "'Touch me and see; for a ghost does not have flesh and bones as you see that I have.' And when he had said this, he showed them his hands and his feet" (Luke 24:39–40). By holding fast to the Risen Lord, those who follow him are led to new life.

But holding fast alone will not suffice; discipleship cannot be reduced to clinging to Christ as a possession. In John, Jesus commands his followers *not* to touch. In his first appearance, to Mary Magdalene, Jesus warns, "'Do not hold on to me, because I have not yet ascended to the Father'" (John 20:17). The Risen One whom Mary wants to embrace, to have and to hold, eludes her grasp. The Risen Christ is not the disciples' property, but goes ahead of them in ascending to the Father.[20] But Jesus' command not to touch is not the final word of John's Gospel. Touch resurfaces in Jesus' appearance to Thomas, where it becomes the means by which Thomas comes to know the Risen One. Jesus here invites Thomas to touch him: "'Put your finger here and see my hands. Reach out your hand and put it in my side. Do not doubt but believe'" (John 20:27). The hole left in Jesus' side by the penetration of a spear is penetrated by Thomas in touch. In penetrating Jesus, Thomas comes to know and believe. The connotations, again, are rife with the physical and sexual. As Graham Ward interprets this scene, "Thomas touches the raw flesh of Jesus, placing his hand into the very wound that in John is symbolic of the vaginal opening through which the community of Christ's body is born (John 19:34). The disciples only see, they only behold. A far greater intimacy is granted to Thomas."[21] We, too, come to know Christ as he makes room for us and our bodies, within his risen flesh.

The resurrection narratives display the fluid nature of touch and letting go.

Disciples touch the risen body but cannot grasp it. Sex in the resurrection community—as a form of touch and being touched—is also characterized by this dynamic. Sex is not a form of possession, but one form of response to the God who touches us in Jesus Christ, where we reach out to one another, but also let go. We are creatures, in part, who are made to touch and be touched. Sex is a dimension of touch, but is not synonymous with it. Another distortion of our age is to reduce touch to sex. As Christine Gudorf writes, "If your sexual partner is virtually the only person allowed to touch you, and if all your emotional needs must be met in sex, you will soon experience every touch as sexual, and come to need a great deal of sex." Men are particularly prone to this distortion of touch, so that sex can become virtually their only way of being touched.[22] While sex is a dimension of touch in the life of the resurrection community, its purpose is not to create a unique possession for each one of us (whether in the form of a spouse or children), but in creating persons renewed by the touch of God in Christ.

Couples also learn of the connections between holding fast and letting go over the long haul of their covenants with one another, as they make love and as they pause from making love. Marriages, to state the obvious, are neither constituted nor authorized by sex. As partners share a history together, their common life is marked by periods of intense sexual attraction as well as periods of abstinence. The rhythm of holding fast and letting go show couples that they are not made for themselves alone, but for God and others. The effect of covenant in both Christian and Jewish traditions is this: exclusive commitment to one person—whether expressed sexually or otherwise—does not lead covenant partners to shut themselves from others, but to a renewed embrace of the world. God's particular covenant with Israel exists not for Israel's exclusive privilege, but as a herald for the world, so that the nations, too, might find a home with God; the coming of God in the flesh does not close the church to the world, but is an opening for the world's salvation; the election of God's people is not for their benefit, but for the sake of all nations. So, too, with sex in the body of Christ: when shared in covenant, the touch of sex can be a sign of God's grace for the world, renewed by the touch of Jesus Christ. This understanding of touch has little to do with gender. As I will claim in chapter four, in the body of Christ, gender, and the supposed "naturalness" of gender-complementarity, fades in light of the new things God is working in resurrection life. What is significant, in covenants of touch, is not whether a couple is same-sex or opposite-sex, but whether the touch shared in covenant is a school of holiness that opens them to the world of God's grace.

RESURRECTION BODIES, SEX, AND COMMUNITY

In the resurrection, the boundaries of bodies become permeable. In sex, as we make room for another within ourselves, our bodies, too, become permeable in response to what God has done for us in Christ. Sex, in this sense, does not prolong resurrection life as much as responds to the new life God has given us, as we become open to the community of faith.

Karl Rahner describes our bodies as "open systems" through which we participate in the world: "We must not get the impression in this connection that our body stops where our skin stops, as if we were a sack containing a number of different things, which clearly ceases to be what it is where its 'skin,' the sacking, stops. . . . In a certain sense . . . we are all living in one and the same body—the world."[23] In the resurrection, in the communion of saints, the body of each person, though distinct, bleeds into the bodies of others and into the world itself. The church's fulfillment is the participation of all persons in Christ's body. In this new life, we are who we are in and through one another so that it becomes increasingly difficult to say where "I" end and "you" begin. Boundaries blur in the risen body.

Much the same can be said about sex. When Genesis describes a man clinging to his wife as becoming "one flesh" (Gen. 2:24), the phrase is more than the author's poetic flourish. The phrase captures something intensely experiential about sex, whether expressed with tongues, hands, or genitals. In sex, it is hard to determine where one body begins and another ends, for pleasure and skin meld amid touch. But sex also blurs boundaries between bodies in other ways: as a means of reproduction, the act of sex also has the potential to open couples to new life. As a child emerges within a woman's womb, it, too, becomes difficult to point where the mother's body stops and the child's begins. The "one flesh" of biblical narratives, however, cannot be reduced to sexual intercourse or biological reproduction. In Genesis, the same phrase indicates broader ties of kinship and the creation of families. When Laban greets, embraces, and kisses his nephew Jacob, he exclaims, "Surely you are my bone and my flesh!" (Gen. 29:14). "One flesh," in this sense, expresses the bond of family.

At its most basic level, sex is a practice of hospitality. Christian understandings of reproduction, procreation, family, and sex are best considered within practices of hospitality. When the church reduces sex to a means of procreation, it risks natalism and ignores the ways in which sex can express promise, commitment, and the building of community. More broadly considered, sex is a practice of hospitality shared with one's beloved that can encourage couples to share other forms of hospitality with the world. Same-sex couples can participate in this dynamic of hospitality as much as opposite-sex couples. Indeed, same-sex couples might even be more aware than most opposite-sex couples of the connections between hospitality and sex: as LGBT partnerships increasingly encounter the inhospitality of wider society (particularly in Christian churches), they find hospitality in the covenants they establish with each other. The bonds of commitment and love shared in these partnerships, celebrated in part through sex, can empower LGBT persons not simply to survive in a hostile world, but to share the hospitality created within those covenants with others.

This understanding of sex as a bearer of hospitality counters another modern temptation: viewing sex as a chiefly private affair that isolates a couple on an island of romantic bliss. Whether captured in the imagery of a vacation on a tropical island, evoked in a bedchamber surrounded by candles, or conceived as an escape from rough-and-tumble everydayness, popular imagination often conceives sex as a practice that sets couples apart from the world: just you and me, nothing else; we'll lose ourselves in one another. Sex in the risen body, by contrast, has a different effect: it opens us to community ever anew. When parents of younger children make love, they often long for a place only to themselves, perhaps a place that captures some of the solitude and time in their lives before the children were born: where they do not have to close the bedroom door, where they do not have to worry about making noise or waiting until after the kids are asleep. Sometimes couples find that place away from home, and sometimes they find it at home: In the shared touch of lovemaking, a few steps away from children's bedrooms, lovers can be swept away, focused only on each other's skin, touch, voice, beauty, person, and the surging energy that draws them together once again. And, again, for a while, they may forget everything else. But in the midst of it all—and often this occurs in afterglow—lovers also feel intense connection: not just to each other, not just to their need to touch and be touched, but to those who surround their bedroom. Sex in the body of Christ is always surrounded by a community, if not physically present, then in the memory of the communion of saints. Parents who make love while children sleep down the hall can represent the interconnection of desire in the body of Christ. In that place, they learn anew what desire, community, and sex are for.

Chapter 4

Eschatology and Sex

Making All Things New

IDENTITY QUESTIONS: A STABLE SEXUAL SELF?

Who am I? In every generation, Christians have asked themselves this question. How is my identity connected to sex? Our (post) modern age seems to be asking this particular question with increasing frequency. Often, the answer to that question suggests a stable sexual self, so that we understand persons as gay or straight in ways that are as self-evident as being male or female. We are who we are at least in part because of our sexualities. In the Christian churches arguments surface over those gendered and sexual identities, often in ways that suggest that these identities are of paramount importance. Policies concerning whom to ordain and whom not to ordain, over what couples may marry and what couples may not marry, fixate on firmly established sexual categories. Sometimes in these debates it seems that sexual difference is the only difference that truly matters.

Christian eschatology, however, suggests otherwise. The answer to the question, "Who am I?" cannot be reduced to a question about gender and sex. Indeed, short of the eschaton, we can never fully answer the question, since we are persons on the way to communion, shaken and being transformed by God's grace. In this chapter I explore some Christian eschatological themes and how they relate to sex: how fixed identities become more fluid, how baptismal promises reorient our identities, and how eschatology points to play as a dimension of sexual life.

Most arguments about sex currently boiling in U.S. denominations involve the distinctions between hetero- and homosexuality and the consequences of those distinctions for marriage and ordination standards. Liberal arguments for the ordination of LGBT persons and same-sex marriage often rely on notions of a stable sexual self: some persons are by nature, by creation, attracted to persons of the same gender, a natural orientation that does not change. Conservative arguments often draw the opposite conclusion: because we are, by nature, oriented to persons of the opposite sex, homosexuality represents an aberration of nature, something that cannot be blessed by rites of ordination or marriage. Despite their differing conclusions, both appeal to a root assumption about the "nature" of human sexuality: one, a natural diversity of sexual orientations that are relatively stable and ought to be celebrated; the other, a natural "straightness" against which all other sexual identities are judged defective.

In most conservative understandings of sexual identity, sex is oriented to procreation, though it cannot be reduced to procreation, since it also exhibits other functions, such as maintaining a bond of fidelity between partners and intimating sacramental union.[1] Procreation, however, requires sexual difference, a difference that is written into the fabric of creation. Genesis 1 often appears as the foundational biblical narrative for this "natural" theology: "So God created humankind in his image, in the image of God he created them; male and female he created them" (1:27). God creates men and women as complements, so the story goes. Without the woman, man stands alone, a faint shadow of the divine image.

When faced with strictly defined patterns that do not fit "natural" heterosexuality, conservatives either tend to endorse a strictly defined toleration of LGBT persons or their rehabilitation as heterosexual. Recent Vatican pastoral documents are examples of the former tack. In a letter composed by Cardinal Joseph Ratzinger, the magisterium tacitly acknowledges same-sex attraction: "Although the particular inclination of the homosexual person is not a sin, it is a more or less strong tendency ordered toward an intrinsic moral evil; and thus the inclination itself must be seen as an objective disorder."[2] Though the "inclination" of homosexual persons is not a sin, acting upon these inclinations is immoral.[3] The dance here is delicate: same-sex orientation must be acknowledged, ministered to, and seen as part of the complex configuration of human life. Though it cannot be dismissed outright, it tends toward disorder. The only solution for those who experience same-sex attraction is chastity, code-speak for celibacy. The homosexual is not singled out for "curing," just singled out for celibacy. Though this approach is most notable among Roman Catholics, it is also the de facto position among most Protestant denominations in the United States, particularly with reference to ordination standards.

Other conservative understandings of homosexuality offer more radical solutions. Some evangelical and fundamentalist churches have well-publicized "therapeutic" programs for LGBT persons. They purport, with varying degrees of "success" to "cure" people of same-sex orientation. The Rev. Ted Haggard, after a scandalous series of liaisons with a male prostitute came to light in 2006, underwent such treatment, and describes himself now as someone who does not have same-sex attractions.[4] Here homosexuality is acknowledged as a reality, but only as a sin, both in orientation and act. Where sin appears, it needs to be extirpated. This understanding claims that human beings should *only* be straight. One size, in this understanding of sexuality, does fit all.

At the other end of the spectrum are liberal Christians who advocate the toleration and celebration of different sexual identities as different experiences of being sexual and faithful. Such accounts also appeal to Genesis creation narratives: "It is not good that the man should be alone; I will make him a helper as his partner" (Gen. 2:18). The fundamental meaning of such texts, in this view, is not biological complementarity, but human community. Sexual desire and attraction is simply one way we express community. John Shelby Spong has popularized this view in church and society:

> Homosexuality is not an orientation that is chosen but rather a reality that is given. . . . Homosexual orientation and the heterosexual orientation in and of themselves [are] neither good nor evil, but only . . . real and true. Both aspects of human sexuality [are] . . . natural. The recognition is growing that there is a majority orientation and a minority orientation and that both have roles in the enrichment of human life.[5]

For Spong, God creates diversity upon the earth, and sexual orientation is one dimension of that diversity. God makes us who we are, and we glorify God by expressing who we are. If the point of creaturehood is to worship and enjoy God forever, our sexuality cannot remain on the shelf, but must be integrated into our entire story of faith. To welcome LGBT persons as they are is to celebrate the diversity of God's creation.

Most of these liberal accounts, like their conservative counterparts, continue to traffic in fixed sexual identities. God makes us gay *or* straight, and perhaps bisexual or transgender as well. The chief commandment here is to be true to oneself. In an insightful book, Miguel De La Torre represents this trend. In provocative reinterpretations of texts that have traditionally been used to condemn homosexuality, he makes the following note on Romans 1:26–27: "In his reference to sexuality, Paul is speaking about heterosexual men who have forsaken 'natural intercourse' to be 'consumed with passion for each other.' Basically, his theme is that it is wrong to change one's nature. Today we can say that it is wrong to change one's orientation."[6] To celebrate sexual difference is to acknowledge that our identities are God-given. Our task in living holy sexual lives is to determine whether we are gay or straight and to live in faithfulness to that calling as we find another to love.

Despite their wide differences in terms of understanding human sexuality, many conservative and liberal approaches share a common notion of relatively

fixed sexual identities. What conservatives construe as problematic sexual identity, liberals cite as cause for celebration. But the identities are firmly in place.
We become who we are most fully in intimate communion with another person,
a communion that involves the mingling of flesh and body in sex. Whatever the
case, however, we should not betray our nature. On this, both conservatives and
liberals agree.

One potential shortcoming of this approach to a fixed sexual identity is that
it may encourage an over-identification with others, a longing for union that
can *only* be satisfied through sexual union. Barbara Blodgett comments wisely on
this tendency, to which adolescent girls may be particularly prone. In a society
that tends to value girls primarily for the spouses and mothers that they might
become, Blodgett warns that our discourse of yielding to others "needs to be
balanced by a discourse that affirms *not* always yielding to others. . . . For one
partner to believe that she is 'nobody' without the other is dangerous in a sexual
context because such a belief makes her vulnerable to tolerating abuse."[7] We
can glorify sexual relationships so much, in other words, that the self disappears
in relation.

The most problematic implication of a fixed sexual self, however, is that
it seems immune to the continuous remaking of self that is part of Christian
eschatology. Who we are, understood eschatologically, is not a fixed thing. The
human person is always *on the way* to fulfillment, as God draws us toward God's
very self in grace. The fundamental truth of Christian life is not a stable series of
markers of personhood, but the instability of all categories in light of grace. The
customary categories of "gay" and "straight," helpful as they are for widening the
welcome of the church, may in the end be somewhat problematic.[8] This is not to
say that customary categories are meaningless or suspect. But when emphasized
as the core to one's identity, they may avoid the more pressing question of living
out one's identity in community with others. As Laurel Schneider puts it, "The
choice at hand, it seems to me, is far more deeply a *set* of choices that has more
to do with *how* we live our lives as gay, lesbian, bisexual, straight, and less to do
with whether we *are* lesbian, gay, bisexual, or straight."[9]

GENDER TROUBLING: ON THE WAY TO GLORY

The trajectory of Christian life evokes pilgrimage more often than a permanent
home, a journey rather than an arrival, transformation rather than stasis. Augustine claimed that one truth of our lives was that "our hearts find no peace until
they rest" in God, or as another translation has put it, "we are restless until we rest
in God."[10] Human persons are made for communion with God and one another.
Christian faith offers hope for this communion but also recognizes the brokenness and incompleteness of our relations. Each of our relationships is marred
by sin, fractured in ways that we cannot heal on our own. Thus, Christian faith
recognizes an incompleteness to the human person—not because he or she lacks

a partner or spouse—but because our relationships with God and one another are not fully redeemed. But, as we are reformed by God's grace throughout our earthly days, we become fitted for communion with God and one another. The process may be slow and painful, sudden and joyful, but it remains unfinished until the end of days. Because God is continually reshaping us, our identity is not fixed. We both participate in communion and are always on the way to communion. The Christian person, in other words, is an eschatological person, whose identity will be fully realized in the glory of God's triune life.

It is fitting that the communion that Christian faith envisions often gets symbolized in the meeting of two bodies in sex and in marriage. The Song of Songs, as we have seen, offers both an extended celebration of sexual love and a symbol of the covenant between God and Israel. Christians also see in this text a celebration of the love between God and the church. The book of Revelation contains similar imagery: "And I saw the holy city, the new Jerusalem, coming down out of heaven from God, prepared as a bride adorned for her husband" (Rev. 21:2). The communion that Christian faith anticipates is akin to a marriage where each of us becomes a bride to Christ. God takes our bodies as God's beloved, a promise realized now and at the end of days. Mechthild of Magdeburg describes the longing of our souls for God (and God's desire for us) in decidedly erotic terms:

> Then the bride of all delights goes to the Fairest of lovers in the secret chamber of the invisible Godhead. There she finds the bed and the abode of love prepared by God in a manner beyond what is human. Our Lord speaks:
>
> "Stay, Lady Soul."
> "What do you bid me, Lord?"
> "Take off your clothes."
> "Lord, what will happen to me then?"
> "Lady Soul, you are so utterly formed to my nature
> That not the slightest thing can be between you and me . . .
> These are your noble longing and your boundless desire.
> These I shall fulfill forever
> With my limitless lavishness."
> "Lord, now I am a naked soul
> And you in yourself are a well-adorned God. . . ."
> Then a blessed stillness
> That both desire comes over them.
> He surrenders himself to her,
> And she surrenders herself to him.
> What happens to her then—she knows—
> And that is fine with me.[11]

Here sex is not incidental to the communion Christians long for; sex expresses some of the longing of Christians in pilgrimage, as they are re-formed by grace. But our sexual identities here are also transformed: we all become, in a queer twist, brides of Christ.

This brief survey of eschatological themes has already suggested how Christian eschatology shakes up gender. If the marriage that Christians anticipate renders all brides, then it suggests that our gendered identities—particularly our "paired" identities—are not permanent. Theological conservatives often claim a centrality for gender, family, and marriage that is rather foreign to the New Testament. Despite the security and meaning that these realities give for earthly life, they tremble in the face of divine grace. Much of Paul's correspondence, in this vein, addresses the continual renegotiation of identity. Reflecting on the purpose of the law, Paul embeds within his discussion a gloss on baptism and how it transforms our customary identities: "As many of you as were baptized into Christ have clothed yourself with Christ. There is no longer Jew or Greek, there is no longer slave or free, there is no longer male and female; for all of you are one in Christ Jesus" (Gal. 3:27–28). One of the ways that we make sense of gender in modernity is via complementarity: Genesis 1, for many conservatives, becomes a proof text for the ways that men and women belong together. But Galatians here stands that reading of Genesis on its head. Note how the NRSV renders the translation more accurate, unlike the RSV's "there is neither male nor female," since the Greek text reads *kai* (and) instead of *oude* (or). What is questioned here is not simply our status as men and women, but the way in which men and women get paired. Stacy Johnson writes:

> In Galatians 3:28, it is not just one's status as male *or* female that is declared irrelevant for one's identity in Jesus Christ; it is also the foundational reality of gender itself, the pairing of male *and* female, that has no ultimate hold on the new community seeking to live out the gospel. Invoking "gender complementarity" or even "gender identity" as a fundamental basis for drawing ethical distinctions of status or worth within the body of Christ has no support in the gospel according to Galatians 3:28.[12]

This does not mean that the ties we make between persons—whether in marriage or other covenant form—are meaningless or disposable. It does suggest, however, that our tendency to pin identity to such pairings is ultimately futile. The final truth of life is not that we belong to our partners, but that we belong to Christ. The natural foundation of gender complementarity turns out to be not a foundation at all. It too, shall pass, as God makes all things new. In fact, it has already passed in the new life given in Christ.

Paul's reflections in Galatians make moot the divisions and distinctions that human beings are prone to make permanent. By claiming that Jew/Greek, slave/free, and male/female no longer hold sway, Paul questions ethnic, cultural and religious identity, legal and economic status, as well as sex and gender. "What the biblical witness is saying here is remarkable: the most basic features of our created human existence—features that are used constantly to define a person's place and significance in the religious, social and political order—no longer define the identity of people who are in Christ."[13] Hardly a defense of traditional marriage or fixed gender identity, Paul's words here shake the foundations of gendered politics and sexual relations. The community of Christ is a community of eschatological expectation, where the bonds that are permanent are not borne by sex or gender, but by Christ's body and blood, given anew in the waters of baptism.

Paul's location of the horizon of hope in a community that is no longer defined by marriage, class, or ethnicity does not mean that difference is obliterated. Rather, it means that the differences of people are no longer obstacles to the communion that God gives in Christ. He does not claim that male, female, Jewish, and Greek identities disappear; he claims, rather, that all these identities are impermanent in relation to the new identity given all in Christ. Notions of complementarity, strangely enough, tend to leave men and women in prisons of difference, akin to the pop-psychology title, *Men Are from Mars, Women Are from Venus*.[14] Difference is fundamental to communion among human persons and between human persons and God, but the ways that we paint difference, particularly sexual difference, do not provide the ultimate truth of our lives. Jesus' own fellowship illustrates the instability of marital and gendered identity. Tradition holds that Jesus was unmarried, a relative oddity for his time in a culture that placed a high premium on clan and familial legacy. We hear relatively little about his followers' families in the Gospels other than the stunning admission that most of them abandoned whatever they were doing to follow him. Furthermore, he gathers around himself men and women in seemingly indiscriminate fashion, allowing a woman to kiss and bathe his feet with her tears and dry them with her hair (Luke 7:38), forming close relationships—but not a marriage—with women who remain with him until his last gasp on the cross. Jesus' own community plays with gender and marital status: what makes his ministry most scandalous is its indiscriminate welcome of married and single persons, men and women, prominent and despised people.

But, still, doesn't biological sex make a fundamental difference? The first question we typically ask when a baby is born is not whether the mother is okay or whether the baby is healthy, but, "Is it a boy or a girl?" From that moment forward, layers of expectation and societal convention begin to pile up. Boys like trucks; girls like dolls. As a parent of both a boy and a girl, I know the weight of these conventions and see them enacted upon the bodies of our children. How much of our son's preference for "Star Wars" is attributable to nature and how much to nurture is a mystery that I will never unravel. Our children are different from each another and much of that difference relates to gender. But the binary of male/female, in many cases, is unable to address the complexity of sex and gender as it is lived. Many children are born who do not fit into the biological parameters of sex and gender that Western cultures view as permanent. Some children are born with genitalia of both sexes (intersex), others display secondary physical characteristics that seem out of sync with their chromosomal make-up. Even at the anatomical level, sexual identity is far from fixed. In U.S. culture, when children are born in this way, the most common "solution" is surgery to remove one sexual part, to make sexual identity neater and more readily classifiable. But ethicist Margaret Farley wonders whether a condition that we render "pathologi-cal" is really pathological: "If a culture were less preoccupied with male/female sexual division and with boy/girl man/woman gender differentiation, would the medical imperative regarding intersexed persons remain as it is?"[15]

Few are ever completely comfortable with the roles and patterns assigned by gender. The eschatological hope of a transformed identity in God's grace finds an analogue in the experience of people who rub against the strain of gendered expectations. Straight couples who co-parent often experience this strain. When men become the primary caregivers of infants in acts of feeding, bathing, and diapering and when women provide the bulk of a family's income, the question of who "nurtures" and who "provides" proves as much a constructed reality as it is built in to biological inclinations. Nearly all of us, from time to time, chafe against the expectations of gender.

Here the work of queer theorist Judith Butler may provide a resource for the Christian reexamination of sex and gender. For Butler, gender—both the societal construction of gender and the biology of sex—is never fully given, but constructed over time through performance and repetition. We become the gender we "are" through repeated enaction of roles and tropes, grasping for an identity, but never really arriving at one. For Butler, "gender is a complex-ity whose totality is permanently deferred, never fully what it is at any given juncture in time."[16] Later in this same work, she writes, "Gender ought not to be construed as a stable identity or locus of agency from which various acts follow; rather, gender is an identity tenuously constituted in time, instituted in an exterior space through a *stylized repetition of acts*."[17] Gender is, for Butler, a "doing" more than a being. "There is no gender identity behind the expressions of gender; that identity is performatively constituted by the very 'expressions' that are said to be its results."[18] Throughout *Gender Trouble* the reader can sense longing for a stable sense of self grounded in gender. But those longings, for Butler, are ultimately misguided, because the stability one seeks in gender never arrives. Against the horizon of human experience, gendered identity crumbles, however much we enact repeated performances of male and female, hetero- and homo-sexuality.

This is not to say that gendered or sexual identity is meaningless. Butler writes, "To claim that gender is constructed is not to assert its illusoriness or artificiality."[19] Our identities, however unstable, affect nearly everything in our experience of the world: men and women *do* have different experiences in the workplace, garden, home, and marketplace. Gender and sexual orientation mat-ter as we encounter and interpret the world, but we also improvise those identi-ties as we move along in the world, with some aspects of our identity enforced by society while other aspects we employ ourselves. How we dress, how we are paid—or not paid—for our work: all are conditioned, in part, by gender and sex. As we improvise, we recognize that others neither impose the patterns of gender for us nor do we make them up wholly for ourselves.

ANDROGYNY AND GENDER
IN CHRISTIAN ESCHATOLOGY

Several currents in the early church also encouraged Christians to play around with gender, or at least imagine gender differently. As God gathers persons for communion, many of the church Fathers pointed to a transformation of gender and sex. Two examples from the early church will suffice here: Gregory of Nyssa, who envisions eschatological existence androgynously, and Augustine, who envisions the abiding significance of gender, albeit in a transformed state. Both, in different ways, envision a glorified existence beyond genital sex.

Gregory ties his account of our androgynous fulfillment to his understanding of creation. For him, gendered differentiation results from the fall. The emergence of gender, in this view, occurs in two steps: first, God creates humanity androgynously in a nonsexed angelic mode; second, humanity enters into physical existence that results in sexual differentiation, a "fall" into physicality, so to speak. Gender as we currently know and experience it is *not* what God intends for eternity. The process of redemption reverses this "fall" into gender. At the resurrection this reversal begins as our bodies lose their sexual differentiation. Though in one sense, for Gregory, we all become female in relation to God, or in Verna Harrison's words, "impregnated with life from God and giving birth to various forms of goodness,"[20] androgyny eventually reigns in the eschaton. Gregory thus plays with gender on the entire stage of salvation history, in the end pointing to a new existence beyond gender, beyond sex. In the resurrection, biological reproduction will disappear, but all will be endowed with procreative power:

> The generative power of nature will be transferred to that work of giving birth in which the great Isaiah participated, saying, From your fear, Lord, we came to be with child and were in labor and gave birth; we were pregnant with the spirit of your salvation on the earth [Isa. 26:17–18 LXX]. For if such an offspring is good and childbearing becomes a cause of salvation [1 Tim. 2:15], as the apostle says, one will never stop bringing forth the spirit of salvation, when once through such a birth the multiplication of good things has been brought forth for one.[21]

Augustine, by contrast, claims that we are created as male and female from the start, and are destined to be male and female for eternity. In his *City of God,* Augustine claims that sexual difference is a procreative blessing: "the difference in sex is quite evident in the physical structure [of man and woman]. . . . It would be a manifest absurdity to deny the fact that male and female were created for the purpose of begetting children, so as to increase and multiply and fill the earth. . . . It is certain that at the beginning male and female were constituted just as two human beings of different sex are now. . . ."[22] Though sexual difference is a procreative good, sex also represents a loss of control, particularly for men. Male erections occur spontaneously, aroused by lust, and not as the result of the human will. Current male sexual experience is a result of the fall, where disordered desire runs counter to the willful, dispassionate sex that Adam and Eve had in Eden.[23] The road to redemption, in some regards, reverses the "problems" of sex and gender that have arisen because of the fall. In the eschaton, we will remain male and female, but our bodies will be ruled by grace and reason, not lustful longings. Though male and female abide in the eschaton, men and women do not have sex, but participate in blessed communion eternally, as persons devoid of lustful desire.

Augustine and Gregory pose different answers to questions of gender and sex. Though both point to an eschatological existence *beyond* sex, Gregory envisions an existence beyond gender, while Augustine claims gender as an abiding eschatological reality. In the centuries that have unfolded since their writings, Christians have reacted in various ways. Generally speaking, the more mainstream groups within the church have held to Augustine's view, where gender abides in some way; others on the margins have opted for Gregory's, playing with gender and subverting it in subtle ways in light of God's grace. Both visions, however, come with costs, particularly for women: "Whereas Gregory stresses the potential equality of women at the price of their sexlessness . . . , Augustine wavers a bit before subordinating women to a place of controlled dependent orderliness."[24] The marginalization of women's sexual experience continues in these eschatological worldviews, where women either lose their sex altogether or submit to a rational order necessary because of a male loss of control in sex.

Does Christian faith, in the end, envision a life beyond gender and sex? I would argue that both Gregory and Augustine claim a bit too much in their respective visions of eschatological existence. Gregory rightly recognizes that gender is unstable in light of divine grace, but his longing for an androgynous humanoid realized in the eschaton suggests that biological differences have no part in eternal communion. This places a significant gulf between the human person *as created* and the human person *as redeemed*, and veers conspicuously close to a theology that redeems part of the person instead of the whole. Augustine, at least, keeps some form of difference intact, but by claiming that sexual desire has no place in heaven, he verges close to the understanding that desire is not redeemed. Why would sex be left behind? It is tempting, as Jo Ind reminds us, "to make an idol out of sex, especially as sex can, at is best, bring us the nearest many of us get to heaven in this lifetime."[25] But banishing sex from heaven is as problematic as claiming it to be heaven, for it removes the ambiguities of sexual life from their fulfillment. Later in this chapter, I will suggest a redemption of sex that does not erase sexual desire. This is something different from either Augustine or Gregory, as well as something different from the suggestion that sexual desire continues to run its current course in heaven.

In short, I want to claim a bit less than either Augustine or Gregory. Christian hope envisions the transformation of all life, all bodies, but we don't know exactly what this will mean for our gendered and sexual bodies. Margaret Farley offers some wise words here:

> We do not know fully what it means that in this world and the next "there is no longer male and female." We do not know, in other words, what transcendence will finally mean for gender. Gender still matters in this world, so we can expect that it will matter in the next. If so, it will not be burdened by this world's stereotypes nor this world's judgments of what we ought to welcome or exclude, celebrate or mourn. In a new world we will not mistake limited possibility for unlimited; we will not make strangers out of our differences; we will not expect either too much or too little from our identities as women or men.[26]

Sex and gender, as currently experienced, lie, like everything else, under the pall of sin. This does not mean that we cannot experience sex and gender as occasions for unbounded joy and love; but it does mean that whatever joy we experience falls short of the fullness of God's intention for us in communion. The good news, however, is that God transforms us and our desire so that we become fitted for that communion. If gender and sex currently exist as unstable, they find rest and transformation in the stability of God's love, promised to each of us in the sacrament of baptism.

BAPTISMAL IDENTITY

Human identities such as male and female, gay and straight, are secondary in relation to Christian baptism. This sacrament renders all children of God participants in the life of Christ and heirs of a reign that is coming, a reign where our allegiances according to tribe and sex pass away: "Do you not know that all of us who have been baptized into Christ Jesus were baptized into his death? Therefore we have been buried with him by baptism into death, so that, just as Christ was raised from the dead by the glory of the Father, so we too might walk in newness of life" (Rom. 6:3–4; see also Col. 2:12). In baptism, we are submerged in the waters in death, and rise, gasping, given new life by grace: dying in Christ, we rise again with him.

Baptism is a mystical rite, in as much as it points to the mutual indwelling of Christ and the believer. John Calvin, not often mistaken for a mystic, writes that in baptism "we are not only engrafted into the death and life of Christ, but so united to Christ himself that we become sharers in all his blessings."[27] The life that we live, the death that we die, is Christ's, and ours through Christ: "As many of you as were baptized into Christ have clothed yourself with Christ" (Gal. 3:27). In baptism, we belong not primarily to ourselves and our kind, but to others and to God through Jesus Christ.

In baptism, God creates a new family where "belonging, not biology" is most fundamental. Stacy Johnson writes, "Baptism bestows on each person a new identity: child of God. Being a child of God constitutes an identity more enduring and more significant than any that we ourselves or others may assign us."[28] But as we journey into the reign that God is bringing, we often behave as if our identities as gay or straight, male or female, make the ultimate difference. Thus, the church permits straight persons to be ordained and married, while denying this permission to others. Current marriage and ordination standards in most churches suggest that sexual orientation, not baptism, is the ultimate marker of a graced life. Such practice fixates on markers of human identity that invariably elevate some at the expense of others. The churches in the United States offer abundant examples of this: African Americans who were "allowed" in white churches, but only in the balconies or in the back rows; women who were "allowed" to teach children's classes but not preach or teach men. History is replete with examples of how Christians place other identities before baptism, an inversion that merits nothing less than the charge of idolatry. Elizabeth Stuart writes of this tendency tellingly:

> Heterosexuality and homosexuality and maleness and femaleness are not of ultimate importance, they are not determinative in God's eyes and in so far as any of us have behaved as if they are, we are guilty of the grave sin of idolatry, and if we have further behaved as if they are grounds upon which to exclude people from the glorious liberty of the children of God, we are guilty of profanity and a fundamental denial of our own baptismal identity which rests in being bound together with others not of our choosing, by an act of sheer grace.[29]

Baptism does not erase this idolatry from our lives; it does not make sin disappear in a magical ablution. But it does fix the reality of hope before our eyes and in front of our lives: in Jesus Christ we are always more than the categories we put ourselves into or that others assign for us. "To be baptized is to be caught up in a kingdom that does not yet fully exist, that is in the process of becoming, it is to be caught up in the redemption of this world."[30]

Baptism, furthermore, does not cause all the differences that mark human life to disappear. The eschatological kingdom does not resemble a eugenics project where all humans wind up looking alike, presenting the same ideals of beauty and the good life.[31] The book of Revelation, tellingly, depicts a scene where the diversity of the nations makes a home in the New Jerusalem: "The nations will walk by its light, and the kings of the earth will bring their glory into it. Its gates will never be shut by day—and there will be no night there. People will bring into it the glory and the honor of the nations" (Rev. 21:24–26). Difference does not disappear in the new city, but difference no longer becomes the obstacle to communion that we often make of it in our day. Difference is fundamental to communion: God's difference with the world makes the world's relationship with God possible; our differences with each other, and our difference with God make possible the Communion of the Lord's Table; difference between partners make marriage the communion of two persons. Such difference, for Christian faith, is also present in our most basic claim of who Jesus Christ is: the communion of human and divine. Christian eschatology does not claim that male and female, straight and gay, do not matter at all; only that they do not matter as the *ultimate* truth of life. In the eschaton, difference remains, but not as a reality that divides and alienates us from each other. Stuart writes that the church's baptismal theology teaches, "There is only one identity stable enough to hope in."[32] Baptism turns division toward the healing of relations, suggesting a desire for communion that intensifies in heaven, a desire that encompasses sex and intimates marriage.

SEX AND MARRIAGE IN HEAVEN?

In the Gospel of Mark, Sadducees ask Jesus some intriguing questions. Tradition has it that the Sadducees denied the resurrection and attempt to trap Jesus with a question about a widow who marries a succession of seven brothers, each of whom dies, leaving her childless. They ask Jesus, "In the resurrection whose wife will she be? For the seven had married her" (Mark 12:23). Jesus' response turns the customary understanding of marriage on its head: "For when they rise from the dead, they neither marry nor are given in marriage, but are like angels in heaven" (v. 25). The ordinary markers of identity, of who belongs to whom in marriage, get blurred in the resurrection life, paling in significance to our belonging to God.

Throughout much of its history, the Christian church has assumed that Jesus' words about the disappearance of marriage in heaven have also entailed the end of sex. Resurrected persons become like the angels, sexless, unable to reproduce sexually, no longer tainted by the stirrings of the loins. But interestingly, Jesus' words say nothing about sex explicitly, either in terms of androgynous bodies or the eclipse of human sexuality. His claim that persons become like the angels bears some resemblance to Paul's notion of a spiritual body (cf. 1 Cor. 15:35–50), a transformed body raised in power and glory (v. 43). Recent interpretations of this passage, therefore, have suggested alternative readings. Evangelical theologian Stanley Grenz offers one example: "Jesus does not explicitly declare that sexuality will be absent, only that marriage will no longer be practiced. Human sexuality will no longer be expressed in genital sexual acts, and the sexually based drive toward bonding will no longer be expressed through male-female coupling. This is not to suggest, however, that the deeper dimensions of sexuality will be eradicated."[33] Though on one read Grenz seems to be denying sex in heaven (as there will no longer be genital sexual activity), he also affirms the reality of sex in the eschaton by expanding the understanding of what sex entails. Sexuality, he claims, will be expressed in the communion that is God's love. It does not disappear, but is fulfilled, though its typical expressions will look different from our current experience of sex on earth. On one level, Grenz takes Jesus' words at face value: denying the existence of marriage at the end of days. On another level, he speculates what the end of marriage might mean: the end of genital sex, but the fulfillment of sexual desire.

Grenz's interpretation of Jesus' words here expands the understanding of human sexuality, but also eyes genital sex with some suspicion. On the one hand, he astutely recognizes how often sex gets reduced to genital motions. Sex is not penile-vaginal intercourse alone, but touching and being touched, kissing and being kissed, holding and being held, longing in desire and the experience of desire's resolution, the purpose of which is to establish communion between persons. Since communion is what God intends for humanity, Grenz claims that sexuality will continue in the new creation, but will be expressed differently. This perspective widens rather than restricts our view of sex. In an age that seems particularly fixated on intercourse, Grenz's words are especially helpful. The genitalization of sex has resulted in elaborate and artificial gradations of what constitutes sex. (Hence, Bill Clinton's denial that he "had sex" with Monica Lewinsky; hence, teenagers pledge abstinence but construe oral and anal sex as "not having sex.") Sex is more than particular body parts fitting in other body parts, and it entails the whole person longing for communion. If the saints do not marry in heaven, their bodies experience communion in ways that draw upon the sexual body.

Grenz falls in line with the strand of the church's history that sees genital intercourse as tied primarily to procreation. Because procreation is no longer necessary in the new creation, the saints no longer have genital sex. But if sex, as Grenz suggests, also expresses the longing for communion, it seems odd that genital sex is automatically excluded from eschatology. I do not want to argue for genital sex as the paramount expression of human sexuality; I do not want to argue that heaven constitutes unending intercourse or the continuation of sex as we know it. Rather, I simply want to leave the question open. If Christian hope envisions the fulfillment of all things, the redemption of our bodies, then genitalia are not somehow exempt. Grenz is right in situating genital sex within a wider view of sexuality than is often assumed in our day. But the redemption that Christian eschatology envisions extends to *everything*: it does not exclude genitalia. If the communion that is God's love redeems all things, then it redeems sexual life, though we may not know what this looks like. It is enough to say that marriage and sex as we know it will end; we claim too much if we say that genital activity ceases. Instead we ought to say that God redeems us as sexual bodies.

One whisper in this direction is offered by Margaret Kamitsuka, who leaves open the question of whether there is sex in heaven. She asks, "What if, in heaven, the immediate presence of the divine so infuses the blessed that they are able to share deep psychic wounds with each other and thus experience the eros of maternal jouissance? Such eros would reverberate, we can imagine, to other interpersonal erotic pleasures, including phallic sex."[34] Here is a vision of the fulfillment of sexual desire that includes the whole body, a vision of sex that intimates mutuality, care and joy, experienced in the quivering of bodies in communion. Kamitsuka's question evokes the possibility of sex marked not by possessiveness, but dispossession, grounded in God's love affair and joyful play with creation.

ESCHATOLOGY, SEX, AND PLAY

Play is an element of God's intent for creation: creation exists for the sake of communion with God, not out of necessity, but out of God's delight and good pleasure. Communion, too, proves delightful *for* creation: The phrase, "And God saw that it was good," reverberates throughout Genesis 1; at the conclusion of the six days of creation we read of further delight: "God saw everything that he had made, and indeed, it was very good" (Gen. 1:31). God's creative activity doubtless involves work; Genesis 2 depicts God as a potter, fashioning Adam out of the dust of the ground, breathing into him the breath of life. But the rhythms of creation are not endless work, for they also include the seventh day of Sabbath rest, which is for God *and* creation. As God delights in creation, so we are made to delight in God and God's gifts. Play, too, is an element of Sabbath rest, where pause from labor allows us to partake in re-creation of the new days that lie ahead.

Sex, at its best, is playful and restful. Many historical Jewish traditions encourage married couples to play with one another in sex on the Sabbath, in the lingering rest that that day promises.[35] Yet for many in our day, sex has lost its playfulness. Sexual addictions seem to be rising, rendering sex a compulsion rather than a delight. Sex also loses much of its capacity for pleasure in a commercial society. The overexposure of sex in media often leads not to the heightening of sexual desire, but its deadening. Increased exposure to pornography can lead to more explicit forms of "erotica," often with subtle or overt depictions of violence. Here play degenerates into violence. Sexual dysfunctions, furthermore, are now the stuff of advertising campaigns, suggesting that sex is a performance rather than way of attending to one's lover. When the stakes are so high (Give her/him the best ever tonight!), it is no wonder that many develop stage fright. Men are enculturated to perform and women to receive, without expressing themselves too much. When play becomes performance, some may lose interest in sex altogether, or slowly become numb to the pleasure and touch of sex. Anorgasmia, or the absence of orgasm, affects about a quarter of American women, by some estimates.[36] Here, an emphasis on male performance can also lead to inattention to one's lover's pleasure.

When sex loses its playfulness, it becomes drudgery, compulsive, and ultimately self-centered. "Unless sex is playful," argues Adrian Thatcher, "it is intolerable." Many Christian treatises on sex—with their serious moralism, solemn pronouncements, and clinical language—have also uprooted play from the fertile soil of sexual love. Thatcher urges the church to recover merrymaking and play in its sexual theologies, the "pleasure, and deep pleasure in our bodies [that] is a precondition of that deep gratitude to God for our sexuality which is itself the key to responsible and passionate loving."[37] The play of merrymaking most typically involves another. Play rarely sustains our interest very long unless we attend to another's delights as well as our own. Even when we play with ourselves, we tend to imagine playing with others.[38] When sex is playful, it enables lovers to attend to one another: to listen to her laughter, to hear his sighs. Playful sex delights in the other simply because she or he is. It seems to have no purpose other than the delight born of mutual love and attentiveness. Sex may involve the three ends that Augustine enumerates: procreation, an increase in fidelity because of sexual union, and an intimation of sacramental covenant. But even these lofty aims become drudgery if not for play and delight. The exhilaration of sex is not in its meeting a goal (whether orgasm or conception), but in the sheer delight of the other found in play, who also finds in us their delight. Moistness on lips and between the legs, breath on the neck, the lightness of touch on navel, slow and fast movements of skin on skin, lingering in the embrace of our beloved: these are forms of play that elicit delight and attentiveness.

Play, in fact, is built into female anatomy. The clitoris serves no "purpose" other than pleasure. It is not necessary for reproduction or any other biological function, but it is finely attuned to play. Glossing on Luce Irigaray, Lisa Isherwood and Elizabeth Stuart claim that "the clitoris symbolizes women's *jouissance*, women's joy, delight and difference that leads to a form of knowledge unafraid of difference and diversity,"[39] a knowledge that comes through play. If play is not part of lovemaking, sex becomes for most women a burden rather than delight. This makes the female genital mutilation in some societies particularly horrifying, for in addition to the physical wounding, it removes play from sex, rendering sex for the man's pleasure but not the woman's. It severs the body from pleasure and play, rendering women the ultimate sexual possession.

John Calvin, a theologian often caricatured for losing sight of pleasure and delight, recognized play as an integral dimension to sex in the marital covenant. In his commentary on Deuteronomy 24:5, "When a man is newly married, he shall not go out with the army or be charged with any related duty. He shall be free at home one year, to be happy with the wife whom he has married. . . . That God should permit a bride to enjoy herself with her husband, affords no trifling proof of His indulgence. . . . He spontaneously allows them to enjoy themselves."[40] For Calvin, the purpose of allowing this year of togetherness is not for the sake of procreation, not for the sake of advancing society, but simply for the purpose of mutual delight, a delight not restricted to sex, but also found within it. Note, too, how significantly the woman's enjoyment figures. Calvin mentions the wife's enjoyment explicitly, while the husband's is mentioned only within the broader sense of "they." Though I wouldn't want to claim too much of this (Calvin was hardly a feminist), it is clear that for him a marriage that does not attend to a woman's delight is impoverished.

U.S. consumer culture tends to commodify play and delight. Play gets sold on the marketplace in the form of adventure vacations and toys that must be had at all costs. This commodification affects sexual lives as well, with sex toys that promise better sex, without which "vanilla" sex becomes plain dull. Pornography, too, twists the play of sexual life into an object for another's consumption. The tragedy of pornography is not only its frequent fusion of sex and violence (as I have explored earlier in this book), but also its exchange of intimacy and mutual pleasure for profit. Others' sexual lives become objects for my consumption, sold on the marketplace for maximum profits, driving a multibillion dollar industry in the United States alone.

Even the concept of "foreplay" can be problematic in our culture. Thatcher writes, "The notion of 'foreplay' as the preparatory sexual activity prior to vaginal penetration already assumes that what comes after the foreplay is the essential thing about the act which the preliminaries make possible."[41] Play, in this sense, becomes a mere stage on the road to the "real thing." Play gets relegated to something that comes before, rather than surrounds, sex. Such notions offer further confirmation of the over-genitalization of sex in U.S. culture and the focus on sex as performance. No wonder so many get anxiety. If sex gets reduced to a particular act, then the particular "quality" of the act becomes paramount. But the notion of play may yet rescue sex from its over-commodification and genitalization. As play turns us toward the delight of the other, sex becomes not the pursuit of a rigidly defined goal, but emerges in the play itself. It's not what lovers achieve, but how they play with each other, that is most significant.

Sex is an expression of the human desire to play. In sex, we glimpse the yearning and the resolution of yearning that are expressions of play in Christian eschatology. Christian life yearns for communion, longs for union with God, but is obstructed from communion because of our estrangement from God. The union that we long for is both promised and given anew each day: Christian pilgrims are on their way to this communion even as God gives us communion by grace. As we journey in faith, we yearn for communion all the more intensely, as intimations of it are offered at Table, in the proclaimed Word, in the waters of baptism, and in the gathered community of the church, Christ's body. Human sexuality expresses one dimension of desire's longing and resolution. Sex is not the pinnacle of our longing or the exhaustion of it, but sex expresses longing in brief moments of intensity and in the narrative of a shared story between lovers that develops over time. In this sexual journey, lovers long for one another: to be with one another, to touch one another, to feel the moistness of the other within oneself. In sex, we long for some kind of union with our beloved, stretching out in anticipation, arching and aching in desire. As we long for our lover and attend to our lovers, we find that they also long for and attend to us. Desire and longing become intermingled: her pleasure becomes mine; my delight is also hers. Their desire for communion, even union, may achieve a momentary resolution in orgasm, in the release of all of the longing and yearning present in the body. Communion does have its ecstatic moments, where one becomes lost in the desire and love of the beloved. But such moments are not permanent: the union is never quite complete, nor is it completely desirable. The sexual journey, like the Christian journey, experiences moments of blissful union and periods of absence, both physical and emotional. The goal of discipleship is not simply one ecstatic moment after another; the goal of sex, likewise, is not endless orgasm. The point is the journey, the play, the movement of grace over time. Our longing is part of our attention to our beloved. The beauty of sex, in light of God's eschatological grace, is not that it arrives at set goals, but that it cultivates delight in the other, which then becomes one's own delight as well. As this delight develops over time, in the long shared story that becomes lovers' lives together, sex becomes a part of life as do shared meals, and all the joys and travails of the journey. Sex then becomes sensuous, sustained in part by the meal that sustains God's people. As we turn toward that Table, we also understand sex as an expression of hospitality and grace.

Chapter 5

The Lord's Supper and Sex

A Sumptuous Banquet

Christian faith is sensual. Its founder, Jesus of Nazareth, was accused of eating and drinking too much (Matt. 11:19). According to the Gospel of John, Jesus' first sign of divine favor occurred when he turned water into wine at a wedding. Apparently it was rather good wine, enjoyed by all who gathered. People wondered why the best wine was saved for last (John 2:1–11). Time and again the Gospels depict Jesus with bread in his hands, breaking, sharing, and enjoying it with others. On occasion he lifts a cup in celebration, as well. Jesus dines with those whom respectable folks would rather ignore, and he sometimes invites himself to dinner at wealthy people's homes (Luke 19:1–10). In Luke's Gospel, Jesus even eats after the resurrection (Luke 24:41-43). Jesus enjoyed a good meal, told stories about sumptuous banquets, and enjoyed the company of those who offered him food. Jesus' ministry often revolves around food, how food is distributed, and the hospitality involved in sharing food. Jesus' teaching is not only heard, but *tasted* as well. Jesus' ministry is sensual because it stresses not simply how we hear the Word, but how we are touched by it (in his acts of healing) and how we taste and see that the Word is good. In Jesus' last meal with his disciples, sensuality is on full display, where Jesus presents himself as host, as the one who dines with and is dined upon. The Last Supper recalls Jesus' earlier words in the Gospel of John: "Those who eat my flesh and drink my blood have eternal life, and I will raise them up on the last day; for my flesh is true food and my blood is true drink. Those who eat my flesh and drink my blood abide in me, and I in them" (6:54–56). The church recalls these words and re-members his ministry when it celebrates the meal of the Risen Christ, the supper given for the world. We, too, are a sensual people that partake of a meal of flesh and blood, invited into deeper intimacy with the One who sets the Table and offers himself in it.

What does this Supper have to do with sex? Sometimes in the history of the church the answer has been rather little. The Supper, according to this inherited wisdom, removes us from the sensual and things of the flesh. This spiritual meal raises us above our nasty mortal coil and becomes contaminated if it is tainted by hints of sex. But such interpretations of the Supper miss the dripping sensuality that is basic to the meal itself: taking another body into one's own, tasting and feasting on the delight of another. The task in this chapter is *not* to show how the Lord's Supper is a sexual meal. Some of the early controversies in the church over the celebration of the Eucharist, in fact, warn against construing the meal as excessively sexual and mistaking communion in Christ for simply another manifestation of sexual ecstasy or the pleasures of dining. Rather, I will explore some of the gestures of this meal that help shape a fuller understanding of sex than has often been the case in the church that celebrates this meal. What are the marks of this meal? How is our understanding of sex affected when we partake of the Supper? It teaches us the intimacy of touch in tasting; it teaches us the importance of gift both in ecclesial and sexual life; it stresses the primacy of hospitality; and it stresses the public nature of bodily communion. Surrounding these eucharistic gestures is a different economy than the one often assumed in sexual life in the United States: an economy of grace and abundance rather than scarcity and competition. The distortions of sex in our time often involve issues of economic exploitation. I will thus explore some of these distortions and their impact on human well-being before exploring the gestures of the Eucharist and how they help recover the sensuality of sex.

ECONOMIC DISTORTIONS OF SEX

Sex and money have woven a tangled web since the dawn of human civilization. People have been having sex for money as long as money has been around. Dowries and other forms of economic exchange appear historically across cultures, indicating that sex and marriage bear economic costs. The Bible, no doubt, records much of this: prostitutes appear in heroic and tragic roles (Josh. 2 contra Rev. 17), and men gain access to marriage in an exchange of property, wealth, or labor (Gen. 29). For much of human history, sex and money go together, with sex appearing as a commodity for sale on the marketplace, whether in the public space of a town center or the supposedly private sphere of a marital bed.

If sex and money have been bound together for millennia, powerful forces in the current global economy have made those connections even more apparent, often with alarming consequences. In the global capitalistic economy, sex translates into big money, crossing barriers between nations, accelerated by the booming growth of the World Wide Web. In nearly all cases the growth of sexual "industries" weaves a treacherous web, grinding up lives, spitting out victims, and demeaning those who become the mere consumers of sex. In nearly all forms of this growth, men continue to exert ownership over female bodies. Yet in purely market terms, the growth of such industries is seen as a positive good, since they create jobs and wealth. Three of the most visible signs of the growth of a global sex economy are prostitution, pornography, and strip clubs.

If prostitution in times of yore was confined to local economies, the world's oldest profession is now a worldwide net of interlocked businesses, some "legitimate," others with deep roots in organized crime. Sex tourism is now a significant source of income in many Asian nations. In the wake of U.S. and Japanese military occupation of several Southern Asian nations, prostitution has boomed, catering primarily to Western and Japanese men. At the end of the twentieth century, the International Labor Organization compiled a report of the economic effects of such tourism and made a conservative estimate that up to 14 percent of the economies of four nations—the Philippines, Malaysia, Thailand, and Indonesia—is generated by prostitution and the sex trade. These economic contributions are hardly unique to developing nations. In South Korea, prostitution contributes 4.4 percent of the GDP (more than forestry, fishing, and agriculture combined), and in the Netherlands, where prostitution is legalized and regulated, the percentage is estimated to be five.[1] Factor into these figures the travel expenses to and from these nations and the percentages increase: prostitution, whether legal or illegal, is also connected to airlines that ferry johns to their destinations, hotels that host them, and a host of other legitimate businesses. Prostitution, to be blunt, translates into big business.

The economic impact of prostitution is enormous, the human costs even more glaring. Who are the women involved in this industry? In most cases, women from poorer nations—who are often forced or sold into prostitution—service the wealthy. Prostitution in Europe, North America, and Southeast Asia, is built upon human trafficking. Though numbers of individuals are difficult to estimate, given the underground nature of trafficking, the U.S. State Department estimates between 700,000 and 900,000 people per year are ferried across international borders. In a sign of how economic desperation breeds desperate measures, women in poorer countries are often sold by relatives, husbands, or boyfriends.[2] In addition to the psychological harm of being sold, the physical costs that the women bear are horrific. A recent study of women trafficked to Europe offers these grim statistics: half were raped, confined, and beaten by their traffickers. Dangers, moreover, did not cease upon arrival. Pimps used psychological and physical coercion to control their "employees:" Twenty-five percent of women in the study reported being "hit, kicked, punched, struck with objects, burned, cut with knives, and raped."[3] A study of prostitutes in the Philippines reports that half experienced vaginal bleeding, almost 70 percent of women suffered broken bones and 62 percent sustained mouth and teeth injuries; while 82 percent report depression, 75 percent rage, and 40 percent suicidal thoughts.[4] STDs and unwanted pregnancies become the norm. Most forms of prostitution are built on violence against women: whether subtle or overt, the women involved in the trade bear wounds on their body inflicted by men.

As gut-wrenching as these statistics and realities are, there are even more haunting truths about the global sex trade as it destroys children's lives. Since child prostitution defies international laws, the numbers of children involved in it is extremely difficult to measure. But, the trade is booming in several corners of the globe, catering to Western men who seek sex with underage girls and boys from the global South. The words of Taiwo, a 13-year old Nigerian, are haunting as they interweave sexism, economic oppression, and prostitution:

> Imagine in a family where there is a boy and a girl, the girl will do all the work in the house. If there is any sacrifice to be made it will be the girl that will suffer it, for instance, when the family income is down the girl will be send [sic] to go and hawk, that is to sell things in the streets and along the highway. Most times they will push her out to an old man or introduce her into prostitution. Even our mothers are also guilty of this act. This is very wrong, people of the world should change their attitude towards girls and women.[5]

If the industrial revolution ground down children in urban factories, the burgeoning global sex trade devours children as victims, costing nothing less than lost lives and lost futures.

If prostitution is the crassest sexual exploitation of women and children, pornography appears in an Internet age as a more socially acceptable outgrowth of the sexual revolution. Though pornography, arguably, has been around as long as people have drawn pictures and taken photographs, the World Wide Web has resulted in explosive growth of the distribution and business of porn. The Internet creates anonymity in the consumption of porn that was impossible before the dawn of the personal computer. Many who would never have set foot into an "adult" bookstore now have access to the same materials in the privacy of their own homes. What is the economic impact of this new way of accessing old material? The total worth of the U.S. porn industry is at least $10 billion and possibly as much as $20 billion. Worldwide, those figures approach $100 billion annually. Revenue from pornography in the U.S. dwarfs the total revenue of mainstream media outlets, accounting for more revenue than ABC, NBC, and CBS.[6]

Porn outdistances Hollywood as a contribution to the U.S. economic engine. The U.S. is the top producer of pornography worldwide, exerting a significant impact on global financial transactions and trade. With demand showing no signs of letting up, porn has become part of the normal course of business for countless other businesses, such as hotels, TV, Internet, and cell phone providers. In 2005, 13,588 new titles of hard-core video/DVD titles were released, a number that has risen steadily year after year.[7]

Though economics of porn are colossal, the human costs are perhaps more drastic. Contrary to the image of porn actresses as women who choose to become involved in movies, are paid a lot, and enjoy it, the reality of a porn career is short-lived, without much money, and subtle and not-so-subtle coercion. Consider the "dialogue" of a video release, and how it represents violence as six men in sequence forcibly enter the star's mouth. The woman is called a "whore" and a "bitch" and is told to "gag" and "choke on it." The scene concludes with the "star" wiping the semen of six men off her face.[8] Who chooses what in this dialogue? The woman chooses nothing and is simply the object of physical violence, even to the point of choking, gagging, and vomiting. What does it say about sex? That sex is an extension of violence against women that men enjoy inflicting. Such visions of violence both tear the bodies of women and distort the psyches of men. Sheila Jeffreys notes how increasing consumption of violent porn has ruptured traditional societies across the globe, "where it has been identified in playing a part in normalizing sexual abuse and prostitution for children and young people," and which socializes adolescent males to believe that women enjoy "being hit during sex because it heightened the women's sexual pleasure."[9] Pornography may desensitize men to accept increasing levels of violence against women and to consume it on a mass market scale.

One final mark of the commercialization of sex in society is the heralded strip club boom. With some strip club chains featured on national stock exchanges, this business is another growing sector of the economy. The industry is estimated to be worth $75 billion worldwide. In the U.S., consumers spend $15 billion per year on strip clubs compared to $4 billion on baseball.[10] National pastime? The economics are rather clear. Profits amass in the owners' hands rather than the dancers'. A study of strip club employees in San Diego documents that most struggle to make $100 a night, and many average closer to half that total.[11] What happens in the clubs, in most instances, is a continuation of practices encountered in prostitution and pornography. Kelly Holsopple, a former stripper who worked for thirteen years in the U.S. industry, reports after extensive interviews and face-to-face surveys with dancers that "customers spit on women, spray beer, and flick cigarettes at them. . . . [they are] pelted with ice, coins, trash, condoms, room keys, pornography, and golf balls," while male customers "pull women's hair, yank them by the arm or ankle, rip their costumes, and try to pull their costumes off." Dancers are "bitten, licked, slapped, punched, and pinched" while men try to penetrate dancers vaginally and anally with "fingers, dollar bills, and bottles."[12] The rhetoric of "choice" here is absurd, as if women choose their own abuse. One of the assumptions of the relative innocuousness of strip clubs is that the women who perform get paid and choose to work in these establishments. The money earned and the choice to earn it in this way makes the sexual exchange permissible and beneficial to both parties involved. The assumption, in other words, is that money makes it all okay, but these assumptions prove more false than true, as women struggle for meager pay and experience workplace coercion in overt and covert ways.

I have already documented many of the human costs of burgeoning sex trades: physical abuse, victimization of children who cannot be said to "choose" sex work, the dehumanization of prostitute and john. Sex industries all too often thrive on violence and perpetuate it. But there is another assumption that has lurked in the background of all of these: that sex is a medium of monetary exchange. Some of this, of course, is irrefutable. As the preceding survey has shown, sex translates into big business worldwide, and its share of the global economic pie seems to be growing. But if, at its core, sex is simply another form of economic exchange, then it becomes a rather mechanical matter of "me" meeting "your" needs and "you" supplying "mine." Sex is fungible on the marketplace because it relates to supply and demand. According to this wisdom, even when we are having sex for free, we really are not. Sebastian Horsley epitomizes this transactional view of sex when he writes, "The difference between sex for money and sex for free is that sex for money always costs a lot less."[13] Sexual access, whether in a marriage, or any other form of relationship, always involves the exchange of money.

If this is the "truth" that our market economy proclaims about sex, then I want to proclaim that this is a distortion of truth. In the Christian economy of grace, sex cannot be reduced to economic exchange, to mutual servicing, to me getting my needs met and you getting yours, or to the selling of sex on the open marketplace. But in developing this alternative account of sexual economy, I have no interest in claiming that sex operates apart from economic concerns or is isolated in a sheltered, private sphere. Whether we like it or not, there is no sequestered bedroom that offers a haven from the rough and tumble economic nature of the world. Economics affects everything: from relations between the sexes to the maintenance of households, to the institution of marriage. Sex operates within the economies that form and shape societies. But a Christian understanding of sex also suggests something more: in addition to being affected by economics, sexual relationships can also suggest a different kind of economy. Christian faith teaches its adherents to treasure taste, gift, and hospitality more than marketplace exchange. Christian rituals carry economic assumptions that affect our understanding and practice of sex, and the Lord's Table enacts many of these assumptions, inviting us to reconceive sex along different economic lines.

TASTE AND SEE THAT THE LORD IS GOOD

Protestant theologies, in general, have stressed the importance of proclaiming and hearing the Word. In the traditions of the Reformation, the Word is spoken and heard. This, of course, is the most common way of understanding words:

they are uttered, listened to, and read. But the Bible offers a more extensive account of how we encounter the divine Word, which we taste and eat as well, at times in a gustatory feast. The Psalms convey this taste in poetic fashion: "O taste and see that the LORD is good; happy are those who take refuge in him" (Ps. 34:8). Words drip from God's lips and the psalmist's pen, inviting those who hear the word to follow and obey not out of compulsion, but out of delight: "How sweet are your words to my taste, sweeter than honey to my mouth!" (119:103). In these accounts, God's Word is sensual as well as auditory, providing pleasures to those fortunate enough to taste.

The Song of Songs captures the sense of taste at its most rollicking. As the lovers linger on one another, they recall what a delight it is to taste one's lover: "As an apple tree among the trees of the wood, so is my beloved among young men. With great delight I sat in his shadow, and his fruit was sweet to my taste. He brought me to his banqueting house, and his intention toward me was love" (Song 2:3–4). As we witnessed in the first chapter, taste appears over and again throughout the Song's pages, inviting us to savor the pleasures of earthly, sexual love *and* the analogue of that love as the way God longs for us (and we for God). These are words that are not simply meant for our hearing; they are meant for our tasting.

The Bible concludes with another vision of tasting—and feasting on—God's Word. In a book rife with questions of purity, of saints distinguished from those who commit iniquity with the whore of Babylon, is a description of the author eating the divine Word: "Then the voice that I had heard from heaven spoke to me again, saying, 'Go, take the scroll that is open in the hand of the angel who is standing on the sea and on the land.' So I went to the angel and told him to give me the little scroll; and he said to me, 'Take it, and eat; it will be bitter to your stomach, but sweet as honey in your mouth'" (Rev. 10:8–9). Here the author of the Apocalypse recalls Ezekiel's eating of a scroll, signaling his divine commission to prophesy (Ezek. 2:8–3:3). But whereas Ezekiel's scroll is sweet, John's is bitter as well, indicating delight as well as anguish. If God's Word is ripe for the tasting, it can also cause the stomach to churn. How very like sex, which is both sweeter than wine and the cause of much anguish, unsettledness, and agony in human life. If the intent is sweet, the practice is often fraught with bitterness.

The Eucharist re-members the sweetness and bitterness of the meal Jesus shared with his disciples. In his last time with those closest to him, he hosts a meal—a gesture of hospitality and celebration. Though its tone is sober, the meal also delights taste buds and belly. Jesus' Last Supper is neither dolorous agony nor bacchanalian revelry. Instead, it is anguished *and* celebratory. It anticipates his betrayal by Judas (who is present at the meal with him) and crucifixion as it also heralds the new age, where many will feast at the banqueting table. It recalls Jesus' radical acts of hospitality to strangers and sinners and claims that those who would follow him must also drink a bitter cup. Neither raw celebration nor begrudging acceptance of companionship marks this meal. Jesus' last meal suggests something more: a God who extends to the depths of human agony and uplifts us to the heights of celebration, of a God who invites us to embrace all of life, and of God's life, simply for the tasting. So in words uttered countless times across the centuries, Christians who gather around the Lord's Table are invited to "taste and see that the LORD is good." At this meal, God's promises are present for the tasting—in the basic staple food across many cultures, bread, and the basic drink of celebration, wine.

When Christ invites us to taste at this Table, he invites us into intimacy. As John Milbank and Catherine Pickstock remind us, taste is a "more intimate mode of touch."[14] Generally speaking, we do not taste many others: lovers do, so do nursing infants at a mother's breast. When God invites us to taste God's very self, the analogues here are appropriate: this is the kind of intimacy that God gives in fullness, where flesh meets flesh and taste buds linger upon skin. The intimacy of the Lord's Supper engages all the senses: tasting the Word in bread and wine, we also see it displayed for the feasting at Table, hear it proclaimed in words of institution and a sermon preceding it, touched as we share the feast with one another, smelled as we prepare to take the Lord in our mouths.

IT BEGINS WITH A KISS

Kisses appear throughout Scripture: in gestures of greeting (Gen. 29:13), in the reuniting of those who have been separated (Gen. 33:4), and as an element of early Christian worship in an exchange of peace (1 Thess. 5:26). But the text that is saturated with kisses is the Song, which begins with a kiss: "Let him kiss me with the kisses of his mouth! For your love is better than wine, your anointing oils are fragrant, your name is perfume poured out; therefore the maidens love you" (1:2–3). As lovers taste, the kisses continue, even in a foreshadowing of the eucharistic banquet: "your kisses are like the best wine that goes down smoothly, gliding over lips and teeth" (7:9). A kiss, like the Eucharist, is an invitation to intimacy, of closeness to the beloved, of taking the beloved into one's self—and one's self into the beloved. This intimacy delights and entices: rolling over the tongue, filling the body with warmth. Eucharist and kiss are delights to the eyes and a pleasure for the tongue. Might the Eucharist also be described as Christ's affectionate kiss of us? The early church may have thought as much, as it incorporated ritual kissing into the eucharistic banquet. But let us linger with the kiss a moment more. A kiss, like wine, can become intoxicating: the mingling of lips and tongue—for lovers—is electric. As kisses mingle, it becomes difficult to distinguish where one lover's body "ends" and the other's "begins." Bodies, pleasures, and experiences are shared as lovers invite each other into themselves. This is why kisses are shared, and why it is well-nigh impossible to kiss oneself. The kiss is an invitation: to knowledge, to sharing, to intimacy.

Kisses are not foreign to Jesus' ministry. Luke records one of the more intriguing episodes of kissing in Jesus' ministry. As Jesus prepares to dine at a Pharisee's house, he encounters a woman from the city "who was a sinner," who brings a alabaster jar of ointment, bathes Jesus' feet with her tears, dries them with her hair, and kisses and anoints his feet (Luke 7:37–38). The language here is suggestive: bathing feet is a sign of hospitality, so too are feet a euphemism for more intimate parts of the body. Certainly the text conveys an opening of intimacy between Jesus and a woman whom the Pharisees condemn: "If this man were a prophet, he would have known who and what kind of woman this is who is touching him" (v. 39). The juxtaposition between Pharisaic condemnation and Jesus' reception of hospitality is striking. Where others would bar the door, Jesus invites in and allows himself to be kissed—on the feet. Gathered together are a woman of the city, a man proclaiming the reign of God and a gathering of those who would condemn their association. She kisses him in a gesture not altogether unlike that between lovers. I am not saying that Jesus and this woman "had sex;" one need not leap to that conclusion to see their mutual affection, the intimacy that results from Jesus' acceptance of her invitation to wash his feet.[15] The contrast with the "hospitality" of those who would dine with Jesus is striking: "You gave me no water for my feet, but she has bathed my feet with her tears and dried them with her hair. You gave me no kiss, but from the time I came in she has not stopped kissing my feet" (vv. 44–45). Here is a gesture of intimacy, conveyed with a kiss: Jesus need not be the only one who kisses us; sometimes we kiss him. The kiss, apparently, communicates a faith that saves, enabling the woman to go in peace (v.50).

Perhaps because they signal intimacy, kisses can also convey falsity and betrayal. A distorted kiss can be a sign of enmity: "Well meant are the wounds a friend inflicts, but profuse are the kisses of an enemy" (Prov. 27:6). The Synoptic Gospels recognize the wisdom of this proverb in their narration of Jesus' betrayal and arrest. In each of them, Judas betrays Jesus with a kiss.[16] Here the kiss turns in on itself; what is meant as a gesture of love and hospitality gets twisted into rejection. Here the mingling of flesh, the invitation of oneself by and into another, becomes the occasion for pushing away. The one we hold close becomes the one we scorn. Judas's kiss is a parody of intimacy: of one who has grown in closeness to another only to reject and attack that one. It mimics the movements of a kiss, but conveys betrayal instead of love. Judas does not mingle and linger with this kiss, but quickly disappears from the scene. Indeed, we do not hear of him again until his suicide. His is the wrong kind of kiss altogether, a reminder of the ways that our kisses can become self-serving if they are not also an invitation to our beloved.

THE KISS IN EARLY CHRISTIAN PRACTICE

The early Christians were aware of the power of kisses, incorporating kisses into the regular patterns of household worship. Justin Martyr records patterns of worship that precede the eucharistic meal: reading Scripture, preaching, prayer, and an exchange of a kiss, which had become "standard practice of all major centres of

Christianity by the middle of the fourth century, if not long before. . . ."[17] In this practice, the kiss immediately precedes the Supper, conveying the peace offered at Table, the peace given by the Lord that disciples in turn convey to one another.

But what is this kiss, and did it resound strangely in those early Christian communities as they distinguished themselves from other communities? Though kisses are not universal, people have been kissing one another since the dawn of time. Was this early Christian kiss simply a modification of kisses in the Jewish or Hellenistic world? Much recent research suggests that the Christian kiss was strange, because worshipers kissed nonrelatives. This kind of kissing was not prominent in Jewish or Hellenic practice prior to its appearance in Paul's letters and Justin's apologies. In the words of Paul Bradshaw,

> The only earlier evidence for such a custom is the reference in several of St. Paul's letters to the exchange of a "holy kiss" between Christians. In the Graeco-Roman culture of the period, social convention usually restricted kissing to very close friends or members of one's own family, and hence for Christians to kiss one another when they were not so related was a powerful counter-cultural symbol, indicating that they regarded their fellow-believers as their brothers and sisters and the Church as their true family. This was reinforced, in some cases at least, by a consequent refusal to exchange kisses any longer with members of their natural family who were not themselves Christians. Such behavior would, of course, have been considered scandalous by outsiders.[18]

In the kissing of the church, the ties of water—not blood—were the ties that mattered, the intimacy that delighted.

We might then ask, where was this kiss exchanged? In the context of worship, of course, but on the body it was exchanged lip to lip. Robert Taft writes that this kiss was exchanged "indiscriminately by those of both sexes."[19] The early Christians did not avoid the intimacy that mouth-to-mouth kissing suggested; instead, they embraced it. In the process, they questioned—at least in the context of worship—some of the rules regarding the expression of affection between genders, between blood family and close friends. It was as if the old rules no longer applied: the intimacy formerly conveyed only to close friends and family was now extended to all the baptized. The kiss was not so much a sign of sexual union or a mark of blood ties as much as the new family that God was creating, by adoption, through baptism. In response to that creation of a new family, believers invited one another into each other with a kiss on the mouth.

Kisses—whether between lovers between the sheets or in the context of worship—are almost never without a hint of eroticism. We understand those early Christian kisses only partially if we see them devoid of the erotic. Some of the earliest sermons that reflect on the kiss are highly charged erotically. Consider fourth-century theologian and bishop Ambrose, who wrote in a homily that when we see the sacrament of the Eucharist, we say along with the Song, "'Let him kiss me with the kisses of his lips:' that is: 'Let Christ give *me* a kiss.' Why? 'Because your breasts are better than wine:' that is, your thoughts, your sacraments are better than wine."[20] For Ambrose, the kiss that begins all kisses is the kiss of Christ, given to all believers in the meal present at Table. Christ invites us to Table with a kiss, and believers respond by kissing one another. Seen in this manner, the kiss of peace is not first and foremost a celebration of sexual love or an apotheosis of the erotic, but a recognition that the One who kisses us claims us body and soul, longing for us in ways akin to a lover's pangs. The erotic, the sexual, is incorporated into Christ's longing for us—not as the most important dimension of life, but as one moment among others. But note Ambrose's language here: Christ's sacraments are like breasts. The gender-bending here is obvious, with a male Christ sporting breasts that symbolize maternal nurturing and sexual arousal, as the breasts taste better than wine. Christ both nourishes us with spiritual food and entices our erotic desire. In kissing us, he invites his breasts to be kissed as well.

Cyril of Jerusalem, another fourth-century theologian and bishop, reflects on the kiss of peace exchanged at the Eucharist. In a sermon, he pays particular attention to what the kiss accomplishes between believers. Reflecting on the deacon's proclamation, "Receive one another, and let us kiss one another," Cyril writes, "Do not assume that this is the customary kiss exchanged by friends in public. No, this kiss joins souls together in search of complete forgiveness from one another. So the kiss is a mark of fusion of souls, and of the expulsion of all resentment for wrongs."[21] In addition to marking desire, the kiss signals reconciliation, so that those who may have been formerly estranged are united in love. The early church placed a high premium on reconciliation before partaking of the Eucharist. Theodore of Mopsuestia writes, "If anyone has wronged another, then, he must do all he can to make amends to the one he has wronged and to effect a reconciliation with him. If the injured party is present, the reconciliation should be made on the spot; if not, the offender must resolve to seek a reconciliation by all the means in his power when occasion offers. Only then may he come forward to take part in the offering."[22] Christians who have wronged another have the responsibility to make amends before they partake of the Eucharist. Though it requires work on both parties, reconciliation, when experienced, is primarily a gift given by the one who first kisses us. To mark this gift of peace, nothing short of a kiss on the mouth will do.

Theodore reflects on the nature and manner of this kiss: "Each of us gives the Kiss of Peace to the person next to him, and so in effect gives it to the whole assembly, because this act is an acknowledgement that we have all become the single body of Christ our Lord."[23] What is shared with one's neighbor thus becomes the possession of the entire church. In kissing our neighbor, we kiss the entire assembly. A mingling of mouth upon mouth unites the body of the congregation in a holy kiss. It is important, therefore, to kiss not only with the mouth but with forgiven and reconciled hearts as well. "We must not be like Judas and kiss with the mouth only, while remaining set on showing hatred and malice to our brothers in the faith."[24]

The kiss of peace, in the early church, emphasized Christ's desire for us, our desire for Christ, and the gift of reconciliation between believers granted by Christ. The kiss orients desire to the gifts of Christ—better than wine—and allows those gifts to be received erotically. The kiss, moreover, was unitive, in that it showed the union of Christ with the believer and believers' fellowship in one body, a mutual participation and interpenetration of lives so that, by grace, the life of Christ becomes the life we live. This kind of intimacy begs for physical expression, the intertwining of flesh and limbs so that it becomes pointless to identify where one person's flesh "begins" and another one's "ends." The life of union is a life of shared intimacy, broken open for another, healed by the touch of another, shared in breath upon skin, tongue upon breast, drinking the fruit of the vine and the milk of the breast. Sex and the Eucharist are not that far apart at all: both bespeak of longing and of union. The question is which has priority in Christian life. For the early church, the Eucharist exhibits priority, suggesting that we understand sex in the context of Eucharist, and not the Eucharist in the context of sex. This priority need not lead to the relegation of sex to the periphery of Christian life; it can lead to a deepening of sexual spirituality, so that sex, too, is an expression of the reconciliation and union given to the entire church in Christ. And, for that, nothing less than a kiss will do.

The implications of this kiss, however, may have proved too much for the early church, as it grew out of favor over the centuries, along with other highly charged erotic practices, such as naked baptisms. By the fourth century, the liturgical kisses were primarily reserved for members of the same sex. Homoerotic connotations notwithstanding, the kiss in its new practice restrained some of the torrents of sexual attraction. But there were exceptions. Taft relates two interesting stories: One of seventh-century St. Mary of Egypt, a former prostitute, of whom we hear ". . . according to custom she gave the monk [Zosimas] the kiss of love on the mouth."[25] Another anecdote concerns fifth-century St. Matrona of Perge, who lived disguised as a man during three years of monastic life and shared the kiss of peace with the men gathered in that community. When the abbot discovered that she is a woman, he inquired whether she had shared the kiss of peace with men. Matrona's response? "As for the symbol of peace and love, I have not shunned it, for I considered that I offered myself not unto human mouths, but unto God's angels and men free of passion."[26] There are kisses and there are *kisses*, but the church became increasingly uncomfortable with kisses shared by members of the opposite sex, even when they were shared, ostensibly, in a passionless way. The passion of the Christ, in this sense, had gathered too much earthly passion.

These early Christian kisses teach us much about desire: how Christ's desire for us is expressed in a kiss of welcome at Table, which we in turn share with one another. When desire is oriented toward the gifts at Table, our earthly desires also find their fullest expression. I kiss my neighbor in Christian assembly and know that this is an expression of reconciliation and not an invitation to bed. But Christ's kiss of peace also displays an erotic dimension—of longing and union that is covered in peace—inviting us to consider the analogues with sex.

In sex, lovers do not kiss as Judas does, but in ways that respond to Christ's kiss and embrace of us: inviting another to inhabit one's space so that the borders between "mine" and "yours" become permeable. In sex we experience some of our greatest vulnerabilities and our deepest acceptance, as lovers embrace, hold, touch, and kiss one another as they are, accepting each other as they are. One task of a theology of sexuality is to consider kisses—liturgical and otherwise—in their proper place again. Part of the point of this chapter has been to explore how liturgical kisses are not invitations to bed, but celebrations of the peace and reconciliation given in Christ, *and* how the kisses of our lover gain even more passion as they are related to Christ's kiss.

TASTE AND EUCHARISTIC INTIMACY

If we take the wisdom of the church's ancient eucharistic traditions to heart, we can reclaim the intimacy of the Lord's Supper. Our most tangible act in the Eucharist is when we take Christ's body into our own, making room for the One who desires us as he penetrates us. Gerard Loughlin writes, "Certainly the Eucharist is as intimate as sex . . . and just insofar as it unites men and women with Jesus, it is gay sex as well as straight sex, gay marriage as well as straight marriage."[27] Though they remember the violence of Jesus' death on a cross and the monetary exchange between Judas and religious leaders that led to the crucifixion, the actions of the Eucharist claim that violence and monetary economies are not the ultimate realities of God's world. The meal, instead, points to an economy of grace and the overcoming of violence in Communion. In the Eucharist, we open ourselves to Christ (taking him in our mouths) as Christ opens to us, and we are opened by him. This movement of opening and closing characterizes the movement of divine presence through human life, not just at Table, but throughout creation as a desiring God pursues our love.

The gestures of the Eucharist bespeak such intimacy that various monastic communities have endowed its liturgy with special solemnity, charged with the erotic. Loughlin remarks on medieval nuns at Rupertsberg who "wore bridal gowns when receiving communion. When they took Christ into their mouths, they were eating not only true flesh, but also the flesh of their bridegroom, their eternal lover. Thus Eucharistic devotions could become ecstatic, passionate consummations of desire."[28] Reflecting on her reception of the sacrament, Hadewijch writes, "After that he [Christ] came himself to me, took me entirely in his arms, and pressed me to him; and all my members felt his in full felicity, in accordance with the desire of my heart and my humanity. So I was outwardly satisfied and fully transported . . . I could no longer recognize or perceive him outside me, and I could no longer distinguish him within me. Then it was to me as if we were one without difference."[29] Notice how Hadewijch does not stress the disappearance of self in the beloved ("I'm lost in you."), but the intertwining of lovers, brought about by lovers' touch. Her identity becomes bound up with his identity, so that she becomes clothed in Christ. Some modern interpretations of these and other writings might stress that the nuns at Rupertsberg were sexually frustrated or maladjusted, projecting their longings for sexual intimacy upon an elusive, spiritual Lover. Instead, I would suggest that their reflections help show us the shape of true intimacy, of a Christian desire that is intensely physical, of desire that is consummated (and not deferred), a desire that shapes our earthly loves. In an age such as ours that is intensely suspicious of celibacy, these celibates offer readings of the Eucharist that teach us how to orient desire not to the exclusion of the erotic, but in affirmation of it. They show us how we are free to love, both our beloved and our Lord and our beloved as the Lord gives her or him to us, tasting God's desire in all of its goodness.

After lauding the taste of Eucharist and how the Table reorients our desire, I need to linger for a moment with a warning, drawing again upon the early church. For, as much as the Mothers and Fathers celebrated taste, they were also aware of its excesses, for taste can lead both to God and away from the good gifts that God bestows. Gregory of Nyssa writes, "Above all be specially watchful against the pleasure of taste. For that seems in a way the most deeply rooted, and to be the mother as it were of all forbidden enjoyment. The pleasures of eating and drinking, leading to boundless excess, inflict upon the body the doom of the most dreadful sufferings; for over-indulgence is the parent of most of the painful diseases."[30] Gregory notes how taste, if left only to itself, can lead to gluttony. What gluttony illustrates is not the sinfulness of taste, but the distortion of taste when it becomes the overriding drive of life. Taste then controls us as we lose the pleasure of taste and are consumed by it. Sexual and eating addictions share a common characteristic: both, in pursuing pleasures of taste eventually lose pleasure, whether at Table or in bed. If taste alone determines the meal, then the gift of Eucharist can become gluttonous and the meal becomes bacchanalian revelry, as we read in Paul's remarks on abuses of the Lord's Supper in Corinth (1 Cor. 11:20–22). The Eucharist and sex do not revolve only around taste, but also express gift and hospitality. When we receive such gifts and hospitality, our eating is less likely to become gluttonous, our experience of sex less addictive. Food and sex are intertwined in daily life and in Christian theology. As Augustine reminds us, "For sexual intercourse is to the health of the human race what food is to the health of a human being, and neither exists without some carnal pleasure."[31] A right celebration of the Eucharist teaches us to distinguish the filling of our gullet from the messianic banquet, sex that is compulsive and possessive from the shared hospitality and gift of making love.

EUCHARISTIC GIFTS

Modern U.S. economic life operates with a fairly prevalent assumption of *scarcity*.[32] Generally speaking, economic life works in this country because we assume that there is rarely enough to go around. Consumers compete for scarce resources, basics such as food staples and shelter as well as more eye-catching luxury items such as cars, household electronics, and exotic vacations. Not everyone can have these things: they cost money, and one must compete with others in order to possess. This assumption of scarcity breeds attitudes of possession: I must have this. I've got to have that. Life becomes a struggle to possess and hold on to things, to clutch them so that one does not lose them. When this assumption becomes engrained, the desire to possess becomes insatiable: if there isn't enough to go around, there's no guarantee that I will ever have enough. Taken to their extreme, the assumption breeds hoarding, where those who hoard are never satisfied, because they can always have a little bit more. Regardless of economic status, many Americans, when faced with the question, "Are you secure right now materially?" will answer, "I need just a little bit more in order to be secure."[33] Year after year we hear the same consumer mantras: hold on to what you can, because there is not enough to go around; crave things that you do not have.

Such assumptions infiltrate our sexual lives as well: we speak of "having" sex, of "getting" a sexual partner. Sexual life can become another manifestation of the insatiable drive that one can never have enough. A reigning assumption in life in the United States is that "more" is always "better," whether one is talking about consumer goods or sex. Recent books have appeared that chronicle couples who commit to have sex every day, such as *365 Nights* and *Just Do It*.[34] The ostensible "result" is a better sex life. When assumptions of scarcity reign, sex gets peddled on the marketplace just like any other good. The results of such practice, as we witnessed at the beginning of this chapter, is that sex gets reduced to a commodity, a medium of exchange between consumers, or at worst, something that one consumes from others by reducing them to a sexual objects for one's enjoyment. In an economy of scarcity, sex is something we *have* to have, clutch, and demand of others for a price.

A eucharistic economy operates with a different assumption: not scarcity, but *abundance*. In a eucharistic economy, scarcity and acquisition do not reign, but gifts, giving, and sharing. At the Lord's Table, it does not matter how many are gathered around it, because there is always enough to go around. In a eucharistic economy gifts are really gifts: they expect nothing in return, but in the strange dynamic of grace, they equip the receiver to give as well. The eucharistic economy is not a zero-sum game, where only a limited number of gifts may be given away, lest the goods become exhausted. Rather, the more we receive at Table, the more we are able to give ourselves. In a eucharistic economy, sex is understood not in terms of "having" and "possessing," but in the contagious movement of giving so that lovers might be fed.

The eucharistic banquet teaches—and embodies—the practice of giving and receiving, of cherishing and releasing, of desire that intensifies in giving. Unlike prominent contemporary attitudes toward sex that stress competition, having, and possessing, where sex is primarily a selfish pursuit, a eucharistic read of sex delights in the other simply because she or he is. Pleasures are not "had" as much as they are shared. We receive our lover as gift, as one who donates her very self, and we donate ourselves in return: not because my gift compensates for hers, but because when caught up in the gift we cannot do otherwise than give.

In *The Interior Castle*, Theresa of Avila writes that God's "riches do not lessen because He gives them away."[35] The divine economy, which propels the eucharistic economy, marks gifts that are given away simply for the sake of giving. In giving, there is life abundant. Whereas hoarding out of scarcity yields insatiability and ultimately the loss and diminishment of life (trapping us in prisons of self), sharing in abundance yields greater life, the sharing of riches so that all might have life in abundance (John 10:10). When sex takes its cues from the Table, it recognizes that the donation of self in making love is also what enables one's lover to donate. And, like the gifts at the Lord's Table, those donations or gifts are never completed, at least short of the eschaton. Both the Eucharist and sex bespeak communion and union: of the person's union with Christ by taking his flesh and blood in the mouth and of union and connection with one's lover as I make room for her in me and she makes room for me in her. But despite all the gushing odes to sex that speak of total bliss and ecstatic union, the union of bodies is never complete; distinctions remain: one's experience is never identical to one's lover's in the acts of making love. Whatever union is approximated is experienced in incompleteness, making the longing for union all the more powerful. This is part of what makes the experience of sex between lovers all the more enticing: the desire for union and connection is not completed in one act, but is carried forth over a history of laughter, disagreement, conversation, sharing in daily toil and celebration, and making love. The Eucharist, likewise, does not offer a union that is completed once and for all, but the continued promise of our union with Christ, as we partake it again and again. We rise from Table both sated and hungry: fed with the body of Christ, hungry to share that body with the world, longing to take part in the Supper again. Rising from our lover's bed, a eucharistic read of sex does not stress the fulfillment of the gift, but the experience of being fed and being hungry again: nourished by the gift of our lover, longing for union again as the story continues to unfold.

If we understand sex as gift then we ought to avoid one potential danger of this position: seeing sexuality as something *external* from ourselves. Sex does not come to us as something other, but wells up from within as we share with our lover. To make sex an external gift is to risk making it a medium of exchange all over again. Progressive church curricula often claim sex as a gift to be treasured. But as Thomas Briedanthal has noted, "The likening of sexuality to a gift is problematic because, without quite intending to, it can suggest that our sexuality is something external to us, a resource that we can use or leave to one side, like the talents in the parable."[36] The giving and receiving in sex is not something external to us, but our very selves, a bodily sharing of who we are with our lovers.

This is why the whole notion of which partner is active and which partner is passive is inherently problematic. Part of what has plagued some theological understandings of sex throughout the ages is the notion of male activity and female receptivity. These notations have led to stereotypes, the sanctioning of male pleasure, the questioning of female pleasure, the condemnation of homosexuality, the tacit assumption that men will seek sex and women ought to receive it from time to time. Notions of one person being active and the other passive express the dynamics of neither the Table nor sex. At Table, I receive Christ's body as I actively eat, and receive God's gift as I actively give in offerings to the poor that accompany Communion. In receiving I am empowered to give and in giving I am open to receive. Lovers, too, experience sex in giving and receiving, in activity and receptivity, in kissing and being kissed, in opening up and being opened.

The eucharistic economy does not show us that sex operates outside economic considerations, in an enclave insulated from the rough-and-tumble financial world. Short of the eschaton, all sex is affected by the dominant economic assumptions of our time; hence, possessiveness and acquisitiveness can invade even the most giving sexual relationships. But the Eucharist also points to another economy, an economy that gathers sex as one dimension of a more abundant life: of giving rather than taking, of donation rather than hoarding. When these assumptions take root in our lives, through participation in the Lord's Supper, they are bound to have sexual effects, evoking hospitality as well.

SEX, THE EUCHARIST, AND HOSPITALITY

One way of understanding the Eucharist is that it is a table set for a select few, a meal for the initiated, a table set in a familiar way, designed for those who are familiar with one another and Christian mysteries. Part of this description, of course, rings true. The early church placed a high premium on catechesis *before* baptism and one's first taste of the Supper. One had to be instructed in holy mystery before one partook of it. The meal, in this understanding, has to mean something, be revered as holy, lest it lose its meaning. Current practices of closed Communion in many contemporary traditions echo some of this sentiment. The rationale for a closed Table is not to claim exclusion, as if God's grace cannot be encountered among people and communities other than the church that practices closed Communion. Rather, the Table is closed because it cannot mean all things to all people: it has a particular meaning and particular gestures that one must learn. One must become a part of a tradition, a story, in order for that story to bear grace.

The danger of closed Table traditions, however, is that they may have the unintended consequence of suggesting that the meal is *only* for the familiar: for those with whom we worship weekly, for those whose theological understandings of the meal correspond with our own. In exaggerated versions of closed Communion, it sometimes appears as if *we* are the ones hosting the meal. But all traditions know this is not the case: at this Table Christ is host, a host who invites us all, and who recognizes that we come to the Table as strangers. The

Eucharist reenacts distinct practices of Jesus' table fellowship, of inviting strangers to dine with him, of inviting himself over to strangers' houses. Jesus dined with nuisances and nobodies,[37] and the meal Christians celebrate in memory of him recalls that hospitality. When practiced over and again, the Eucharist does not insulate Christians in a cocoon of familiar friends and fellow initiates, but teaches us to welcome the stranger, the rejected, the forgotten, to Christ's Table. The Eucharist invigorates us to share bread with a hungry world. This is why after receiving the elements of Communion, most ecclesial traditions have a prayer that stresses going forth into the world to share what is offered at Table: "Help us who have shared Christ's body and received his cup, to be his faithful disciples so that our daily living may be part of the life of your kingdom, and our love be your love reaching out into the life of the world."[38] The Table, in other words, is set for strangers.

In its hospitality to the stranger, the Eucharist reenacts Israel's privileging of strangers in their midst. In torah, the treatment of strangers corresponds to Israel's acceptance or rejection of the Law and their worship of God. "When an alien resides with you in your land, you shall not oppress the alien. The alien who resides with you shall be to you as the citizen among you; you shall love the alien as yourself, for you were aliens in the land of Egypt: I am the LORD your God" (Lev. 19:33–34). Loving God and rejecting the stranger are contradictory. By dining with strangers, Christians recall that God is the One who welcomes the stranger, regarding them as God's own. God calls us to do likewise.

The hospitality of the banquet recalls the procreative dimensions of sex. One common misperception of sex in our hyper-romanticized age is that sex only concerns two people: it is part of what insulates a couple from the designs of an increasingly hostile world. It is something private shared by two people to the exclusion of all others. And of course, part of this sentiment rings true. Sex without some degree of privacy diminishes gift; sex without some degree of exclusivity devalues covenant. But privacy and exclusivity do not insulate couples from others; they also demonstrate how our lives are opened to others. Procreation illustrates how sex can open us in surprising, radical, and often disruptive ways to others in our midst. The birth of children, no matter how anticipated and longed for, or unanticipated and not longed for, introduces the radical claim of another upon us: an other who at the beginning of life is utterly dependent on us for every physical need. The child's survival—and flourishing—is linked by birth to our life. Counter to many modern assumptions, procreation in sex is less about passing on one's genetic material or family lineage and more about the call to hospitality. It is less about what we pass on and more about how we are opened to the others we welcome as children.

Why do Christians have children? Part of the answer, obviously, is because Christians have sex. One age-old attitude about children is that they help ensure our family legacy. Modern medicine has accelerated this attitude in some ways. Recent advances in infertility treatments, such as in vitro fertilization, now make it possible for couples who could not conceive a child naturally, through sexual intercourse, to now have their "own" biological children. The customary language about biological children is telling, with a child marked by possessive language. These advances in medicine, of course, are welcome, especially for those who struggle with fertility. But they may also come with unintended consequences, fostering views of children as possessions, where we become increasingly able to mold children in *our* image (by selecting genetic traits and excluding others), where we are encouraged to dispense with "undesirable" children through genetic testing. If having children is simply about passing on genetic material, then childbearing can become a rather self-centered practice.

Evangelical theologian Rodney Clapp suggests another view: "*Christians have children so we can become the kind of people who welcome strangers.*"[39] Children are not ours, but given to us, and they come to us as strangers. Spend any length of time with a child and one quickly discovers how different each child is, how different each child is from each of his or her parents. "Whose child is this, anyway?" we may ask ourselves, even about those children we know best. Children wake us up at night, interrupt comfortable routines, and bug us for food, clothing, and shelter. Each one introduces something unexpected in our midst. As parents grow in the knowledge and love of their children, they realize that there is always more to know and love about them. The child also comes to us as mystery, given to us by God. By opening our lives to the unexpected, surprising movements of the children under our roofs, we can also become more adept at welcoming the strangers in our midst. The procreative dimensions of sex, in other words, recall the patterns of hospitality at the Lord's Table, of setting a table so that more can dine.

Having children, in other words, is less about biology and more about adoption. The primary image of children of God in Scripture, after all, is not biological, but adoptive. Christians are not children of God by birthright, but by adoption, by being engrafted into the covenant that God establishes with Israel (Rom. 11). The Table reminds us of this: all who gather are children of God, adopted by God. When we make love, then, we bear in our bodies the gestures of hospitality to strangers. Good sex, in this view, is not merely dependent on the number of orgasms, but the ways in which sexual relations open us to others: children and strangers.

Providing hospitality to children, as an expression of lovemaking, puts love to the test. As David M. McCarthy writes, "Bearing children turns love into hospitality and, in doing so, fulfills it."[40] Couples who have children struggle with time and how to continue the path of love together. Few occasions remain for hour upon hour of uninterrupted conjugal bliss. From time to time, couples will long for dinners that aren't punctuated by spilt milk and demanding petitions—and at times they may find it. But these interruptions are also an experience of grace, and examples of the ways in which love grows. Love remains not closed in upon itself, but grows as it is shared with others, as dinner conversation welcomes other voices and as couples are changed, surprised, and transformed by their children. Interruptions are also occasions for laughter, all made possible—in part—because sex establishes practices of hospitality.

In terms of procreation, however, one clarification is important. I am not claiming that sex *must* be procreative or that the central purpose of sex is procreation. Various traditions within the church often suggest as much. The understanding I am putting forward is that hospitality is more important than procreation, that procreation is a dimension of hospitality, a hospitality that we learn at Table. Thus considered, procreation is one dimension of sex, but not its end result or overarching aim. What is important is not whether individual sexual behaviors result in the conception of a fetus, but whether the story of shared sexual relation over time results in increased hospitality. A mark of bad sex is that it leaves couples trapped to themselves (even if that is endless oceanic bliss); good sex, by contrast, shares a story of lives and is marked by how we welcome our beloved *and* others. I know of no better illustration of this than the attestation given by many lovers that the experience of making love, over the long haul, can make us more welcoming than we might otherwise be. For those called to marriage, this is typical. When I experience myself as one who is able to forgive and to have compassion, I attribute much of this not to something innate within me, but to the long, slow growth of forgiveness, compassion, and understanding that I share with Molly and experience with her every day of my life. Making love is part of what gives this story its shape, and we have learned part of what it means to be accepting and forgiving by making love. This does not make sex somehow essential to Christian life—those called to celibacy are also, in perhaps even more radical ways, opened to the claims of others—but it does show us that sex can instruct us in gestures of hospitality.

The important insight here is not whether couples conceive children, but whether they can welcome outsiders. "What is ultimately pleasing to God about sexuality is the quality of its hospitality. This is not to say that every stranger must be offered sex, but that sex must cultivate an openness and warmth to strangers, it must open our hearts, break down our boundaries, and push us beyond ourselves,"[41] as sex builds up the body of Christ. Whether gay or straight, childless or the parents of twelve children, couples over the long haul can cultivate hospitality or turn in on themselves. At its most basic level, sex is one of the ways we show our beloved hospitality: by opening ourselves, our skin, and our lives to him. But those same acts can display inhospitality, when conceived mainly for self-gratification. Kathy Rudy offers a helpful distinction: "If our sexual relations help us to open our hearts and homes to lost travelers and needy strangers, they are good. And if they cause us to be aggressively territorial and abusive to outsiders, they are evil."[42] When sex takes its cues from the Table where strangers and outsiders are welcomed, we more readily embrace those who come to us as surprises, just as we are surprised by the grace of making love. This, in part, is what I mean by the public dimension of sex.

SEX, PRIVACY, AND THE PUBLIC

It may seem surprising that I close this chapter with the claim about the public dimensions of sex. There is much that can be contested about this particular claim. In some ways, I have anticipated my concluding argument throughout this chapter. The Eucharist is not simply a private meal for the initiated, but results in distinct public postures of hospitality and welcome. It is a meal for the baptized that releases the baptized for the world. As such, the Eucharist is a public meal. But public sex? Clearly I don't mean that. Most modern interpretations of sex stress the importance of privacy: part of what makes sex sacred is that a couple makes love in the privacy of their own bedroom, as something shared by them alone. I do not want to deny the importance of such moments. Part of the sacredness of sex is that it does focus on our beloved and no one else. But sex is not *only* private.

Our market culture purveys a faux version of sex's public dimension. Glimpsed most clearly in pornography, this understanding of public sexuality claims that one can view others' sexual behavior for the sheer enjoyment of it, for a price. The sex trade in its varied manifestations—Web sites, sex tourism, strip clubs—has a decidedly public face as it publicizes private sexual acts that are sold to the highest bidder. But that kind of public face is simply the reach of consumer culture into our sexual lives. To claim that sex has a public dimension is not to make all sexual behaviors and relations public or to claim that we make love in public. One of the problems with the pseudo-public nature of the sex trade is that it renders intimacy another commodity. In the vision of public that I am suggesting, public is not synonymous with visibility or the marketplace. Intimacies remain intimate, even private, but they redound to public postures. Sex, in this sense, connects us to wider communities.

Another problem with discussions of sexuality that stress privacy is that they render sex another mode of performance. Women have particularly felt the burden of this, though men are not immune either. Patricia Jung notes how the sexual revolution, and its privatization of sexual pleasure, yields an ambiguous legacy for women:

> Contemporary accounts portray female sexual pleasure as if it were a purely private or individual matter; this legitimizes performance anxiety and the American tendency to turn sex into work. For women exhausted by the work associated with their double shift (on the job and at home), enjoying sex becomes "just one more damn thing to do." Her woeful failure at it is simply one more indicator of her individual inadequacy and her marital and/or relational maladjustment.[43]

When confined to an artificial private sphere, sex can become oppressive in its expectations: more is better, longer is preferable, you better enjoy it or else. The e-mails that wind up in my junk box invariably concern sexual performance: promising readers the magical elixir that will render a man a stallion in the privacy of his bedroom. We have made, in this consumer culture, even the delights of sex yet another performance that requires plenty of work for it to come off right.

Instead of the public advertisements that promise orgasmic magic in the privacy of one's own domain, the public nature of sex that I stress centers on the life of communities. Sex is public because it is one phenomenon that connects us to the power of life itself. As Wendell Berry writes, "Sexual love is the heart of community life. Sexual love is the force that in our bodily life connects us most intimately to Creation, to the fertility of the world, to farming and the care of animals. It brings us into the dance that holds the community together and joins it to its place."[44] The shared practice of making love is a reminder that we are never alone or abstracted from the earth. Making love involves taste and touch, fluids and breath, the possible birth of new life and the experience of all things new again in one's lover's arms. Because sex connects us to life, to others, societies across the ages have issued regulations for sexual behavior. The point of these regulations is not simply to control or to enforce arbitrary standards; rather, the point is to remind its adherents that sex is a powerful life-giving and life-sustaining force. Regulations simply recognize that if left without any guiding principles, sex can teeter toward the chaotic, just as all life-sustaining forces can (religion, economics, politics, family). Regulations do not trammel those forces; they simply are attempts to make the channels of these forces more fruitful for the good of community. Of course, many of the attempts to maintain sexual regulations are notoriously flawed. Misogyny, homophobia, and racism have often lurked behind self-evident sexual codes. But the failure of past attempts at regulating or guiding sexual behavior does not mean we should scrap them altogether. The final chapter of this book will offer one such framework. But for here, suffice it to say that because sex has a public dimension, and because it can foster public good, there are some general guidelines that we might follow in maintaining its goodness for the public.

Christians begin to understand whether their sexual relations fulfill the public dimension when we situate them in the context of the church. Christians are people not called to a private cocoon of coupledom. When marriages are celebrated in the church, they involve the entire community of faith (all unity candles aside!). Couples make promises to one another, to God and to the church, while the church, as witness to those vows, makes promises to support the couple in their life together, as they are called to serve church and world. A Christian marriage is a public affair where promises are made all around so that partners are bound to one another, God, and the community of faith. This means that the first question we ought to ask of sexual behaviors is not whether they conform to past mores, whether found in the Bible or otherwise, but whether the sexual love shared by Christians helps foster the common life of the church or whether it inhibits that life. Elizabeth Stuart phrases this powerfully:

> The Church has a long tradition of affirming that sexual relationships must
> be unitive, which is to say that they break the boundaries of the self and

propel people out of individualism into *koinonia*. . . . The Christian aim is to achieve a permanent porousness that can only be achieved with considerable practice—a lifelong practice in fact—and therefore requires stability and a presumption of permanence on behalf of the couple and the community around them. But Christians are not called into a sexual community but an ecclesial one. Sexual relationships must themselves be permeable to the Church and spill over into the Church.[45]

The questions here that are paramount are not: "Is the couple straight?" "Are they married?" or "Do they intend on having children?" but rather, "Does their love isolate couples or free them to be children of God?" "Is their love a response to the love given by God, mediated through the church, and does it call them back to the church?" These are questions that *all* Christian couples should ask themselves, not simply at the beginning stages of their relationship, but throughout their lives together. And, though the answers to those questions are known most intimately by the couples themselves, the effects of those questions and those relations are felt throughout the community of faith. This is why the condemnation of homosexuality and cohabitation before marriage in so many churches does not build up the life of the *ecclesia*, but tears down the body of Christ. Couples that are called to the church instead experience rejection, moral condemnation, and sermonizing when they walk through the church doors. These couples experience their shared lives as expressions of grace, as responses to the life God gives to the world, and are called to the church only to have the church shut its doors. The surprise, given this state, is how the church that has routinely excluded them continues to be a place that queer Christians feel called to. Perhaps it offers further witness that the church, in the end, does not belong to its members, but to Christ alone.

Belonging to Christ alone means that Christian lovers do not belong only to one another, shutting out the din of the world. Wendell Berry writes: "Lovers must not, like usurers, live for themselves alone. They must finally turn from their gaze at one another back toward the community."[46] Here attentiveness to one's partner and concern for the world do not exist in inverse proportion, as if the more couples fall in love, the more they enclose themselves from the world. The Christian practice of sex is not a series of endless retreats, secluded getaways, and lingerie purchases meant for his eyes only. Rather, the attention cultivated with one's partner in sex occurs as part of the everyday tasks of maintaining a home, planning budgets, cooking and dining together. These domestic tasks connect us to the neighbors with whom we share sidewalks and yard work, the communities that provide schools for our children, the fertile earth that yields bountiful harvests. This is not to say that the Christian practice of sex leaves neither room nor time for romantic getaways, but rather that whatever getaways are planned occur in connection with the daily fabric of quotidian life, and not in escape from them. Attentiveness to quotidian realties, in fact, might be sustained through occasional respites from them. The Sabbath reminds us as much.

Over the years of marriage that Molly and I have shared, the quotidian realities have remained, even when we have been too exhausted and spent for sex. Like most couples, I suspect, there have been seasons in our sex life. Early on in our relationship, I tended (like most men) to equate more with better: that the quality of our relationship was directly proportional to the amount of love we were making. But as I look back on it, the quantity often had little to do with the level of attentiveness. When I thought I was paying attention to her, I often really was not, and at those times I often felt cut off from community. And, though bouts of inattention do reoccur, I have discovered how greater attention to Molly—her passion, her desires, her pleasures—has made me a more attentive person in general. When I lose the capacity to pay attention, all of life suffers. I have become more aware of how our tenderness and attentiveness to each other connect with our sense of finding a place in community. The long story of our marriage has shown me how the experience of nurturing love with Molly also finds room for others: in children, in community, in allowing others (neighbors, fellow worshipers, friends) to have a claim on us as well. Sex occurs in the context of these wider commitments and loves, and is part of what allows lovemaking to flourish.

In this way, the privacy of love making becomes a factor in public flourishing. This seems to be a consistent biblical refrain. The varied writers of Scripture are not interested in the sexual life because of titillating interest, or for exposing the peccadillos of the powerful, or for enforcing arbitrary rules. Rather, these writers—in varied ways—each suggest that the ways sexual love is shared reflect the larger question of communal flourishing. Paul's injunctions against various sexual behaviors, we have seen, are condemnations of idolatries that have the potential to tear Christian community; the Torah's regulation of sexual behavior is part of what distinguishes the Israelite community from others. And, the Song's pointed eroticism recognizes the goodness of sexual love, its power as strong as death, that intimates something of the relationship between God and Israel. Commenting on the Song, Robert Jenson writes: "In the Song, the necessity of concealment is experienced as a burden and impediment: the woman and Israel are passionate to conduct their love openly. . . . However private the act of sexual union may indeed be, its existence and character is vital public information."[47] One question we should ask ourselves is whether our sexual lives contribute to the building up of the body of Christ, which involves the building up of each other's *bodies*. Christian faith teaches us to attend to the body, and one of the ways we cultivate that attention is through our lover's body, who also attends to our own, in the process putting flesh on the claim that the well-being of one body is bound up with another.

When conceived along eucharistic lines, sex cultivates attentiveness to the senses: to tastes and touches, the lingering of tongue on skin, to kisses of peace and kisses of passion. But that same meal teaches us that our shared meals have public consequences, that the ways in which food, wine, and love are shared intimately bear fruit (or refuse to bear fruit) as that meal is opened (or closed) to the world. The Eucharist teaches us that a regularly shared meal, reserved for the baptized, issues forth in bread for the world. When sex takes its cues from that meal, shared lovers' delights can also become impetus for renewed commitments to the flourishing of the world, just as the lovers' delights are possible through the promises and commitments of community. The task of the next chapter is to chart some of the relationships in community that cultivate sexual life, where the delights of this meal might flourish with others.

Chapter 6

Vocation and Sex

Living in Light of Desire

Visions of Christian life often promote or prohibit sexual behavior: whether or not to have sex; how much or how little to have sex; with whom to have sex or with whom not to have sex. Sex figures into Christian faith because the faith that we profess is not exhausted by our speech, but informs the life of the body. God's claim upon human life encompasses the whole of that life: in life and in death, where no aspect of life is removed from God's blessing and claim. Our lips can express Christian faith, then, in our proclamation and our kisses.

Christians have argued about the significance of sex for Christian life since the calling of the disciples, those people who suddenly left their families and occupations in order to follow a single and—as tradition would have it—celibate savior. Christians have seen in sex both the antithesis to life in the Spirit and an analogy of beatific union with God. Christians have considered sex to be both the primary obstacle to the Christian life as well as one of the fundamental blessings of that life. This chapter explores sex and Christian life in light of the doctrine of vocation, which claims that God's calling upon each person is unique and takes shape differently for each person. Amid the diversity of vocations, however, are three patterns of sexual life—marriage, celibacy, and singleness—that are sustained by the God who calls each one of us.

CONFLICTED UNDERSTANDINGS OF SEX
AND THE WISDOM OF VOCATION

Christian suspicion of sex dates from the earliest traditions of the New Testament. Paul's first letter to the Thessalonians (perhaps the oldest text in the New Testament canon), for example, considers illicit sex an impediment to sanctification: "For this is the will of God, your sanctification: that you abstain from fornication; that each of you know how to control your own body in holiness and honor, not with lustful passion, like the Gentiles who do not know God" (1 Thess. 4:3–5). Though Christians have argued over centuries in the wake of Paul about what constitutes fornication (see chapter 1), the early church discouraged many sexual practices that were prevalent in the Greco-Roman world. Paul even deems licit, marital sex suspect if it expresses too much passion. Marriage, instead, ought to extinguish inordinate sexual desire: "But if they are not practicing self-control, they should marry. For it is better to marry than to be aflame with passion" (1 Cor. 7:9). Over time, the church developed increasingly suspicious narratives of sexual desire, and developed hierarchies that valued abstinence from sex above other forms of sexual expression. The highest form of Christian discipleship, in this view, was celibacy, as an "abstinence-only" form of catechesis began to take root. Hence, the church considered the path of the ascetic desert hermit more exemplary for Christian life than the mother and father who cherished the marital bed as well as their six children. By the fourth century, Christians who suggested otherwise—such as the Roman Christian Jovinian, who considered marriage and virginity morally and spiritually equal—were not only deemed suspect, but were considered as heretics.[1] The assumption here is clear: sexual desire is dangerous; therefore the more we can contain it by grace, the better for blessedness. Best of all for Christian life was the complete restraint of celibacy.

U.S. consumer society offers almost the reverse message. In the wake of multiple sexual revolutions, repression of sex is out, while celebration is in. These revolutions have bred much good, as women have gained access to birth control and overt hostility and violence toward gays and lesbians has gradually morphed into greater societal acceptance. But beneath these positive developments lies a frequent assumption: that our capacity for happiness and fulfillment increases the more sex we have. More is always better, and the most fulfilled lives are those where all vestiges of sexual repression have disappeared. If the wisdom of the ancient church was that sex impeded sanctification, the wisdom of a consumer society is that more sex makes us blessed.

Both assumptions are problematic and potentially misleading for a theology of human sexuality. Christian understandings of vocation, however, provide some resources for critiquing either of these extreme positions because they show us that God's call on human life is diverse. We should expect the sexual lives of the saints, therefore, to be varied. Vocation teaches us that there is no singular path, sexual or otherwise, in Christian life. The elevation of one sexual path over and above all others violates the image of the church as the body of Christ, knit together in the different gifts of each member. Paul writes, "Now there are varieties of gifts, but the same Spirit; and there are varieties of services, but the same Lord; and there are varieties of activities, but it is the same God who activates all of them in everyone" (1 Cor. 12:4–6). The church has long recognized celibacy and marriage as Christian vocations, even though it has often emphasized one at the expense of the other. To these two vocations, I add a third: singleness that does not entail sexual abstinence. Each one of these vocations builds up the body of Christ, each one is holy, each one is a response to a gift of the Spirit, and each one draws something from and depends on the others, so that no one stands normative or preferable in Christian life.

SEX AND PRAYER

Prayer knits together all Christians in a bond of love. Despite our variety of vocations, God calls all Christians to pray. Often prayer seems remote from sexual life. Prayer, in this view, stills the body and muffles its desires. In Protestantism, such views of prayer run especially deep. Other strands of the tradition, however, understand prayer to animate the body. Toni Morrison's *Beloved* offers one compelling vision, coming from the lips of ex-slaves who have fled plantations that have broken body and spirit:

> "Here," she said, "in this here place, we flesh; flesh that weeps, laughs; flesh that dances on bare feet in grass. Love it. Love it hard. Yonder they do not love your flesh. . . . This is flesh I'm talking about here. Flesh that needs to be loved. Feet that need to rest and to dance; backs that need support shoulders that need arms, strong arms I'm telling you. . . ." Saying no more, she stood up then and danced with her twisted hip the rest of what her heart had to say while the others opened their mouths and gave her the music. Long notes held until the four-part harmony was perfect enough for their deeply loved flesh.[2]

In the midst of a wider, racist culture that neither honored nor protected their flesh, at a time when their bodies were regarded by that wider culture as dispensable machines to produce a maximum yield through whips and chains, these ex-slaves celebrate their bodies and pray for flesh that needs to be loved. This dancing, touching flesh is both a praise of hard-won freedom and a prayer to the Maker of all flesh. It is nothing less than bodily prayer. Morrison's novel invites the reader to consider prayer as something more encompassing than private conversations with God, stilled by the quiet of folded hands and bowed heads. The experience of prayer can also allow bodies that have been broken and abused to slowly become themselves again. New life in the Spirit gives life to the body.

Sex also enlivens bodies. For many, sexual intimacy offers another way of recovering the body's grace: to be touched by another, to open oneself to the gift of another. The dynamic of sexual arousal, plateau, orgasm, and afterglow is accompanied by palpable changes of the body: the quickening of pulse, a heightened sensitivity of skin, engorgement of erogenous zones, an increase in their moisture, the deepening of breath, the intensification of movement, tensing and releasing of muscles, the throes of climax, the melting of oneself in another, and the rest after release. Awareness of embodiment and the body's pleasures, no doubt, increases during sex. Many experience sex not only as pleasurable but also as healing touch in the warmth of embrace, in flesh that is loved. Lee Butler has claimed that people often use the same words to describe afterglow and worship, leading him to conclude, "Spirituality and sexuality are not only related, they have the same purpose as the end goal, that is, to integrate human persons with one another and the Divine through the harmony producing activities of communality."[3]

Sex not only offers parallel responses and postures to prayer, it may also condition us to pray. Prayer and sex both cultivate the discipline of attention, though their focus of attention differs.[4] In prayer, our attention is drawn to God, so that those who pray participate in God's life, as the Spirit intercedes on our behalf with sighs too deep for words (Rom. 8:26). Sex also orients our attention upon our beloved: in thanksgiving for her embodiment and the exquisite detail that makes our beloved unique. The shape of her hips, the taste of his tongue, the feel of her skin, the arch of his neck. The texture of our beloved's body that is typically hidden from public view becomes the subject of our undivided attention, just as ours becomes the site of our beloved's attention. In this mutual give and take, in the sharing of pleasure and the delight of eye and tongue, sex can focus our attention, both as the intensification of desire and as we turn our attentions to the beloved. Because it nurtures attention, sex can prepare us to pray.

Given their connections—theologically and physiologically—sex and prayer can inform each other. Christians can pray over sex, and when we do, sex and prayer both become transgressive acts. Common wisdom understands sex and prayer at arm's length from each another, especially when it comes to questions about gay, or queer, sex. Queer sex, supposedly, represents the departure from a prayerful posture. This understanding also tends to equate queer sex with promiscuity. But as Mark Jordan claims, "Unbridled sex is hardly the most transgressive queer act. That is only what queers are scripted by public imagination to do. Praying over queer sex—now that transgresses."[5] This is why the case for gay marriage ought to be particularly strong in the Christian church: marriage understands that sex and prayer have a place together, that they make room for one another in the ebb and flow of a common life of a couple and their connection to a community of faith. To deny marriage to those in the church who seek it is to allow stereotypes of sexual behavior to trump theology.

If sex resembles and informs prayer (and vice versa), then the experience of each exhibits highs and lows. Intimacy and the dark night of the soul are present in the life of prayer. Sex, likewise, can cultivate deep intimacy in attentiveness, as well as detachment and compulsiveness. Simply "going through the motions" of prayer and sex is no guarantee of the benefits of either. Nearly identical words, nearly identical touches, can convey vastly different meanings—or lack of meaning—depending on the level of attentiveness or the availability of intimacy. Dennis O'Brien writes,

> Prayer adopts body language: rhythm, posture, music to acknowledge ontological dependence, to bridge the split between the independent self and the body which is forever in "fusion" with the mother/the Father. Proper sexual behavior immersed in body and its language negotiates the split between independent selves and ontological "fusion.". . . That our sex life may be no more successful and secure than our prayer life should be no surprise.[6]

O'Brien suggests that physical postures are not enough for intimacy in prayer or sex. The life of the Christian is not an endless chain of advances in deepening intimacy with God. Rather, it is the experience of presence and absence, deep pleasure and painful loss. Even the duration of time spent with our beloved is no guarantee of the benefits of prayer or sex. The dark night of the soul is common to those who have devoted a lifetime to prayer (as in Mother Teresa's case) and the loss of meaning in sex can be found in couples who have been married for decades. Familiarity sometimes can breed inattention. But the Christian pilgrim is also hopeful, discerning grace even amid loss, knowing that absence is not the final word, that communion is promised each day anew and at the end of days. Whether in prayer or in sex, Christians long for this communion.

THE VOCATION OF MARRIAGE: HISTORICAL ROOTS

As Christians pray, some will be called to marriage. But marriage has a complicated history in the Christian church. Early Christians were often suspicious of marriage, particularly if perceived as a mandate for all people. In the New Testament world, perhaps even more than today, men and women were expected to marry, but the early Christians resisted this expectation. In the New Testament we find more arguments *against* marriage than for it. Paul, for example, prefers singleness to marriage throughout his writings. Christians' primary responsibility, in this view, was not to the institution of marriage and families that resulted from marriage, but to the new family inaugurated in Christ that transcended the bonds of blood and kin.

Paul's suspicion of marriage continues in the patristic period. Tertullian interprets Paul's lukewarm endorsement of marriage as impetus to become free of sexual passion: "Scripture says: *It is better to marry than to burn* [1 Cor. 7:9]. What sort of good is it, I ask that is commended only by comparison with an evil, so that the reason why marriage is better is because burning is worse? How much better it is neither to marry nor to burn!"[7] Tertullian here offers some concession for the necessity of sex (and marriage) for procreation, but the new covenant inaugurated in Christ renders even that concession suspect.[8] The path of the Christian disciple, in this line of thought, ought to increase sexual restraint. The only two paths worthy of distinction are marriage and celibacy, and it is clear, for Tertullian, that the latter is more honorable than the former.

Amid suspicious attitudes toward marital sex appear some robust defenses of it, not in terms of a concession for procreation, but for the good of couple and society. John Chrysostom, for example, understands eros not in opposition to agape, but as an expression of yearning for communion in Christian life. In a homily on Ephesians he writes, "Deeply implanted in our nature there is a certain desire (*eros*) that, without our noticing it, knits together these bodies of ours."[9] Coming together in the flesh is a boon, a gift. The desire that draws a couple together in love and in marital sex is a creation of God and the highest form of human love.[10] Though Chrysostom also upholds chastity as a virtue, he does not uphold it at the expense of marriage. For him, marital sex is also holy.

Medieval liturgies of marriage tended to convey more of the holiness of marital sex than patristic suspicion of it. One example of this positive view is the *Hadrianum*, an eighth-century text sent by Pope Hadrian to Charlemagne. It claims that "generation adds to the splendor of the world," and includes the following blessing: "O God, you have consecrated the conjugal union with so excellent a mystery in order to signify the sacrament of Christ and the church in the bond of married persons. O God, by your agency woman is united to man, and society is ordered from the beginning by the gift of that blessing, which is the only decree that was not removed either by the penalty of original sin or by the flood."[11]

Another seventh-century document, the *Verona Sacramentary*, contains the following affirmation: "Because of this sharing of the marriage bed has been decreed for the increase of all people, so that these unions may link the whole world together and bind together the alliances of the human race."[12] In this liturgical tradition, marital sex is a good when it reflects sacramental bond and procreative blessing. Eventually, this tradition helped lead to the establishment of marriage as a sacrament in the Western church in 1215 at the Fourth Lateran Council.

The Protestant Reformers inherited conflicting attitudes toward marriage and sex. On the one hand, the Augustinian tradition interpreted sex primarily in light of original sin and saw marriage as a remedy for unbridled sex in a fallen world. That trajectory (and other more suspicious attitudes) tended to view marriage as a vocation inferior to celibacy. On the other hand liturgies of marriage often celebrated the bond and gift of marital sex. Calvin stands as one example of this mixed inheritance, as he writes: "The Lord sufficiently provided for us . . . when he established marriage, the fellowship of which, begun on his authority, he also sanctified by his blessing. . . . The companionship of marriage has been ordained as a necessary remedy to keep us from plunging into unbridled lust."[13] For Calvin, the sexual *restraint* of marriage is also a joy, since it encourages marriage partners to focus attention on their beloved.

Following Calvin, the Westminster Confession of Faith contains a clear endorsement of marital union as a public good:

> Christian marriage is an institution ordained of God, blessed by our Lord
> Jesus Christ, established and sanctified for the happiness and welfare of
> mankind, into which spiritual and physical union one man and one woman
> enter, cherishing a mutual esteem and love, bearing with each other's
> infirmities and weaknesses, comforting each other in trouble, providing in
> honesty and industry for each other and for their household, praying for
> each other, and living together the length of their days as heirs to the grace
> of life.[14]

Notably absent from this ringing chorus are injunctions of procreation. The good of marriage is not tied directly to the rearing of children. Its underlying purpose is neither to propagate the species nor to establish a seal of sexual union. In this sense, Westminster demystifies both sexual intercourse and the raising of children, anchoring both in the public goods of happiness and human welfare. Sexual union and children are the fruits of that wider good rather than their source. They are gifts that may occur in the context of a marriage. Indispensable gifts, however, they are not. One consequence of this more effusive understanding of marriage, however, is that celibacy and singleness began to fade from Protestant view over time. If the early church was often suspicious of marriage, Protestants became increasingly suspicious of those called to a single life.

One way of connecting marriage to other vocations in sexual life is to claim it—like all other vocations—as a gift of the Spirit. Marriage shows us that desire for God and desire for partner can exist in direct, rather than inverse, proportion, so that love of God can grow as a partnership grows. Marriage is not the *only* vocational path for Christians and sexual life, but it does make a distinct contribution to those called to other vocations. Marriage shows how promises to one another take visible, tangible, embodied form, and that these promises are particular. One pledges in marriage not to an ideal of someone, but to a particular person, in all his warts, in all her wisdom and shortcomings. Marriage offers one example of how promises become incarnated in Christian faith—when couples pledge body and soul to be with each other, where these pledges then become a gift to the church, showing us the ebb and flow of faithfulness in embodied life.

MARRIAGE AS MUTUAL SOCIETY

How does marriage express the longings of couples, the eros of relation? One of the prominent interpretations of marriage in our time focuses on marriage as a resolution to the longing for completeness. In Valentine's Day cards and in some strands of theology, two halves make a whole. These sentiments can run from the saccharine to the profound, but share one thing in common: persons are not complete until they find a soul mate. This view of marriage is suspicious theologically, since it claims that we are incomplete as created. It also can heap enormous expectations upon a marriage or even encourage the loss of self in one's partner.

Language of mutual society, prominent in some Reformation theologies, is less likely to lead to these suspicious theological ends. In his commentary on Genesis, Calvin claims the chief aim of marriage not to be procreation or sacramental union, but the well-being of each other and community. "In creating the woman . . . there should be human beings on the earth who might cultivate mutual society between themselves."[15] Calvin does not assume that marriage *necessarily* creates mutual benefit and promotes the common good. Indeed, as an institution entered into by human beings marred by sin, marriage often can result in enmity and discord. But even this marring does not negate the original intent or aim of marriage, and "amidst many inconveniences of marriage, which are the fruits of degenerate nature, some residue of divine good remains."[16] In this context, Calvin understands sex as not only procreative, but also for the mutual benefit—and enjoyment—of the couple. "Thence it will follow that the children of God may embrace a conjugal life with a good and tranquil conscience, and husbands and wives may live together in chastity and honor."[17]

Current Reformed liturgical practice reflects much of Calvin's theology here. A service for Christian marriage contained in the Presbyterian *Book of Common Worship* contains these words: "God gave us marriage for the well-being of human society, for the ordering of family life, and for the birth and nurture of children."[18] The ordering of these benefits is significant: first marriage is for society at large; second for family life; and, third for children. The prayer of blessing in this same service reflects this hope: "Make their life together a sign of Christ's love to this sinful and broken world, that unity may overcome estrangement, forgiveness heal guilt, and joy conquer despair."[19] Marriage, in this view, represents not the longing for completion, but the desire for others to flourish: one's partner in marriage as well as the society in which that marriage takes root. As it radiates outward, the blessing of marriage can also become a delight.

This context is helpful for understanding the place of sex in marriage. Certainly the eros for union is prominent in sexual desire, but as married couples experience sex over the long haul, they recognize that union is never fully achieved. When sex flourishes in the context of marriage, however, attentiveness can increase as couples spend time together: in cooking and cleaning, in saving and spending; in dreaming and planning; in arguing and supporting. When couples spend time together, they typically aim not for beatific union, but for mutual flourishing. This flourishing, moreover, can become real. Marital sex might best be seen not as a longing for ecstatic union (which no sexual experience can sustain over any lengthy period of time), but as a practice that enhances mutual society and delight. None of this is to deny that moments of union do occur, from time to time, but those moments in marriage are often fleeting—whether experienced in orgasm or in delight of a common commitment to a shared dream. Over the long haul, what makes marriages endure is not the permanence of union or even the longing for union, but a shared commitment to mutual flourishing.

WITH MY BODY I THEE WORSHIP

One of the strongest, and sexiest, endorsements of lovemaking in Christian tradition occurs in the Church of England's liturgy of marriage, penned by Thomas Cranmer: "With my body I thee worship." This is perhaps the one instance in Christian liturgy where worship is oriented to something other than God. Here couples proclaim to one another that what they do with their bodies, shared with each other, is an act of worship. What does this phrase mean? Is it an instance of ecclesial-endorsed idolatry? As Cranmer uses the term, it connotes "to count as worthy." To worship one's spouse is to pay honor to, to give thanks for, to recognize the claim that the spouse has upon oneself. Episcopal bishop Paul Marshall writes: "Consider the possibilities of physical intimacy as worship of a spouse. The expression *making love* takes on new possibilities when we see ourselves giving pleasure as an act of worship—affirming the worth—of the other, doing what we have learned to do to move as *one flesh* to a repeated experience of ecstasy."[20]

We worship, or count as worthy, our partners with whom we share domestic life. Martial sex, in this view, gets domesticated. Domestication most often connotes a draining of vitality, a sapping of vigor, a confining of what had once been ribald. That is not the meaning of domestication in this case; rather, it means sharing a domicile, occurring within the flow of a household's rhythms, which is part of what makes married sex a comfort. Lauren Winner writes, "Married sex does not derive its thrill from the possibility of the unknown. Married sex is a given. It is solemnized and marked in ritual. It is established. It is governed by vows. It becomes a ritual in itself; it becomes a routine."[21] To proclaim "with my body I thee worship" is to recognize that one shares one's body with the one who knows it better than anyone else, better, in some regards, than oneself. Domestication makes sex ordinary, but in Christian vocabulary only the ordinary becomes sacred: water, essential and basic to life, becomes the promise of new birth in baptism; bread and wine, the basic food of sustenance and the basic drink of celebration, become the body and blood of Christ; ordinary, broken people become the church, the body of Christ in a broken world. Sex is an ordinary practice in marriage that sometimes happens frequently and sometimes only after a long period of abstinence. But over the course of a story shared together, this ordinariness is part of what makes sex holy, and one's partner worthy of worship.

Robert Jenson reflects on marriage liturgy in a similar way: "The blessing of marriage by the church brings sex within the gate of heaven, within the gate of the coming new and transformed Eden, and so restores its innocence."[22] Perhaps the current manifestation of the fall is not shame over sex, but the rampant commercialization of sex, which reduces sex to a commodity or transaction. Sex loses its innocence in modern times because it is one more thing to be sold or pursued on the open market. Sex in marriage, as celebrated in liturgy, is a restoration of innocence because it places the couple before God and the church in the midst of the everyday ebb and flow of desire and living together.

Sex in marriage is a mixture of exultation and restraint, the deepening intensity of physical pleasure and the withholding of that pleasure for a time, of fulfilling desire and postponing desire's fulfillment. Marriage has its sexual seasons. Calvin remarks that sexual relations within marriage do not hinder prayer any more than eating and drinking hinder fasting when appropriate. In his commentary on First Corinthians, Calvin counsels his readers to find the appropriate seasons for each: "It is the part of believers to consider wisely *when* it is time to eat and drink, and *when* to fast. It is also the part of the same wisdom to have intercourse with their wives when it is seasonable, and to refrain from that intercourse when they are called to be engaged otherwise."[23] Married couples know well the ebb and flow of sexual life: it is hardly all sex, all the time. There are household chores and bills to pay; parents and children to care for; struggles over finance and work outside the home. Desire runs hot as well as cold. Even when sexual desire is strong within a marriage, it can often remain unfulfilled because of the multiple other concerns that occupy a couple's attentions. Sometimes desire gets intensified, and at other times it's obstructed.

In this sense, the movement of eros in marriage can reveal surprising similarities with that of celibate persons. Sarah Coakley remarks,

> A realistic reflection on long, faithful marriages (now almost in the minority) will surely reveal periods of enforced "celibacy" within marriages during periods of delicate pregnancy, parturition, illness, physical separation, or impotence, which are simply the lot of the marital long haul, realistically considered. . . . The reflective, faithful celibate and the reflective, faithful married person may have more in common—by way of prayerful surrendering of inevitably thwarted desire to God—than the unreflective or faithless celibate, or the carelessly happy, or indeed unhappily careless, married person.[24]

One mistake of many contemporary understandings of eros is that eros gets reduced to sex, and sex is always found: more is better, and desire is always quenched. Most married persons know, however, that desire experiences its seasons and in some senses is *never* fulfilled. The more one comes to know one's partner, the more there is to know; the more physical or emotional closeness is achieved, the more one is aware of what separates the beloved from oneself. Here the path of Christian mysticism is again of some help: for the mystic's desire is not to have God—the subject of desire—completely, but rather to be formed by that desire as one grows into deeper relationship with God.

Desire in marriage is not the desire to possess. As Paul Lakeland has noted, "the opposite of desire is not its absence but possession."[25] When desire degenerates into having, eros loses its grip. But the true things of eros are not capable of being possessed: God and one's spouse, the divine and the earthly beloved. When eros becomes possession, idolatry is the inevitable result, so that God becomes an object to be manipulated and the partner exists for one's own instrumental, emotional, or physical needs. When that happens, the relationship disappears, and desire becomes turned in on itself. Don Juan misconstrues desire with possession and therefore is left with an endless pursuit of conquests that do not satisfy. But sex in marriage can point to a different trajectory of desire: where eros grows and subsides, where persons seek the flourishing of the other, where companionship (not possession) marks the continuing sexual journey.

CHRISTIAN MARRIAGE, GAY MARRIAGE

The theology of marriage that I have outlined here applies equally to gay and straight couples. The Reformed churches, in particular, ought to celebrate gay marriages because they, like all Christian marriages, (1) are examples of covenant; (2) express mutual society; and, (3) anticipate the new creation God is bringing about in the world.

Covenant is an expression of promise: God covenants with us, pledging to be with us, to sustain us, to give us new life. In response to the God who gives life, we respond with promises of our own. The Bible records this giving and receiving of covenant time and again. God gives and people respond with gifts of their own. The promises we make to one another are part of what it means to live in faithfulness to the God who gives life. Marriage is one of the ways we witness promises made to other human beings most clearly. In marriage we see promises that two people make to one another in the company of the community of faith, promises made first and foremost between *persons*, not between genders. These promises are not simply words; they are lived over time. When persons covenant with one another in marriage, they are not promising that they will always be understanding, or always be happy, or always be sensitive. But they do promise to be with and for another person, to journey with that other person under God's grace and to learn hospitality and forgiveness with that person. These promises, no doubt, are countercultural. In a commercial culture that often treats relationships as disposable commodities, the church blesses a covenant between persons that endures under God, sustained by Christ's marriage to the church.

Marital covenants represent one of the ways that we respond to God and to others in love. When we consider this dimension of marriage, it is highly unusual that some churches expend so much effort trying to prohibit gay marriage, in effect keeping people from making promises of commitment to one another. Many, ironically, are arguing *against* enduring relationships when the church ought to be fostering the hope that relationships can endure by God's grace.

Marriage, as we have seen, also expresses hope for mutual society. Same-sex marriages may even offer opportunities for reexamining mutual society throughout Christian marriages. Because they are composed of couples of the same sex, by their very nature same-sex marriages question the common gender roles that many straight couples fall into. Parenting, work outside the home, cleaning, and cooking, for example, do not fall to one person in the marriage simply by gender. If what makes a marriage valid is the mutual pledge of fidelity before God and community and the mutual sharing of life and joy, then gay marriages offer one example of how life can be shared, where gender roles are questioned in the name of common flourishing.

However, the celebration of gay marriages in the church doesn't give same-sex couples something they do not already have. If mutual consent is one of the oldest marks of marriage in Christian tradition, then gay couples might *already* consider themselves married. Church weddings do not magically render a couple married any more than the absence of particular ceremonies render them unmarried. Consider Karl Barth here: "Two people may be formally married and fail to live a life which can seriously be regarded as married life. And it may happen that two people are not married and yet in their precarious way live under the law of marriage."[26] The witness of same-sex couples in the church, the body of Christ, may suggest that these couples already live in marital covenant, even when church practice and societal law refuse them access to it.

Marriages are also signs of hope; gay marriages anticipate the communion and reconciliation God brings to the world in Jesus Christ. The words Christians proclaim at weddings offer hope for the world: of unity overcoming estrangement, of forgiveness healing guilt, of joy conquering despair. In a world infected by violence and hatred, people struggle against one another in fits of combat. Marriages, too, often contribute to such conflict, as couples learn to fight as well as forgive in them. Marriages are never perfect, yet they are signs of God's grace—even in brokenness—and responses to the love God gives to the world in Christ. Marriage is a sign of hope not because two people together will always make the best choices or always be considerate to one another; they are signs of hope because they point to the new creation God is establishing, a creation of communion and reconciliation, where we exist in communion with others and with God. Marriages are signs of hope because they draw us toward one another, never leaving us alone. Marriage, in much of the tradition, has little to do with gender differences and everything to do with the promises people make to one another in light of God's grace and promises to us. Marriage, in this tradition, is not mandated for anyone, not discouraged for anyone, but celebrated as one of the ways God blesses human persons made for community. Whether gay or straight, marriages are for the people of God.

Christian marriage is one response the church makes to the God who claims us—body and soul—as God's own. In Christ, God's body, none are alone, whether married or single. Communion is established not because persons find each other and form partnerships, but because God desires us and embodies that desire in Jesus Christ. Our desire for another, our covenant with a partner, is a reflection of God's desire for us. To pledge, body and soul, to live the length of one's life uniquely with that other is one response to the God who desires us. Marriage, however, does not exhaust the possibilities of responding to God's establishment of communion.

Christian marriage revolves around bodies: how the bodies of two persons are brought together before the church, the body of Christ. The celebration of marriage ought to nourish bodies lavishly. Weddings figure prominently in the

Gospel narratives: in John, Jesus performs his first sign at a wedding celebration where wine flows freely; in parables wedding banquets anticipate the reign of God. Because weddings nourish and sustain bodies, the Eucharist is rightly celebrated within them, signifying the communion of Christ with the church. When Christians marry, they are caught up in a communion far wider than the romantic fusion of two souls. In marriage, partners do not meld into each other, but respond to the God who is continually gracing creation by becoming open to the mystery and depths of another human being. Without others, marriage partnerships would soon collapse. Because marriages are incomplete without the witness of others, without the promise of the body of Christ, the ever-incomplete journey of a marriage throws couples outward into the presence of single persons and other married couples, gay and straight. No marriage accomplishes all things, but wherever marriages are celebrated as a dimension of the church's life, the church responds to the God who desires us—in our imperfection—as God's own. Thus Christian marriages point to other possibilities in life, including celibacy.

THE VOCATION OF CELIBACY

I have spent a large portion of this chapter exploring the vocation of marriage, considerably more than my exploration of the other two vocations—celibacy and singleness—that compose the remainder of this chapter. That is no accident. I write as a married person: it is the path where the Spirit has called me and Molly, and it is the most familiar to me, with all its joys, struggles, celebrations, and tears. Because I have written more on marriage than celibacy or singleness does not mean that these vocations are not equal. The amount of space devoted to each simply reflects my own vocational life at present. Others who have taken vows of celibacy are better equipped to write about it; and persons who are single have a more immediate sense of that path. When I write about singleness and celibacy, readers should keep in mind my own experience with these vocations is once-removed. I have never taken a vow of celibacy, and though I spent a decade of my adult life as a single person, the length of time I have spent in marriage now outlasts that experience. But my lack of an immediate experience of a particular path does not mean that I cannot write about that vocation. Each of these vocations, I have already argued, needs the others to glimpse some of the fullness of life in the Spirit.

Celibacy is not fashionable these days. In a sex-saturated society that purportedly celebrates all things sexual, celibates are seen as aberrations, strange, sexually frustrated, infantile, and even maladjusted. Protestant polemics against celibacy have been part and parcel of the tradition since the Reformation: celibacy represented an unnatural development in church history that led to the undervaluing of marriage and the forced stunting of the sexual drive. Popular fascination with persons who have taken vows of celibacy but then become parents to children, moreover, echoes obsessions with the sexual lives of celibates that have been around for ages, "proof" that the vow, in the end, is unsustainable.

What is celibacy? How is it a gift of the Spirit? How as a distinct vocation does it contribute to the well-being of Christian community? Celibacy is the willing restraint from sexual relations with another person, so that the celibate symbolizes in his or her body humanity's ultimate desire for God. Celibacy cultivates a reserve of desire, which for married people is oriented sexually toward one's partner and finds bodily satisfaction (sometimes ecstatically) in eros for God. This posture is a gift to the community because it shows us that our ultimate fulfillment is found in God's life, and that all of our other commitments, promises, and desires ought in some way to reflect God's desire for us and our desire for God. Celibacy is also a gift to the community because it can represent possibilities for deep, erotic friendships between genders and between persons of the same gender that do not necessarily lead to sex. Celibacy refutes the wisdom of *When Harry Met Sally*, where Harry (played by Billy Crystal) claims that men and women cannot be friends because sex always gets in the way.

One misunderstanding of celibacy is that it represents the absence or frustration of sexual desire, that it points to a unique gift that is comparatively rare in persons, akin to asexuality. To the contrary, the witness of celibates is quite desirous. Instead of the absence of sexuality, celibacy is an expression of sexuality, an expression that refuses to reduce eros to sex. Celibates have passionate friendships, even what might be described as love affairs. The qualification is that these love affairs do not lead to sex. They point to slow growth of love that does not rush headlong into the bedroom. Janie Gustafson, a member of the Sisters of St. Joseph, calls this a witness to all our loves: "All of our love-making, regardless of who we are or what we are committed to, should be purposeless and leisurely. In an erotic relationship involving singles, vowed religious, or two people not married to each other, abstinence from intercourse can be one expression of such leisurely love."[27] Intriguingly, the sexual restraint of celibates can allow erotic friendships to grow and flourish. This movement points to the realization that eros must not always be satisfied sexually, that it can find fulfillment, release, and ecstasy in relationships with other human persons in nonsexual ways.

Celibacy often has figured in Christian theology as a foretaste of heaven. Gregory of Nyssa, in his treatise on virginity, represents this strand: "The Life of Virginity seems to be an actual representation of the blessedness in the world to come, showing as it does in itself so many signs of the presence of those expected blessings which are reserved for us there."[28] For Gregory, these blessings are not expressed chiefly in sexual abstinence, but in the celibate's refusal to be conformed by worldly values, demands of family, and concern with status, honor, and worldly recognition.[29] Celibacy offers a foretaste of heaven not merely through sexual restraint, but through conformation to heavenly values that center one's life in the life of God. Celibates thus show all persons where our ultimate loyalties and life reside. Sexual abstinence is a dimension of one's conformation to heaven, but not its totality. Celibates avoid sexual relationships because sexual relationships are prone to idolatry, even though they also tend toward worldly ties that are good. To be sure, celibates are not absent of worldly ties, but their bodies witness another way, a way bound not to power, status, and family lineage, but to the God who gives life abundantly.

Celibates witness to the community of faith through their cultivation of what Thomas Aquinas reportedly called "vacancy for God."[30] One temptation of married life is to fill this vacancy with the presence of one's partner. The cloying sentimentality of "you complete me" in Valentine's Day cards only adds to this temptation. Single persons, according to this view, are missing a piece that will not be made whole until they find their soul mates. Sex, then, becomes one of the ways the person is completed. Partnered and married persons can be tempted to become everything to one another—the very definition of idolatry—promising to fulfill what they never can fulfill. The cultivated practice of vacancy for God by celibates, however, offers up the truth that only God completes persons made in God's image. The vacancy visibly present in celibate life is a vacancy that needs to be present in different forms in every Christian life, as God makes room in our bodies to make God's self known. Elizabeth Stuart claims that the celibate offers two truths for the entire church: "The first is that heterosexuality, marriage, and family life, are not identical with Christian discipleship. The second is that all desire is ultimately oriented towards God. Our desire for the other is ultimately desire for the Other and will not be satisfied until it reaches its *telos*, its end in God."[31]

Despite its communal focus, celibacy has often been misconstrued by Protestants as an essentially selfish practice, as something that cuts the person off from intimacy with others, as a practice that vaunts itself as superior to marriage by avoiding sex, as a practice that chiefly focuses on the self's spiritual development at the expense of the community of faith. Yet the primary value of celibacy is not what it offers the celibate, but the church. As Lisa Cahill notes.

> The worth of celibacy itself, in Christianity today, must also be measured in communitarian terms, not in those either of personal perfectionism or of a new sexualization of the celibate state. Part of the value of celibacy is its witness to a transcendent fulfillment of all human strivings and the relativization of all human loves; part of it is even a testimony that sexuality is not as deep and definitive a component of human identity as it seems for post-Freudian Westerners or was socially for premodern women. But surely another test, even a more important one, is its role in building up discipleship community.[32]

Celibacy contributes to the community's life because it shows—in its unique way—that persons are made for community, and not chiefly the microcosm of community that marriage provides. Vacant for God, the celibate also cultivates a vacancy for other persons—a vacancy that is often not possible for married persons to cultivate, especially those with young children, where the demands of the microcosm of community can occupy twenty-four hours a day.

The lives of celibates also present a seemingly novel possibility for male-female relations (among straight people) and same-sex relations (among queer people), the possibility of erotic friendships: "The man-woman relationship that is erotic but not coital could be the greatest single witness to society of the inadequacies of mere libido."[33] Celibates refute Harry's conventional wisdom in his conversation with Sally. Celibate passionate friendship suggests that the deepening of desire need not become sexual. Desire, in passionate friendship, is for the other to flourish, to have life abundantly. Friendship itself is a decidedly underdeveloped theme in Christian theology, despite Jesus' naming his disciples as friends during the Last Supper (John 15:15). In our day , friendship points to possibilities of relationships that are free, mutual, and as Sallie McFague has suggested, "potentially the most inclusive of our loves."[34] While marriage invariably involves negotiations of finding mutuality amid the legacy of patriarchy, friendship may more naturally incline toward freedom and mutual flourishing.

The life of the celibate, however, is not a life beyond sex. The celibate too is a sexual person, but finds sexual satisfaction in ways that differ from marriage. Eugene Rogers writes, "Monasticism is for people who find a bodily, sexual sanctification first and foremost in the desirous perception of God. Marriage is for people who find themselves transformed by the desirous perception of another human being made in God's image."[35] The celibate shows the community that the love of God can also be sexual love: hence the mystics talk about union with God in ways that would make many blush, indicating that the sexual ecstasy found in divine communion is juicier than pomegranates. This is not sexual sublimation: rather, it points to a fulfillment of sexual life as it is gathered together in God's life. "The married need the celibate to tell them what sex is really for. It is for the experience of the body as gift. It is for the taking up of human beings by means of their bodies into the life of the One whose life is a perpetual movement of gift. It is for making the other an occasion of joy, as the life of the Trinity takes the other as an occasion of joy."[36] Human persons find their ecstasy in God: sexual ecstasy mirrors this, and whether it results from the exchange of pleasure with one's lover or the intense practice of prayer, monastics show married Christians where ultimate ecstasy lies.

Married and celibate persons are meant for community, though openness to community is not a guarantee of either path. Married couples can turn in on themselves, and celibates can become so engrossed by their own spiritual pilgrimage that others fall by the wayside. Monasticism and marriage, then, have more in common than what might first appear, for both involve restraint. "The 'choice' between the vocations of marriage and monasticism is not a choice between asceticism and non-asceticism but between different types of asceticism. Marriage is a form of asceticism in which denial and restraint is practiced for the purposes of sanctification. Monasticism is also a form of marriage. Both involve the obligation to welcome the stranger."[37] This hospitality, this welcome of the other, whether in the covenant partner of marriage or the other to whom the celibate is summoned in love, are reflections of the divine Other who welcomes us and shows us hospitality. Marriage and celibacy show us that in welcoming the other, we also welcome Christ, even if they manifest that welcome in different ways.

But what of those persons who do not take vows of celibacy or enter into the covenant of marriage? This has been a gray area in the history of the church, either glossed over a preparatory phase in advance of marriage or one assumed to have the same general sexual rules as those that constitute celibate life. The contemporary path of most Christians, however, suggests something else: the single state is neither a state free from sex nor merely preparatory for marriage. Singleness also is a calling, and it also has something to offer the church.

THE VOCATION OF SINGLENESS

Compared to the volumes upon volumes that Christians have written on the estate of marriage and the call of celibacy, singleness has occupied little theological attention across time. By singleness, I mean the vocation of persons who have neither entered the covenant of marriage nor made the conscious vow of "vacancy for God" that celibacy entails. Singleness covers a whole range of persons: from teenagers to elderly people; from divorced persons to widows and widowers. In many stages of the church's history, the sexual lives of singles was assumed (or at least urged) to be celibate. Sex belongs to marriage; those who are not married should not have sex. In many cases, such wisdom continues to have relevance. Premature entry into sexual relations may contribute to lessened self-esteem. Adolescent boys and girls often feel significant pressure to engage in sexual behavior, thus blurring the boundaries of consent. In many cases, it makes more sense for teenagers to be abstinent than sexually active. Adolescents may not be aware of the long-term implications of their sexual decisions. Delaying sex, indeed, can allow opportunities for the development of an integrated sexual and spiritual life. Since, historically, the early onset of sexual life was often connected to marriage, it may be advantageous for many to delay marriage. Women, for example, have made enormous gains in the workplace, education, and society, because of avoiding marriage at an early age. Voices that have not been heard in the past are beginning to be heard because women are marrying later in life. Many young people postpone sexual relationships rather than rushing headlong into them. But to assume that the sexual behavior of fifteen-year-old single persons ought to be the same as twenty-five-year-old single persons is problematic; let alone the sexual behavior of a forty-year-old widower or a sixty-year-old divorcee. What of the sexual lives of these singles? How is the vocation of singleness also a gift of the Spirit? How are their lives a gift to Christian community?

Singleness, in its varied manifestations, is a gift of the Spirit because it shows how Christian life is an itinerant pilgrimage that requires discernment. The Christian is always on the way; so, too, is the single person, the one who is not bonded to another in marriage or fixed to a vow of celibacy. The single person cultivates—perhaps more intently than many others—the gift of discernment:

whether to enter into an intimate relationship with another person, whether to end an intimate relationship, or whether for a time to maintain vacancy for God by avoiding sexual intimacy. Single persons date, and single persons refrain from dating; single persons ponder marriage, and single persons ponder a life without marrying; single persons have sex, and single persons remain celibate—all of these are dimensions of the vocation of singleness. Discerning where to be and with whom to be in the midst of pilgrimage is part of the gift and challenge of single life. This discernment is a gift to Christian community because the single person shows the church that we belong ultimately to God, not to our marriages or monastic communities. The single person shows us all that we are all single, alone before God, *and* partnered, bound to other persons in the Christian church.

The vocation of singleness reminds us that each person is unique, standing before God. Most visions of the last judgment throughout the church's history entail some recognition that persons are responsible for their own actions; we are formed, of course by our communities and our histories, but we are also accountable for our own behavior. Much Christian prayer cultivates some time of solitude. In order for the pilgrim to grow in the life of God, the pilgrim needs to cultivate occasional times of aloneness; otherwise, the pilgrim drowns in a sea of other concerns. Solitude is not inimical to Christian life, but an enhancement of it.[38] Jesus's own ministry suggests as much. The Gospels portray Jesus as perennially responsive to others: he heals, he breaks bread with sinners, he preaches, he touches and is touched. But the Gospels also present him withdrawing in solitude to pray. This interplay of serving others and withdrawing from others for a time is integral to his ministry. Jesus is not a "quivering mass of availability,"[39] but a person who grows in intimacy with God as he serves and prays, as he gives himself for others and as he cultivates a practice of solitary prayer.

The lives of singles show the community that Christian life, too, has its own sense of solitude and that if solitude isn't found from time to time, the spiritual life suffers. Singles experience chosen solitude and imposed solitude. Sometimes persons choose singleness as something essential for spiritual and physical well-being (for example, after a difficult marriage ends in divorce); at other times singles long for companionship but are not able to find it. Single persons, in their bodily experience, show us that we are made for God and stand before God on our own.

The paradox, of course, is that in Christian community no one is ultimately alone. As Stuart writes, "in the church no one is actually single, no one is alone, all are bonded together in the body of Christ."[40] The life and witness of singles show that we belong to one another in the church. One of the oddities of contemporary churches is that single Christian adults often experience marginalization in parish life: churches host plentiful programs for parents, children, and married couples, but approach single adults as an afterthought. Church growth is often predicated on recruiting young families. Compare the welcome of a family with two or three children to a single forty-year old, and one quickly discovers how imbalanced the church's ministry toward married persons is. Thus,

Christian community often betrays its own moorings, suggesting that we belong together as couples and not as a new family in Christ Jesus. But the persistent, embodied witness of single persons can serve as a gift to the community: that marriage or vowed celibacy does not make us who we are. In the end, only our baptism identifies us, a new birth that marks us as belonging to God, bonding us to our brothers and sisters in the church who are not related to us by blood. As single Christians do not couple themselves to other persons, as they refrain from sexual relations, they remind us where we really belong.

But the life of singles is not characterized by constant abstinence or perennial vacancy for God. Single Christians date; single Christians have sex; they enter into relations with other persons, often with great hope for the future. Dating is a reality of single life and it ought to be seen as a component of Christian life. Jason King and Donna Freitas have attempted to outline how dating might be conceived theologically, chiefly by comparing it to those persons who are affected by Jesus' ministry but do not become the itinerant disciples who follow him. Many figures in the Gospels are changed by Jesus' message for good, but do not leave their homes, possessions, or livelihood like the disciples do. King and Freitas call these persons "hospitality disciples."

> Such "hospitality disciples" were models that the Christian community could imitate. Even though their physical interaction with Jesus was temporary and their encounter with him did not lead to a radical change of life like that of the twelve apostles, their contribution was still valuable and an ideal for the Christina community. By making a comparison between the hospitality disciples and dating, we argue that we can view dating as part of the larger story of God's redemption of humanity, even if dating involves a temporary encounter between two people. Dating is a component of redemption valuable in and of itself regardless of whether it leads to marriage, just as believers who stayed home contributed to the building up of the kingdom even if they did not leave behind their work or family.[41]

Dating changes the lives of persons. Two people who are initially on separate journeys travel for a time together, and this encounter and journey together changes them for good. Coming together is a good for the dating couple, even if only for a time. The journey together may turn sour; it may blossom into a covenant. But the journey, regardless of its length, can be an expression of the togetherness and being made for one another that is also a dimension of Christian life. Togetherness can, but need not necessarily, lead to sexual intimacy. Sex can be an expression of togetherness, of promise to be with, but it is not an indispensable component of the desire to be together. Thus dating may involve sex, but it does not require it.

Dating might even be called a school for the single person, a school that focuses the discipline of discernment, whether the single person might be called to marriage. This does not mean that dating is mere preparation for marriage, but that it can serve as an apprenticeship for marriage. Persons often learn, through dating, whether they are called to marriage or not.

Singleness is a vocation of Christian life. It is not an anticipation of marriage or celibacy, but it can help persons discern whether or not those callings are theirs. Many will discern a call to singleness as a lifelong call, a call that involves neither the covenant of marriage nor the vow of celibacy. This call will then cultivate attention, of how, when, and whether to enter into sexual relationships with another person. This vocation, no doubt, entails risk and blessing. The risk is that dating relationships become disposable, that relationships are only for the good of the individual, and that as soon as they prove challenging, they get dumped. But that is the distortion of dating rather than its promise. Another risk is that sexual relationships, in single life, can become casual, that the bodily promises of sex slowly come to be seen as something other than promises. Sex then becomes transactional rather than relational. But marriage and celibacy also have their own pitfalls, perils, and risks. Marriages can become enclosed upon themselves to the exclusion of community; celibacy can become a narcissistic preoccupation with individual spiritual development. Each vocation in Christian life gives rise to distortions of the life they offer.

Singleness also expresses promises and gifts to the community: it reminds Christians of the itinerant pilgrimage that is Christian life; it emphasizes that we stand alone before God and are made for community. Sex in single life is part of this promise and gift. Sex for the single Christian always involves a risk: a risk that the promise of the body is not returned, a risk that relationship can prove more destructive than constructive, a risk of sex becoming more transactional than relational. But sex in married and celibate life also entails risks: of promises in marriage that get broken; of the possibility of betrayal; of the risk that celibacy really was not one's calling in the first place. All of our promises, as Christians, are fragile ones. Only God's promise to us is irrevocable. As we make promises as single persons, as married persons, and celibate persons, we witness to the promise that God makes to the church in Jesus Christ: that we are made for God and made for one another. Each vocation—marriage, celibacy, and singleness—bears witness to that promise in its own distinct way.

Chapter 7

Ethics and Sex

Flourishing Desire

ACTS AND CONTEXTS

What constitutes good sex? American consumer culture has offered many answers to this abiding question: Good sex involves novelty, pleasure, self-fulfillment, and the liberation of self from outdated mores; good sex is frequent sex. One of the messages that Americans encounter on an almost daily basis is that sex makes us happy. In a consumer culture, good sex, as it fulfills us, chases an endless supply of sexual goods and partners, all in the name of a better life. The church has also ventured several answers to this question across time, sounding chords that are dissonant from many of these modern-day assumptions. Frequently, the markers of good sex in the church boil down to specific acts: some acts, such as marital sex, are condoned, while others, such as gay sex, masturbation, and premarital sex, are taboo. Sex requires restraint, not liberation, in order for it to be good. Otherwise our sexual desires run riot. Sex thus needs an ethic to help persons perceive what is right and wrong. Typically, this ethic claims that sex needs the discipline of marriage in order for it to flourish. In some of what follows, I will follow suit, since marriage situates sexuality in a context of mutual promises, fidelity, and trust. But the marital norm also has its limitations, because it often excludes sexual behaviors based on *acts* rather than *contexts*. The alternative that I offer in this chapter is to view Christian sexual behavior in the larger story of God's redemption of creation, the story of God's love spilled out for the world. Sex is not the most important part of that story, but it is shaped by that story. Our attitudes and behaviors regarding sex thus help show how we are living as part of that broader story.

Before I develop this alternative account I need to examine an influential stream of Christian sexual ethics, the approach advocated by Thomas Aquinas. Though Aquinas's approach is not strictly act focused, he dubs some sexual acts as morally acceptable and others as aberrant. His approach is an example of Christian natural law, where everything exists for a purpose that can be discerned through the proper use of reason.[1]

Aquinas teaches that sexual desire is not intrinsically evil. Sexual desire is found throughout the animal kingdom and is part of God's design for the world. Our natural desires, however, ought not run their course wherever they may lead. In order to discern desire's proper course, we have to know what sex is for. Aquinas enumerates three purposes to sex in descending order of importance: First, sex serves a procreative purpose. Since reproduction is essential for life, procreation might be described as the essence of sex. But this is not its only purpose, for sex also can strengthen the bond of marriage and serve as a pledge and marker of fidelity. Third, the pleasure of sex is also part of its purpose: "The exceeding pleasure attaching to a venereal act directed according to reason, is not opposed to the mean of virtue."[2] These three ends of sex, for Aquinas, find their fulfillment in human marriage, a place where sexual desire can find a home.

Marriage provides the proper context for sex, which means that sexual acts that occur outside of marriage run contrary to God's design. But the list of sexual sins that represent departures from marital sex are not all equal departures. Some sexual acts, for Aquinas, depart from the norm more than others. The least serious sin is premarital sex or fornication. It is least serious because it fulfills two of the purposes of sex (procreation and pleasure), but departs from the purpose of marital bonding. Premarital sex can offer a foreshadowing of the sexual bond that occurs in marriage, but because marital promises are not yet present for the couple, it ultimately fails to fulfill the ends of sex.

Adultery is more serious, because it represents an outright violation of marital promises rather than the mimicking of a promise present in premarital sex. Even though procreative potential and pleasure may be present in an extramarital affair, adulterers break the vows that they have made with their spouses and thus betray one of the purposes of sex. Even more serious is rape, since it violates all the purposes of sex except the first, its procreative potential.[3] But the most serious sexual sins for Aquinas are what he calls "sins against nature," acts that depart from the primary procreative intent of sex. Included in this category are masturbation, sodomy, and bestiality. The only criterion that such acts fulfill, according to Aquinas, is pleasure, the lowest purpose of sex. This grouping is rather odd since it considers some sexual acts that are consensual, such as masturbation and homosexual intercourse, to be more serious sexual "sins" than rape, which is a violation of consent and freedom. It places bestiality—a sexual act that is never consensual—alongside masturbation (which modern psychology and theology views as more or less innocuous and a normal—indeed, to use Aquinas's language, "natural"—part of human sexual development). Here the problems of Aquinas's approach are evident: a focus on specifically taboo acts can obscure wider concerns of human freedom and creaturely integrity.

The idea that sex belongs to marriage, however, is not the exclusive property of medieval theologians. For most practical purposes, it is the most common way of talking about sex in the Christian churches today, even if its teaching is often not embodied in Christian practice. The marital norm is a tried "rule" to Christian sexual behavior that has often served the church well. It teaches that Christians are made for covenant; it can teach us to honor the body; it affirms intimacy and recognizes that sexual intimacy can become a parody of itself in promiscuous sex; it honors the significance of promises and vows. But is the only Christian practice for singles abstinence before marriage? Does the marital norm offer a fixed standard for all time? In an essay on marriage, Martin Luther makes an intriguing observation about biblical laws: "Moses' law cannot be valid simply and completely in all respects with us. We have to take into consideration the character and ways of our land when we want to make or apply laws and rules, because our rules and laws are based on the character of our land and its ways and not on those of the land of Moses, just as Moses' laws are based on the ways and character of his people and not those of ours."[4] In other words, customs of marriage and sexual life vary culture to culture. What the Bible offers is not a static mold in which all marital practices are formed, but broader patterns that orient varied cultural practices toward faithfulness. Marriage is not the same for Moses as it is for Luther as it is for us. The age of first marriage, for example, has changed dramatically over centuries, with betrothal happening typically in late adolescence in Luther's Germany to the age of first marriage approaching thirty in twenty-first-century America. This shift has given rise to a significantly longer period between the onset of puberty and the age of marriage, perhaps longer than at any other time in history. What this means for sexual ethics is often not addressed in traditional approaches that see sex as *only* reserved for marriage. Luther's observations about the nature of people, culture, law, and land open the door to something other than an "abstinence-only" approach to sex before marriage. What laws we have, Luther claims, exist "for the sake of the conscience, not the conscience for the sake of the law. If one cannot help both at the same time, then help the conscience and oppose the law."[5] The letter of the law, in the worst cases, can sometimes bind the conscience oriented toward the good.

A rigid interpretation of the marital norm can also invest sex with a quasi-magical meaning. This occurs when the church interprets sex as the consummation of marriage. Adrian Thatcher sees problems in this language that "invests a single act of sexual intercourse with power to achieve a crucial transformation in the relationship in the sight of God. . . . 'The sexual and sacramental automatism contained in the first-night-consummation concept recalls . . . the sympathy magic found in the fertility cults which the Judeo-Christian Tradition opposed from the outset.'"[6] Sex, of course, represents one of the ways in which married couple's express commitment to one other. Language of consummation isolates sex from other marital activities, as if sex were the apex of the marital pledge. The case and experience of many Christian marriages, especially as they extend over time, is not that sex is the highest form of marital commitment. Marriage is sealed not in an instantaneous act of intercourse that gets repeated again and again, but over the long haul, as couples negotiate responsibilities and share domestic duties, as they learn to live together, as they cook and clean, show and receive hospitality, build a home, pay bills, and learn forgiveness amid laughter and tears. Time, commitment, and promise, rather than sex, seals a Christian marriage. Sex, in this context, is a bodily expression of promise rather than the act that seals a marriage. In its concern for establishing the proper context for sex (which is a legitimate concern), the church has sometimes hyped sex so much that it promises more than it can deliver.

Stanley Grenz, though his conclusions about marital and nonmarital sex differ from my own, offers wise words about sex and its context:

> Sex is not something that happens "out there," at a distance from the person who participates in the act. Rather, like human actions in general, the sex act is an expression of the intent of the actor who creates a context for the action, from which, in turn, the act derives its meaning. Just as there is no "brute fact of history" and thus no "brute act," so there is no sex act apart from the context in which it transpires. To attempt to separate the sex act from the personhood of the participant, then, is doomed to failure. Instead, the participants must engage in the act cognizant of what this specific act of sex is intended to declare.[7]

Sexual acts are not isolated bits of behavior that can be held up for examination apart from the context in which they are practiced. Sexual behavior is never just "mere behavior," for the actions involved communicate meaning. Sex, in other words, is never "just sex," for in sex we communicate (or withhold from communicating) our deepest selves. Thus sex can occur in contexts that facilitate communication or obstruct it from ever happening. Determining the context, therefore, rather than the act itself, is usually the primary ethical question. The approach that I am offering takes into account Aquinas's account of the purposes of sex without leading to the conclusion that certain sexual acts (most notably, premarital sex and gay sex) are excluded from the realm of the good.

Indeed, some scholars have argued that the church's often obsessive concern with premarital sex runs counter to the cadences of Scripture itself. Miguel De La Torre notes, "The Hebrew Bible contains many sexual constraints, yet nowhere is premarital sex forbidden. Likewise, there is no explicit prohibition of sex prior to marriage in the New Testament. Indeed, there are a few examples in which premarital sex is accepted without a hint of outrage or moral indignation," such as the Song of Songs and Ruth.[8] De La Torre's point is that sex occurs in contexts that may inhibit or enhance human flourishing. Marriage often provides a context for that flourishing, but it is not guarantee of it. The move among many contemporary Christian ethicists, therefore, is to focus on principles that allow for the flourishing of human persons in sexual relationships, or to identify characteristics of contexts that promote human well-being.

Three Catholic approaches to sexual ethics serve as representatives of such moves. The earliest is a jointly authored report commissioned by the Catholic Theological Society of America in the early 1970s, which identified seven characteristics of sexual behavior that allows human beings to flourish. Good sex, in this view, is (1) self-liberating, (2) other enriching, (3) honest, (4) faithful, (5) socially responsible, (6) life-serving, and (7) joyous.[9] Though this report implicitly criticizes the Vatican's procreative norm for all sexual behavior, it resulted in no substantive change in magisterial Catholic teaching on sex. More recently, Lisa Cahill, has argued for four fundamental markers or values of good sex: (1) equality between the sexes, (2) reproduction, (3) pleasure, and (4) intimacy, with the "most complete and morally attractive experience of sex . . . at the intersection of . . . the pleasurable, the interpersonal, and the parental."[10] Finally, Margaret Farley has argued for sexual ethics to be framed by justice, or "justice *in* loving and in the actions that flow from that love. The most difficult question to be asked in developing a sexual ethic is not whether this or that sexual act in the abstract is morally good, but rather, when is sexual expression appropriate, morally good and just, in a relationship of any kind."[11] In the process of answering that question, Farley suggests seven norms for sexual justice: (1) do no unjust harm, (2) free consent of partners, (3) mutuality, (4) equality, (5) commitment, (6) fruitfulness, (7) social justice.[12] Sexual ethics, in each of these perspectives, involves more than a checklist of appropriate sexual behaviors. In identifying these markers of good sex, each approach seeks to situate sexual behavior in context. Good sex refers less to isolated acts than it does to the pattern of how acts are carried out over time. The approach that I would offer, in some ways, draws on each of these attempts to identify appropriate norms for good sex. But it also amplifies the theology behind the norms that the aforementioned approaches do not. Some of the norms that I highlight are identical to norms from these other approaches. All, however, are connected in a more sustained way to the broad patterns of the Christian understanding of redemption that I have outlined in the earlier chapters of this book. The point of Christian sexual ethics is not to develop the ideal list of characteristics that mark moral sexual behavior, but to show how our sexual lives intersect with and are informed by the story of God's redemption of the world. Christ comes so that we might have life and have it in abundance: good sex takes its cues from the pattern of how that abundance is shown for the life of the world.

Any attempt to identify norms, however, risks oversimplification or the flattening of the Christian story of redemption into a tidy list. The norms that I offer are not immune from that risk. They are not meant as a handbook that validates or invalidates all sexual behaviors, but they are meant as general guides. As I write them, I am especially aware of my own children. The messages about sexual development and behavior that they are bombarded with on a daily basis are often destructive. In a culture that often assumes that frequent, early sexual initiation is a prerequisite to the good life, charting an alternative path is difficult. I thus write these out of a spirit of frustration that the sexual messages of commercial culture are especially destructive toward adolescent girls' sexual awakening and exasperation that the church sometimes has fostered an "abstinence-only" message for unmarried young adults that often places sex in a quasi-magical realm. If commercial culture teaches us to treat sex casually, ecclesial culture sometimes reveres it as a holy of holies. A Christian vision of good sex, I am convinced, traverses these extremes and implicitly critiques both. Historically, church and culture have both overestimated and underestimated its significance. In the Christian story, however, sex is one part of the abundant life given us in Christ. As we respond to that life, five markers can signify how sex fulfills its purposes for life: (1) consent, (2) mutuality, (3) covenant/trust, (4) community, and (5) joy. In isolation none of these markers establish the parameters for good sex or exhaust the possibilities for Christian sexual expression; together they paint some patterns in the Christian story of redemption. The markers, in other words, represent not a place to end a discussion of good sex, but a place to begin.

CONSENT

Free consent of persons to engage (or not engage) in sexual behavior is the *sine qua non* of Christian sexual ethics. If consent is present, Christians can begin to determine the shape of good sex; if consent is absent, we cannot even begin a discussion. But what is consent? Consent means that persons engaging in sexual decision making are free to say yes and free to say no. Consent means that persons making sexual decisions have a voice and that their voice is heard, valued, and honored. The presence or absence of consent often determines whether sexual behaviors are healing or harmful. When consent is present, making love is possible; when consent is absent, movements that can be instances of lovemaking become rape instead. Rape is the most harmful sexual behavior because it ignores consent and treats the one who refuses to grant consent as an object.

Consent does not occur at one time and then authorizes all subsequent sexual behavior. In the story of sexual life, consent develops over time. Adolescent boys in the United States are often socialized to trivialize consent: when a girl says yes to one thing, she implicitly says yes to further sexual intimacy. Thus a kiss becomes license to fondle; or a fondle provides license to intercourse. "No," boys are often told, means "yes." Here "consent" is gained once and never revisited. But consent is not achieved once and for all; it is, rather, "a moment-by-moment gift,"[13] whether in adolescence or in a forty-year marriage. Marriage does not license consent, but provides a ground where consent may flourish. Societal laws have not always recognized this. Most states, for example, did not recognize the crime of marital rape until the latter part of the twentieth century.

How is consent related to the Christian story of redemption? Free consent reflects God's creation of the person in freedom, a freedom that fits us for relationship with one another. Most theological accounts of creation stress divine freedom.[14] The God of Christian faith is not compelled to fashion a world because of external necessity, but creates out of sheer grace. God brings a world into being in abundance and diversity, and this is good. We who are creatures thus experience creation as gift, as a continuous testament of grace. We persons who are created in God's image are also free. Human persons are not compelled to act out of necessity or because of the brute force of fate, but have choices. God creates not automatons who must love the God of creation, but creatures who are capable of loving and capable of spurning that love. Yet Christian faith also recognizes that many things impinge on creaturely freedom. The long course of human life is a struggle against things that inhibit creaturely freedom. Often the things that enslave and snare human persons appear at first set us free. Reformed Christianity has consistently addressed this dynamic of idolatry: where good things of creation—such as family, sex, honor, and possessions—become the source of our enslavement. But the good news of Christian faith is that God in Christ breaks these various forms of self-imposed bondage. God creates us in freedom, fits us for freedom, and when we impose bondage upon ourselves (or when others attempt to bind us), God frees us in Jesus Christ to be in relation to God and others.

One distortion of freedom in a consumer context is libertarianism, where freedom means that I am bound by nobody and may do whatever I want, as long as I do not harm others or infringe on the freedom or property rights of others. But the Christian view of freedom forms us *for* relations, honoring and respecting others who are equally children of God, fitted for freedom. Laurie Jungling has written eloquently how freedom is connected to faithfulness: "Erotic freedom requires erotic faithfulness for embodied relationality to reach its full potential in creating, sustaining, and empowering the abundant life of all creation."[15] She also notes how faithfulness and freedom mutually inform each other. Freedom without faithfulness, in sexual life, "reverses the spirit/body dualism to make the body's needs lord over all. Freedom without faithfulness is 'radical individualism.'"[16] Yet faithfulness without freedom is equally problematic. When persons experience faithfulness as an excuse to disrespect the freedom of their partner, faithfulness parodies itself, and relationships meant to sustain life wind up draining us of life. Faithfulness alone can trap persons in rigidly defined gender roles and "demand that erotic relations be confined behind walls of simplistically gendered bodies and abusive social orders."[17] The Christian vision of freedom recognizes that the person develops and grows in freedom with another. When relationships become characterized more by manipulation, bitterness, or constricted roles than by nurture and growth, then the relationship begs for transformation, or in the worst cases, termination. Faithfulness does not mean that one stays in relationship whatever the costs to oneself or others.

Much of this language of consent states the obvious. Of course, persons in sexual relationships must heed consent; good sex means, at minimum, noncoercion, that one does not manipulate another into sexual relations. Yes means yes and no means no. But the language of consent is still countercultural in North America because much of what masquerades as consent is really not consent. Advertising in North America constantly purveys images of sex, and the images tend toward the endless sexual availability of women. In this unsubtle form of marketing, the message is not simply "buy this and you'll have sex," but that consent is not important at all. Rather, the message is that men want sex, that they should have it, and that there are plenty of women available to have sex at any time. Men want sex and women are there to provide sexual release. Much of North American consumer culture blurs consent or renders it unimportant. One of the first tasks of Christian ethics is to reestablish its prominence as the first touchstone of good sex. We are created for freedom, and meant to enter into relationships freely. Without consent, there is no such thing as ethical sexual behavior, Christian or otherwise.

Consent, however, is not wholly sufficient for a Christian understanding of sexual ethics. For, two persons may freely consent to sexual behaviors that, in the long run, drain life of its vitality and intimacy. Sustained extramarital affairs, for example, often become the embodiment of lies—lies to one's partner, lies to one's affair. Persons can consent to sexual behavior and betray themselves and the promises that they have made. As Cahill notes, "A new generation of sexual attitudes and practices in liberal democratic societies presents mutual consent as practically the sole behavior-guiding norm, and hardly encourages ongoing responsibility for one's sexual partner, or for the procreative potentials of sex."[18] Consent, in other words, requires complements for freedom to flourish. If the Christian vision of freedom is freedom *for* another, then markers that further underscore our obligations to others are especially important.

MUTUALITY

Good sex revolves around giving and receiving: intertwining bodies in passion and delight, giving and receiving deep pleasures, sharing intimacy over time, both in and out of the bed. Christian sexual ethics also recognizes mutuality, the sharing of one's body and life with another. Sex expresses one of the ways persons communicate intimacy with each other; indeed, in sex we get as close to one another as physically possible. Sex mingles flesh: where I open myself to receive my lover within me, and she opens herself to receive me. This opening and receptivity is part of what can make sex such a mutual delight, for these very openings are also the sites of the body's deepest pleasures and sensitivities. Part of what makes mutuality so important is that these very places that accommodate others can also be sites of intense pain: when they are unprepared for receiving another, the physical acts of sexual intercourse can become painful. Sex is delightful as partners experience mutual arousal: engorgement and lubrication, moistness and the quickening of pulse. Without mutual arousal, sex becomes painful. But at its best, sex can represent one of the heights of mutual sharing, where in the throes of arousal, the intensification of pleasure, plateau, and climax, the pleasures of one's partner become one's own pleasures as well. In the mingling of pleasure and touch, we can bring one another to pleasurable heights that can seem remote one one's own.

Mutuality involves more than the sharing of physical pleasures and flesh. It also focuses our attentions on each other. As close as bodies and flesh become in sex, we never inhabit our beloved's flesh. We will never know *exactly* what our partner feels, but we are called to attend to what she or he feels. Stephanie Paulsell writes, "Sex, like all moral activity, requires us to imagine what another person feels, to seek what will give pleasure and avoid what will not."[19] Good sex involves the imagination, both in the making known of what gives one pleasure, and imagining oneself in our lover's shoes. In good sex, we listen to one another, and are claimed by one another as we grow in relationship together.

Mutuality is essential for Christian faith because Christians stress communion. Communion cuts to the core of our incarnational, ecclesial faith. Jesus Christ is God for us, the one who comes to share his life with others so that others might have life in abundance. Jesus, God's son, enters into the depth of human flesh, sharing God's life intimately with human life. Jesus of Nazareth is the communion of divine and human, the one who is fully human *and* fully divine, the one who shows us that God's intent is not to remain unto God's self, but to share the divine life with humanity, fully and without restraint. Jesus' human flesh is the revelation of God's very life, the communion given for the world. As the communion of humanity and divinity, Christ also invites us to share in his body at Table: "Take, eat; this is my body" (Matt. 26:26b). In the Lord's Supper, communion gets extended as Christ gives of himself—in the flesh—so that we might receive him in our lives and that we might, in turn, give to others. At the Communion table Christ feeds us with his presence, his life given for the world, as we take the body of Christ into our mouths. Here is intimacy at its greatest physical proximity. As we taste Christ, the community gathered around the Table also becomes the body of Christ for the world. We are fed at Table, but rise from it to share with others, to make Christ's love and sacrifice for the world known, so that others, too, might taste and see that the Lord is good. Mutuality in sex, therefore, is not simply a good ethical idea, it reflects the way a people of Table are called to live. Good sex responds to the rhythms of Christ's gestures at Table, recognizing that intimacy is shared, that giving also involves receiving.

This message of mutuality is countercultural in North America for several reasons. First, it contrasts to the rampant language of possession that permeates popular parlance about sex. Slang expressions for sex in a consumer culture often revolve around "taking," "having," and "getting." Possessive attitudes about sex ultimately leave the self alone, for in taking there becomes little to share, and in *having,* one often becomes lonely. Language of possession also reveals the narcissism that accompanies many attitudes about sex in popular culture and the endless chain of self-gratification that eventually leaves us empty. Mutuality also counters attitudes of performance that often accompany sex in U.S. culture. Sex, in this distorted view, becomes something I stage for another, something I "do" *to* someone else. An endless array of products promise increased performance, more fulfilling array of techniques, stamina and libido increasing concoctions, and devices that will make our partners never forget. But performances can quickly become tired and most become quite forgettable. The language of mutuality and communion situates sex not in the realm of performances that soon become banal, but in the practice of sharing, becoming close, and becoming vulnerable with and for another. Mutuality makes sex as much about one's lover as oneself, countering the narcissism and performance anxiety that permeates the North American landscape. Good sex stresses mutual sharing in the name of a God who fits us for communion.

COVENANT AND TRUST

A Christian understanding of covenant focuses the mutuality of sex. Good sex, in this vision, involves the promises we make with our words and bodies. Covenant means that persons involved in a sexual relationship make a pledge of faithfulness to one another. Christian theology has long recognized the importance of fidelity and covenant. The traditional sentiment that sex belongs to marriage is one instance of this stress, where the meaning of sex becomes clearer as couples share their bodies' pleasures with one another amid the ebb and flow of domestic life.

In contemporary society, commitments and covenants often seem strange. Good sex, in consumer culture involves an endless series of sexual highs, ideally achieved with new partners. Good sex involves novelty in consumer culture: when desire grows cold, one must move on to the next partner. A glance at grocery store check-out aisles often reveals the same assumption in men's and women's magazines: tricks for the most mind-blowing orgasms yet, tips on how to bed the man or woman of your dreams, how to grab your fantasy's attention in a new way. Affairs tap into this mentality because nothing other than novelty can sustain affairs. Without commitment and the shared planning of meals and bill paying, only sexual escapes will give an affair life. Good sex gets boiled down to a user's manual rather than a story of promises and embraces shared over time. In such an environment, covenants appear strange and uptight.

But covenant is central to the Christian vision of abundant life and the God who makes all things new. From start to finish, the Bible tells a story of covenant, of a God who extends God's self in love to particular people and to the entire creation by making promises. God chooses a people, Israel, to be God's own, and promises never to forsake them. God sinks an anchor of flesh into the world in that people and extends that covenant to the whole world in Jesus Christ. God's promise to the world is a promise to be with God's people, whatever may come.

From that promise, we as a people and as a church gain life, and are able to make promises to one another. As people who respond to the God who chooses us, we become equipped to make promises to one another. Even though the promises that we make are always fragile and may even break, we make them nonetheless. We make them because they draw their life from a promise that will never be forsaken: God's promise to us in Christ.

Is covenant restricted to marriage? Many would say yes. I would suggest, however, that we understand marriage not as equivalent to covenant, but situate marriage within a wider understanding of covenants, marital and nonmarital. We as a people learn to make covenant as we grow together in relationship with one another. Sex can be part of the journey of growing together. In an era in which the age of first marriage for North Americans is approaching thirty, it is important that the Christian churches offer guidelines for discussing responsible sexual behavior in a nonmarital context.[20] The age between the onset of puberty and the late twenties is an age in which many people experience sexual intimacy before getting married. Others will remain single for the rest of their lives. Between these years, most persons will learn much about trust and promises, and sex will be part of the story of how persons learn to trust and not to trust. Yet to say, as is often the case in popular culture, that "love" is enough to warrant a sexual relationship is a vast oversimplification. In an important study of adolescent girls and sexual ethics, Barbara Blodgett recognizes the limits of popular discourse: "Love alone does not ensure safety and . . . love can be seriously misconstrued."[21] Talk of love can mask manipulation. "Adolescent relationships are too often disingenuous and sometimes even coercive, which by no means indicates that all adolescent boys are manipulators and all adolescent girls dupes. The real issue at stake in the morality of a trust relationship . . . is the extent of unwarranted reliance on the other."[22]

For a covenant to begin, love alone is not sufficient. Blodgett suggests that a sexual ethic for adolescent girls rely more on the development of trust and friendly distrust: "The more a girl can trust herself and her partner, the better she will be able to tolerate the remaining ambiguity about the meaning of sex."[23] Trust develops over time; it is not something that is automatic to a relationship and may take years to grow. Especially for young people, who may not have lengthy experience of what it means to trust and be trusted, caution about entering sexual relationships is important, not because sex is dangerous (although it can be) or that adolescents are immature (although they may be), but because sex is an expression of trust and is a mutual donation of our deepest selves. "When we have sex, all of who we are is on the line. Any attempt to deploy our bodies in a sexual encounter while holding back the rest of ourselves damages us; the impossible attempt to divide body and spirit does violence to both."[24] Sexual restraint, for adolescents, may be part of the way in which trust is learned. It can be part of how we learn to make promises, and to be people of covenant. In the Christian story, after all, covenants are scandalously particular. God makes a promise to the people Israel not to forsake the world, but to show God's love for the world; God becomes incarnate in Jesus of Nazareth not to the disparagement of all other bodies, but to uplift all bodies as participants in God's very life. By learning restraint, adolescents and adults learn that particularity rather than promiscuity is the way in which God shows love for the world and we respond in love for the world. The Christian understanding of covenant does not close in on itself, but shows us that we learn to love the world by loving a particular part of it, by making unique promises to a particular beloved.

Part of learning trust, Blodgett suggests, also involves "friendly distrust." This kind of distrust, she claims, is not the absence of trust, but "a different relational choice that still allows two people to act in concert but with more safeguards erected around their relationships. In relationships of friendly distrust, partners acknowledge the ambiguities of their situation and realize that neither may know the full meaning of what they seek to achieve from it."[25] Trust, in other words, takes time to grow.

But as we grow and learn in relationships, we often become more capable of responding and honoring sexual commitments. The church has often taught that marriage authorizes sex, but it has not often recognized that the decision of whether or not to marry takes a long time, and often becomes clearer (or muddier) as we grow, as we date, as we develop friendships. Adrian Thatcher notes,

> Learning *whether* to marry may take a profound effort of self-knowledge, discovering *who* to marry may take a decade or more of cautious and painful experiment; and for people of faith, learning the full potential of the marital sacrament for the pursuit of holiness, and, learning this with one's prospective partner, deserves the equivalent of a catechumenate or school for marriage where personal, relational, and spiritual discovery can be safely made, within a supporting community which itself seeks to grow into the fullness of life which it knows in Jesus Christ.[26]

Sex can be a part of this process of learning what it means to make covenants, just as sexual restraint is. But here, there are no guarantees of safety: for, in opening oneself up to another sexually, there is always the risk that one may become injured emotionally or betrayed. Marriage does not remove these risks, but it does place those risks within the parameters of public vows and promises. Persons can learn what it might mean to make such vows by pledging—in word and in flesh—privately to one another. This is the case for countless couples in the church and outside of it. The experience, which is now the norm in Western societies, is that premarital sex can be a good part of the way in which couples come to know and be known, to trust and be trusted, to promise and be promised to. Indeed, the lengthy arguments against premarital sex, in a strange way, depart from much of the witness of Scripture. The unmarried lovers of the Song, for example, experience erotic passion and the fulfillment of it (or at least the anticipation of its fulfillment) as an unambiguous good, as part of what it means to know and be known. Instead of policing premarital sex, the church ought to recognize how and in what ways it may be a good, especially for persons in early adulthood, who are beginning to know the language of trust and covenant. This does not mean that premarital sex *must* lead to marriage. Many are called neither to marriage nor to celibacy. Instead, it means that the church should not see marriage as what authorizes sex, but rather that sex occurs in the body of Christ in the context of promise. Thatcher voices some of this hope: "I am more sanguine that within the community of faith, sexual awakening and sexual experience might one day be seen and understood more positively as an opportunity for learning and discerning the values, and acquiring the virtues, that Christian marriage requires."[27] This does not mean, of course, that all who have sex must one day marry. Rather, it shows that the values of marriage are not restricted to marriages authorized by the church. Sexual relationships, when conceived as bodily, faithful promises, may be one of the ways Christians learn more intimately what it means to be a people of promise.

Sex within and before marriage can cultivate practices of attentiveness and responsiveness. For sexual relationships to flourish, we are required to pay attention to our beloved, what pleases him, whether she simply wants to be held and whether a kiss is enough. If much of U.S. consumer culture impresses the attitude that sex is about self-gratification, the shape of covenantal sex shows us that sex involves giving and taking, expressing need and responding to our beloved's need. None of this, of course, is guaranteed. Sex within and before marriage can revert to patterns encouraged by consumer culture, leading to bitterness and possessiveness. But the hope of covenant is that relationships become sources of life rather than draining us of life. Sex represents a way in which we respond bodily and attend to the pleasure and vulnerability of our beloved. The lovers in the Song know each other's bodies intimately, as if every crevice, fold, and mound of the body matters. To lovers, every inch of flesh *does* matter, because every inch makes us unique, makes us who we are to one another. As the church takes its cues from this Song, we can claim the same for Christ's relationship to the church: each of us, every inch of our flesh, matters to the life of God, as we are incorporated into divine life in Christ's incarnation. Sex becomes lovemaking when it cultivates the attentiveness and responsiveness that covenant makes possible. And this gives hope to the body of Christ.

This presence of attentiveness and responsiveness is part of what makes extramarital affairs so damaging—not simply to the couple, but also to the body of Christ. Extramarital or extra-covenantal sex, as it frequently occurs in our culture, involves the breaking of covenant. Such affairs occur in secret, with one partner unaware (at least temporarily) of the dalliances of the other partner. Affairs are the bodily violation of covenant whose damage is often unforeseen. Through them, the promises that partners make to one another devolve: secrecy rather than openness begins to reign, trust devolves into distrust that is not friendly, the sharing of oneself becomes mocked in the feigned trust of a one-night stand. A consumer culture encourages (or at least tolerates) affairs because they represent a roaming desire that needs to find new objects of desire. But covenants for Christians are important because we are a people formed by covenant, sustained by promises that God makes to God's beloved. Christian faith maintains that no one is worthy of absolute trust other than God, but the promises we make to one another are ramifications of our trust in God and God's trust in us. Thus, Christian faith encourages the establishment and nurturing of covenants—in marriage, before marriage, outside marriage—in order that we might better live as persons of the covenant God establishes with us.

These marks of covenant are significant for all persons in the church, gay or straight, single or married. We learn what it means to be people of promise not because one gender complements our own, but as we make promises in voice and body with our beloved. The argument against gay marriage that has so often vexed the churches often proceeds from a rather odd assumption that only the opposite sex can complement me. But the promises of Christian faith often proceed along queer lines, irrespective of gender: of Christ taking the church as his beloved bride, making all in the church "female." Persons learn what it means to be people of promise and covenant not because of gender, but because of the promises themselves, the pledge made with another. Sex is one of the ways we express covenant, and it knows no gender lines, only the shape of desire itself, and the pledge in which desire can flourish as it focuses on a particular beloved.

COMMUNITY

One of the ways North American consumer culture talks about sex—despite its near ubiquitous public presence in advertising and entertainment—is as a "private matter." Sex concerns, and should only concern, the two persons who choose to tango. Good sex, in this read, is not anyone else's business. Romantic getaways, secluded islands, and lengthy periods of uninterrupted lovemaking then become the markers of good sex. At one level, some of these assumptions about privacy and intimacy are important and true. It is not simply good taste to make love in private, it respects the intimacy of covenant. Just as there are words that I say only to my beloved, and there are aspects of my psyche only known to my beloved, there are parts of my body that I do not show to or share with anyone other than my beloved. Intimacy gets adulterated if it becomes a public show. Likewise, covenantal attentiveness can be enriched when couples share time alone with each other, and sometimes this time can only be found in retreat. But privacy is not the final word on sex for Christians, because sexual relationships, in the Christian story, do not converge in upon themselves, but become open to the wider story of God's investment in creation. Good sex, in this story, involves communal as well as private considerations. Good sex redounds not simply to a couple's romantic bliss or personal covenant, but to the wider community's good.

In many traditional versions of sexual ethics, the focus on community turns immediately to questions of reproduction. Good sex, as it echoes the divine command to "be fruitful and multiply" (Gen. 1:28), is at least *potentially* open to procreation. Thomas Aquinas, as we have seen, is one exemplar of this perspective, as he considers procreation the chief end of sex. Current Vatican restrictions on contraception reflect much of this tradition: if we divorce sex from the cycle of reproduction, we risk objectifying others and ourselves in sex as we consider it a means of pleasure. Though I quibble with the way that many Vatican pronouncements focus the concern chiefly on the reproductive ends of sex, I appreciate their concern with the communal dimensions of sex. For that reason, I want to expand the Vatican's concern. Good sex, in the view I am advocating, can render a couple more receptive to the love of community and more capable of showing love to community and world. The primary public marker of good sex is not how many children are produced through sexual intercourse, but the degree to which the sexual relationship is an animating factor in extending the circle of love and justice beyond the couple to the wider world.

Another version of good sex involving community that is often present in our culture is that good sex involves multiple partners. According to this interpretation, monogamy is unnatural, outdated, and inhibits the flourishing of persons. Sex columnist Dan Savage, who has fostered frank, straightforward, and open dialogue about sexual relationships, echoes this sentiment. He routinely describes the hypocrisy of religious leaders who tout monogamous marriage (between a man and a woman) and have extramarital affairs as the natural result of an ethic that runs counter to our sexual nature. Most of us, he claims, are not hard-wired for strict monogamy, but for "monagamish," or negotiated non-monogamy relationships. Monogamy is difficult, and in some cases extramarital sex can strengthen the marital bond; without occasional other partners, sex in marriage can become stale or even resentful.[28] Marcella Althaus-Reid offers a similar, more explicitly theological justification of polyamory, as she describes monogamy and compulsory heterosexuality as fostering a loneliness that more fluid sexual relationships do not.[29] Elsewhere she grounds more promiscuous sexual relations in the Trinity. God's triune life emphasizes not a binary, coupled love, but the extension of that love to other partners. The Trinity, in this sense, signals the death of the mono-lover.[30] Just as Trinitarian love does not close in on itself, but envelops others in fleshy embrace, our sexual lives ought to expand beyond restrained repetition of acts with one person only. Triune love is promiscuous; when extended to sexual life, promiscuity is hardly a vice, but a virtue.

The problem with this read of sexuality is its somewhat tendentious understanding of triune love. I applaud her argument that triune love *is* promiscuous, that the nature of divine love extends to all, so that all are enveloped in love. But her reading of triune love holds little room for the unique relationships that constitute the Trinity. Augustine's analogy for triune love is the triad of Lover (Father), Beloved (Son), and the Love shared between Lover and Beloved (Spirit), where each person is distinct, where Father loves the Son in a unique way and Son loves the Father uniquely.[31] But the uniqueness of triune love does not mean that the Father withholds love from all of creation, as if no love is left over after loving the Son. Rather, the promiscuous and profuse love for the world is made possible because of the Father's unique, reserved, covenantal love for the Son. God loves creation profusely at the same time that creation is *not* the Son. Althaus-Reid's understanding of the Trinity suggests that all loves must multiply and, when appropriate, include sexual love. However, Augustine's understanding preserves unique relationships that result not in the withholding of love, but an extension of love to others, albeit in different ways. The triune life offers a pattern for sexual relationships: of a unique covenant between persons that reflects the sharing of love between lover and beloved (life in the Spirit) that avoids narcissistic enclosure of lovers upon themselves and extends love to a wider circle. Yet this extension of love to others avoids sexual intimacy in the name of the uniqueness of covenant. Lovers do not have sex with anyone else, not because they cannot love others, but because that is one way they learn to love others. Thus conceived, the Trinity offers clues to a sexual ethic that is somewhat conservative in its honoring of sexual covenants between persons, but liberal in its extension of love beyond the covenant. For Christians it should come as no surprise that triune love finds reflection in our sexual lives.

In the end, however, monogamy and marital covenants hardly need more arguments. Theology ought not perpetuate old polemics that argue for the superiority of the marital state or that view other sexual covenants as licit because they approximate marriage. Such arguments invariably view other states (such as singleness) as deficient. Some in life are called to marriage, others to singleness. The only proof of covenants is the path that they provide, the journey together. But even the journey offers no guarantees, as people who make covenants also fall into bitterness and loss of affection, experiencing their covenant as a diminishment of life rather than its enrichment. When covenants consistently drain its members of life, there is good reason to end them. But the failure of covenants is not an argument against them either, for people can also find in them hope, acceptance, and an impetus for a wider love of the world.

Christian theology suggests that good sex takes place in relation to the maddening crowd, so that we may find the crowd to be not so maddening in the first place. Good sex involves others and the couple's relationship to others. The most obvious of these relationships is the child that can emerge from the sexual love of two partners. Here the bodily promises shared between lovers, the intimacies that are only known to one's beloved, open the couple to another person, who is introduced somewhat abruptly, changing the life of that couple for good. Children, even when they are anticipated, emerge on the scene with a wail and massive interruption of sleep. They may come to couples as longed-for gifts, but they surprise them with their uniqueness and even strangeness. Lovemaking can result in the creation of new life, causing us to extend hospitality and care to new members of the family. Here, in visible fashion, private intimacies lead to public care for others. Here, good sex does not turn in on itself, but enables a couple to participate in wider circles of love, which may even result in stronger bonds of love between lovers themselves.

What is crucial is not the sheer number of children that sexual unions create. If that were the criterion that mattered, then only those relationships that resulted in the greatest possible number of children would constitute the greatest good: a stance that appears ecologically unsustainable. What is important, rather, is whether the pattern of sex leads couples to greater acts of compassion and hospitality for others instead of inward obsession and privatized seclusion. Many experience sex as something that fosters compassion: the promises and pleasures reserved only for one's beloved can allow one to extend oneself in different ways to those who are not one's lover. Binding promises made to one's partner can lead one to act more freely in response to others in acts of compassion, because one will *not* enter into sexual relations with them. The oft-cited sexual tension that always exists between people can actually be experienced as a newfound freedom to relate to others (without sex) more fully in Christian love. Countless people, because of the sexual love shared with a partner or spouse, are able to glimpse the world with a bit more compassion, or be opened to the beauty of the world a bit more fully. Sex is not the only thing capable of opening us to the wonder and beauty of the wider world, of course, but it can accomplish those things just the same.

Christians can claim that good sex contributes to the building up of the church, fostering the greater well-being of the members of the body of Christ. Sex is public not because our sexual relations are plastered on big screens across the land, but because it can foster greater loves and deeper compassion. The question of community is not "how many children does sex produce," but "does the pattern of sex foster the kind of hospitality and compassion that characterizes the reign of God?" Good sex, in other words, cares about community.

JOY

Good sex also involves pleasure, delight, and passion. To say as much seems to state the obvious: of course sex is pleasurable and fun. One way of describing this dimension of sex is to say that sex is an expression of the joy of life itself. U.S. culture purports to celebrate this aspect of sex more than any other, but on closer examination, it fosters less joy than it claims. Never in our history have we had so much sexual information available at our fingertips: information about technique, about the physiology of pleasure, about the ebb and flow of sexual desire. We also have spent millions on drugs, gadgets, and products to enhance sexual pleasure. At nearly every turn in the grocery check-out line or with nearly every click of the computer mouse, we get bombarded with sexual information, glimpsing overt and disguised sexual messages. But the result of this bombardment of information and imagery is hardly greater happiness and joy. Instead, sex for many has become more compulsive than joyous. Addictions to pornography seem only to have increased now that such images are only a Web site away. Given the amount of advertising spent on enhancement products, sex is also laden with its own dose of performance anxiety. In this consumer realm, sex has become yet another product that requires countless consumer interventions. It has lost much of its joy.

Good sex, by contrast, evinces delight. It rejoices in the gift of the beloved and the lingering attention that comes with our beloved. Sex, as an expression of joy, delights in one's lover simply because she is who she is. Nowhere do we see this attention and joy in Scripture as clearly as in the Song of Songs, in lines that evoke the joy of love and life:

> I am my beloved's,
>   and his desire is for me.
> Come, my beloved,
>   let us go forth into the fields,
>   and lodge in the villages;
> let us go out early to the vineyards,
>   and see whether the vines have budded,
> whether the grape blossoms have opened
>   and the pomegranates are in bloom.
> There I will give you my love.
> The mandrakes give forth fragrance,
>   and over our doors are all choice fruits,
> new as well as old,
>   which I have laid up for you, O my beloved
>   Song 7:10–13

Here is attentiveness, here is joy, here is delight. Here we see sex not so much as that which creates joy and happiness, but sex as an expression of joy and delight. In fact, the lovers in the Song speak more of the anticipation of sex than they do of its consummation. But their speech remains joyous. The lovers of the Song show us that joy is not the direct result of sex, but that sex is an expression of joy. The question the lovers ask is not "how often do we make love?" but "how is our sexual love for each other is an expression of joy?" The joy that the Song expresses evokes spontaneity (the lovers express themselves without restraint, showing how their expression of love cries out in the streets), attention to the body (the lovers know each mound and crevice of each other's body and compare them to choice fruits), and the pleasure of making love. Full joy indeed, in the incomparable arms of one's beloved.

Joy is a hallmark of Christian life. In an age that claims to celebrate joy in sex, but often fosters its opposite, Christians should recover joy as a mark of the good life. In Philippians, Paul's letter of friendship to a congregation that he loves, we hear the apostle's plea: "Make my joy complete: be of the same mind, having the same love" (Phil. 2:2). Paul connects his joy with the love of community, a love shown forth in Christ's love for the world and as members of the church in Philippi look after each other's interests. Consumer culture in the United States can assume that joy is synonymous with happiness, or that it is an emotional state brought about by the satisfaction of individual desires. The joy that Paul expresses here is characterized more by relationship in Christ and the journey-ing of persons with one another. Joy is existential, rooted in God's contagious love for the world, where promises we make to our beloved arise out of God's initiating love. Joy does not mean we are happy all the time, but it does indicate postures of thanks and praise for the gift of life itself. When we recognize God as the source of all joy, then joy can accompany each dimension of life, in work and in play, in labor and in rest.

More sex does not necessarily make people happier or more joyous. One word that Christians can offer in a consumer culture is that sex can be an expression of a joyous life, expressed in thanksgiving to God, in gratitude for the mystery and delight and uniqueness of one's partner in lovemaking and in times of withdrawal and distance from one's beloved. The lives of the celibate and the betrothed are not at as separate as we often suppose. Both can be expressions of joy, as they are rooted in God's abundant love. The good news of Christian faith is not that more sex makes us more joyous, but that our sexual lives are expressions of joy. Christians find new freedom in Christ, a freedom that questions the ways that our culture and our church often views happiness. If culture assumes that more sex is better, the church often assumes that less sex is more virtuous. But for the one who finds joy in life given by God, sex is less the source of joy and more the outgrowth of it. As each person finds joy in Christian discipleship, the sexual paths will not look identical for many. But along each of these paths is joy aplenty, orienting Christ's beloved to the fulfillment of joy as Christ takes each one of us as his beloved. In the mean time we eat and pray, work and rest, fall in love and make love, and find in each expression of life a dimension of the joy given to us in baptism. If Christ's joy makes us complete, we also find joy as we journey together, especially as desire flourishes with our beloved.

Conclusion

I began this book with a claim that sex is an expression of Christian faith. I close with similar words: the saints of the Christian church have sexual lives, and these lives draw their rhythms from the God who desires us as God's beloved. Sometimes the church has assumed that saints are uniquely holy: that only a few, in the end, are called to sainthood and that their sexual lives are paragons of chastity. The New Testament, however, tends to use the language of "saints" to refer to all members of the body of Christ. The saints of the Christian church, in this understanding, reflect the call of God in diverse ways, though each of these ways ultimately is directed back to God. In this understanding, the saints of the church are married and single persons, young and old, gay and straight, celibates and noncelibates. The lives of these saints do not conform to a single script. Their lives, instead, unfold as unique narratives, each cherished and sustained by the God who gives life to the world in Jesus Christ. A Christian understanding of human sexuality does not expect the sexual lives of the saints to be identical. But amid these multiple stories is a narrative that gives shape to all our lives: a God who desires us as God's own, a Christ who encounters us in the flesh, a banquet that invites us to taste and see intimacy, a passionate vocation endowed by the Spirit, Scriptures that bespeak a desire more powerful than death, and a consummation of life where all things are made new. When we pay attention to this story, we can better discern how our sexual lives reflect God's desire for us and how they fall short of that desire.

Notes

Chapter 1: Scripture and Sex

1. Stanley J. Grenz, *Sexual Ethics: An Evangelical Perspective* (Louisville, KY: Westminster John Knox, 1997), 84.
2. See also Mark D. Jordan, *The Ethics of Sex* (Malden, MA: Blackwell, 2002), 24–31. Jordan claims that Paul's "lists give us very little evidence about the exact meanings of the terms in them. . . . So, too, the Pauline texts may be using *porneia* metaphorically or symbolically, not intending to refer to specific sexual acts at all." Ibid., 27–28.
3. Robert A. J. Gagnon, *The Bible and Homosexual Practice: Texts and Hermeneutics* (Nashville: Abingdon, 2001), 138-42. Gagnon's interpretation of this text offers a view of "gender complementarity" that may be questioned in Paul's letter to the Galatians, that in Christ "there is no longer Jew or Greek, there is no longer slave or free, there is no longer male and female" (Gal. 3:28). In W. Stacy Johnson's words, "The pairing of male *and* female . . . has no ultimate hold on the new community seeking to live out the gospel. Invoking 'gender complementarity' or even 'gender identity' as a fundamental basis for drawing ethical distinctions of status or worth within the body of Christ has no support in the gospel according to Galatians 3:28." *A Time to Embrace: Same-Gender Relationships in Religion, Law, and Politics* (Grand Rapids: Eerdmans, 2006), 150.
4. In Jordan's words: "The prohibition has nothing to do with women and—in 18:22 at least—nothing to do with the 'passive' or receptive partner. It would also not prohibit same-sex erotic activities other than anal intercourse: the phrase does not include oral sex, or mutual masturbation, or a number of other practices." Jordan, *Ethics of Sex*, 30.
5. Jordan, *Ethics of Sex*, 23.
6. Adrian Thatcher, *Liberating Sex: A Christian Sexual Theology* (London: SPCK, 1993), 16.
7. Ibid., 21.
8. L. William Countryman, *Dirt, Greed, and Sex: Sexual Ethics in the New Testament and Their Implications for Today* (Philadelphia: Fortress, 1988), 265.
9. Ibid., 241.

10. Ibid., 243.
11. Anne Bathurst Gilson, *Eros Breaking Free: Interpreting Sexual Theo-Ethics* (Cleveland: Pilgrim Press, 1995), 96.
12. Ibid., 112.
13. Grace Jantzen, "New Creations: Eros, Beauty, and the Passion for Transformation," in *Toward a Theology of Eros: Transfiguring Passion at the Limits of Discipline,* ed. Virginia Burrus and Catherine Keller (New York: Fordham University Press, 2006), 286.
14. Here I interpret Thomas' disbelief not as skepticism over the resurrection, but disbelief over the catastrophic loss of his teacher and beloved, a "love that cannot come to terms with loss." For this reading, and for some of the thoughts related to Thomas and Mary, I am indebted to Graham Ward. See Ward, "There Is No Sexual Difference," in *Queer Theology: Rethinking the Western Body,* ed. Gerard Loughlin, 77–81 (Malden, MA: Blackwell, 2007).
15. See "The Gifts of God for the People of God," in *Feminist and Womanist Essays in Reformed Dogmatics,* ed. Amy Plantinga Pauw and Serene Jones (Louisville, KY: Westminster John Knox, 2006), 217. See also John Milbank and Catherine Pickstock, *Truth in Aquinas* (New York: Routledge, 2001), 71–83.
16. For an example of feminist musings on Revelation, see Catherine Keller, *Apocalypse Now and Then: A Feminist Guide to the End of the World* (Boston: Beacon, 1996).
17. Dale Martin has noted about Revelation, "Although actual sexual intercourse is *supposed* to be absent from the eschatological community, desire and the erotic, especially the erotic of the eye, is everywhere." *Sex and the Single Savior: Gender and Sexuality in Biblical Interpretation* (Louisville, KY: Westminster John Knox, 2006), 110.
18. Robert W. Jenson, *Song of Songs* (Louisville, KY: Westminster John Knox, 2005), 13.
19. See Martin, *Sex and the Single Savior,* 116–18.
20. Richard Kearney, "The Shulammite's Song: Divine Eros, Ascending and Descending," in *Toward a Theology of Eros,* 339.
21. George Lindbeck, *The Nature of Doctrine: Religion and Theology in a Postliberal Age* (Philadelphia: Westminster Press, 1984), 117.

Chapter 2: God and Sex

1. Lisa Sowle Cahill, *Sex, Gender, and Christian Ethics* (New York: Cambridge University Press, 1996), 95. My critique of the biological reductionism of human sexuality owes much to Cahill. See ibid., 90–97.
2. Kelly Marages, "Talk Her Clothes Off," *Men's Health,* October 2007, 130–31.
3. "Bust Out of Your Romance Rut," in ibid., 70.
4. "Pick-Up Tricks," in ibid., 52.
5. John Grogan, "Marley & Me & Single Women," in ibid., 194.
6. See also David Matzko McCarthy, *Sex and Love in the Home,* New Edition (London: SCM, 2004), 33–49, for an account of the commercialization of sexual desire.
7. Denise L. Carmody, *Christian Feminist Theology: A Constructive Interpretation* (Cambridge, MA: Blackwell, 1995), 225.
8. Ronald E. Long, "Toward a Phenomenology of Gay Sex: Groundwork for a Contemporary Sexual Ethic," in *Embodying Diversity: Identity, (Bio)Diversity, and Sexuality,* ed. J. Michael Clark and Michael L. Stemmeler (Las Colinas, TX: Monument Press, 1995), 70.

9. Ibid., 104.
10. Ibid., 105.
11. Anders Nygren, *Agape and Eros*, trans. Philip S. Watson (Philadelphia: Westminster Press, 1953), 30.
12. William Madges, "Love," in *New and Enlarged Handbook of Christian Theology*, ed. Donald W. Musser and Joseph L. Price (Nashville: Abingdon, 2003), 314.
13. Karl Barth, *Church Dogmatics* IV/2 (New York: T. & T. Clark, 2004), 734–35.
14. Ibid., 744.
15. Augustine, *Confessions*, trans. R. S. Pine-Coffin (New York: Penguin Books, 1961), 21.
16. Karen Baker-Fletcher, "The Erotic in Contemporary Black Women's Writings," in *Loving the Body: Black Religious Studies and the Erotic,* ed. Anthony B. Pinn and Dwight N. Hopkins (New York: Palgrave Macmillan, 2004), 202.
17. Wendy Farley, *The Wounding and Healing of Desire: Weaving Heaven and Earth* (Louisville, KY: Westminster John Knox, 2005), 101.
18. Ibid., 2.
19. One of the best of these critical examinations is Barbara J. Blodgett, *Constructing the Erotic: Sexual Ethics and Adolescent Girls* (Cleveland: Pilgrim Press, 2002).
20. Rita Nakashima Brock, *Journeys by Heart: A Christology of Erotic Power* (New York: Crossroad, 1988), 26.
21. Ibid., 40.
22. Ibid., 41.
23. See Blodgett, *Constructing the Erotic*, 48–50.
24. Christine E. Gudorf, *Body, Sex, and Pleasure: Reconstructing Christian Sexual Ethics* (Cleveland: Pilgrim Press, 1994), 91.
25. Ibid., 118.
26. Ibid., 33.
27. Stanley J. Grenz, *Sexual Ethics: An Evangelical Perspective* (Louisville, KY: Westminster John Knox, 1997), 83.
28. David Matzko McCarthy writes poignantly of domestic desire, as contrasted with the roaming desire of popular imagination: "In a popular view, it is thought that domestication deadens sexual desire, but the household economy actually 're-socializes' and transforms it. . . . Hands and face, hips and arms are invested with common endeavors, joys and pains, with who we have become, and with our being—claimed by another. Our desires are satisfied in belonging." *Sex and Love*, 239.
29. Pseudo-Dionysius, "The Divine Names," in *Pseudo-Dionysius: The Complete Works*, trans. Colm Luibheid (Mahwah, NJ: Paulist, 1987), 75.
30. Ibid., 79.
31. Ibid., 77.
32. Ibid., 79.
33. Teresa of Avila, *The Interior Castle*, trans. Kieran Kavanaugh and Otilio Rodriguez (Mahwah, NJ: Paulist, 1979), 118.
34. Ibid., 70. Later in this same work, Teresa writes, "The soul desires to be completely occupied in love and does not want to be taken up with anything else, but to be so occupied is impossible for it even though it may want to; for although the will is not dead, the fire that usually makes it burn is dying out, and someone must necessarily blow on the fire so that heat will be given off." Ibid., 146. The flourishing of desire in love, in other words, is not the result of human will, but a gift from God.
35. Ibid., 108.

36. Ibid., 115. Later, Teresa claims, "This action of love is so powerful that the soul dissolves with desire." Ibid., 116. For Teresa, love is not disinterested and general, but particular and passionate, at times drowning the soul in desire.

37. For a similar indictment of modern wedding culture in the United States, see Mark D. Jordan, *Blessing Same-Sex Unions: The Perils of Queer Romance and the Confusions of Christian Marriage* (Chicago: The University of Chicago Press, 2005), 6.

38. Teresa, *Interior Castle*, 178, 211. In the final version, she changed the wording to "between two who can no longer be separated."

39. Bonaventure, *The Tree of Life*, in *Bonaventure*, trans. Ewert Cousins (New York: Paulist, 1978), 167–68.

40. Pseudo-Dionysius, "The Divine Names," 82.

41. Teresa, *Interior Castle*, 74.

42. Sarah Coakley, "Pleasure Principles: Toward a Contemporary Theology of Desire," *Harvard Divinity Bulletin* (2005): 31.

43. As Benedict XVI has written, "*Eros* and *agape*—ascending love and descending love—can never be completely separated. The more the two, in their different aspects, find a proper unity in the one reality of love, the more the true nature of love in general is realized." *God Is Love: Deus Caritas Est*, Encyclical Letter (Washington, DC: United States Conference of Catholic Bishops, 2006), 11.

44. Sebastian Moore, *Jesus the Liberator of Desire* (New York: Crossroad, 1989), 18.

45. Ibid., 11.

46. Eugene Rogers, *Sexuality and the Christian Body: Their Way into the Triune God* (Malden, MA: Blackwell, 1999), 83.

47. Ibid.

48. Rowan Williams, "The Body's Grace," in Eugene F. Rogers, ed., *Theology and Sexuality: Classic and Contemporary Readings* (Malden, MA: Blackwell, 2002), 311-12. Emphasis in original.

49. Rogers, *Sexuality and the Christian Body*, 212.

50. Ibid.

Chapter 3: Christ and Sex

1. Thomas Aquinas, *Summa theologica*, supplement q. 81, a. 3. (New York: Benziger Brothers, 1948). "Since to eat, drink, sleep, beget, pertain to the animal life, being directed to the primary perfection of nature, it follows that they will not be in the resurrection." Ibid., q. 81, a. 4.

2. "Statistics," www.rainn.org/statistics, accessed December 13, 2010. RAINN is the acronym for Rape, Abuse and Incest National Network, the largest antisexual violence organization in the United States. It administers the national sexual assault hotline and sponsors programs throughout the United States to help prevent sexual violence.

3. See Miguel A. De La Torre, *A Lily among the Thorns: Imagining a New Christian Sexuality* (San Francisco: Jossey-Bass, 2007), 162. Statistics from Federal Bureau of Investigation, *Crime in the United States 2004: Uniform Crime Report* (Washington, DC: U.S. Government Printing Office, 2005), 23.

4. Jan Oberg, "The New International Military Order: A Threat to Human Security," in *Problems of Contemporary Militarism,* ed. Asjorn Eide and Marek Thee (New York, St. Martin's, 1980), 47.

5. *The State of America's Children* (Washington, DC: The Children's Defense Fund, 2001), xiv, 81, 100.

6. See Robert Jensen, *Getting Off: Pornography and the End of Masculinity*

(Cambridge, MA: South End Press, 2007), 93. Dialogue from *Big Booty White Girls*, DVD (Los Angeles: Evil Angel, 2004). Another, more shocking, explanation of a film includes these remarks: "Lizzy Borden, who runs Extreme [a pornographic video company] with her husband, Rob Black, described one of their controversial films this way: 'A girl being kidnapped, being forced to have sex against her will, being degraded. Being called "a whore, a slut, a piece of shit." Then being butchered at the end, and spit on. She's being degraded.' Borden explained that the woman who performed in the scene is a good friend. 'I know she can take it. She's a good actress. And I can abuse somebody that I know, but I can't abuse somebody that I don't know. So it's like, I know that I can hit her harder. . . . And at the end I give her a hug, I take her out to dinner, and we go shopping.'" Jensen, *Getting Off*, 191. See "American Porn," *Frontline*, February 7, 2002, http://www.pbs.org/wgbh/pages/frontline/shows/porn/interviews/borden.html, for full interview, accessed November 28, 2012. Here hugs and consumer goods provide "compensation" for violence against women.

7. William C. Placher, *Mark* (Louisville, KY: Westminster John Knox, 2010), 229, 238.

8. J. Denny Weaver, *The Nonviolent Atonement* (Grand Rapids: Eerdmans, 2001), 32–33.

9. St. Symeon the New Theologian, "Hymns of Divine Love, 15," in *Theology and Sexuality: Classic and Contemporary Readings*, ed. Eugene F. Rogers Jr. (Malden, MA: Blackwell, 2002), 100–101.

10. James B. Nelson's theology tends in this direction: "The fleshly experience of each of us becomes vitally important to our experience of God. Then the fully physical, sweating, lubricating, menstruating, ejaculating, urinating, defecating bodies that we are—in sickness and in health—are the central vehicles of God's embodiment in our experience." *Body Theology* (Louisville, KY: Westminster/John Knox, 1992), 31.

11. *The Constitution of the Presbyterian Church (U.S.A.), Part I, Book of Confessions* (Louisville, KY: Office of the General Assembly, Presbyterian Church (U.S.A.), 2004), 7.197.

12. Karl Rahner, "Resurrection of the Body," in *Theological Investigations*, vol. 2, trans. Karl-H. Kruger (Baltimore: Helicon, 1963), 211.

13. Origen, *De principiis*, in Alexander Roberts and James Donaldson, eds., *Ante-Nicene Fathers*, vol. 4. (Peabody, MA: Hendrickson, 2004), 348.

14. The phrase is from the rite of Christian marriage in the Presbyterian Church (U.S.A.). *Book of Common Worship* (Louisville, KY: Westminster/John Knox, 1993), 848.

15. These polarities are not simply remnants of Paul's era; they continue in our time. When popular imagination celebrates esoteric religious traditions as a means for better, more frequent, and wilder sex, or ascribes to celibates a unique closeness to God, we perpetuate these polarities. What we seem unable to do is to celebrate sex in the ordinariness that most people experience. Popular sexual saints are either holy abstinent or wholly active in ways that exclude most of us from the communion of saints.

16. Irenaeus, *Against Heresies*, in *Ante-Nicene Fathers*, vol. 1, 551.

17. Intriguingly, however, the visual arts are less prone to this charge when depicting Jesus' sex and sexuality. Many Renaissance painters, in particular, portrayed Jesus' nudity and sexuality openly and frankly. See Leo Steinberg, *The Sexuality of Christ in Renaissance Art and in Modern Oblivion*, 2nd ed. (Chicago: University of Chicago Press, 1996).

18. Roland Boer, "Yahweh as Top: A Lost Targum," in *Queer Commentary and the Hebrew Bible,* ed. Ken Stone (London: Sheffield Academic Press, 2001), 78.

19. Eugene Rogers, *Sexuality and the Christian Body: Their Way into the Triune God* (Malden, MA: Blackwell, 1999), 206.

20. In Mark, the risen Christ goes ahead of the women to Galilee, eluding their grasp (Mark 16:7), returning to the place where his ministry began. The "ending" here draws readers back to the "beginning."

21. Graham Ward, "There Is No Sexual Difference," in *Queer Theology: Rethinking the Western Body,* ed. Gerard Loughlin (Malden, MA: Blackwell, 2007), 78.

22. Christine E. Gudorf, *Body, Sex, and Pleasure: Reconstructing Christian Sexual Ethics* (Cleveland: Pilgrim Press, 1994), 89.

23. Karl Rahner, "The Body in the Order of Salvation," in *Theological Investigations,* vol. 27: *Jesus, Man, and the Church,* trans. Margaret Kohl (New York: Crossroad, 1981), 87–88.

Chapter 4: Eschatology and Sex

1. One foundation of this understanding of sex is found in Augustine's *On the Good of Marriage,* in *Nicene and Post-Nicene Fathers,* First Series, vol. 3 (Peabody, MA: Hendrickson, 2004), 399–413, which offers a threefold defense of marital sex as fidelity, procreation, and sacrament.

2. Congregation for the Doctrine of the Faith, "Letter to the Catholic Bishops on the Pastoral Care of Homosexual Persons," in *Theology and Sexuality: Classic and Contemporary Readings,* ed. Eugene F. Rogers Jr. (Malden, MA: Blackwell, 2002), 250.

3. Ibid., 256.

4. Stephanie Simon, "Humbled Haggard Climbs Back in Pulpit," *The Wall Street Journal,* online edition, http://online.wsj.com/article/SB100014240527487042 49004575385170843908594.html, accessed October 25, 2012.

5. John Shelby Spong, *Living in Sin? A Bishop Rethinks Human Sexuality* (San Francisco: Harper & Row, 1988), 83, 85.

6. Miguel A. De La Torre, *Lily among the Thorns: Imagining a New Christian Sexuality* (San Francisco: Jossey-Bass, 2007), 148.

7. Barbara J. Blodgett, *Constructing the Erotic: Sexual Ethics and Adolescent Girls* (Cleveland: Pilgrim Press, 2002), 37. Emphasis in original.

8. Marcella Althaus-Reid points to another potential problem in customary ways of viewing heterosexuality: it ultimately leaves persons alone to themselves. "Heterosexuality makes people's lives lonely and produces unnecessary suffering because in reality relations are more fluid than fixed, and we are confronted with that elasticity and sometimes uncontrollable lack of boundaries which exists between bodies and communities." *Indecent Theology: Theological Perversions in Sex, Gender and Politics* (London: Routledge, 2000), 76.

9. Laurel Schneider, "What If It Is a Choice? Some Implications of the Homosexuality Debates for Theology," in *Sexuality and the Sacred: Sources for Theological Reflection,* 2nd ed., ed. Marvin M. Ellison and Kelly Brown Douglas (Louisville, KY: Westminster John Knox, 2010), 203.

10. Augustine, *Confessions,* trans. R. S. Pine-Coffin (New York: Penguin Books, 1961), 21.

11. Mechthild of Magdeburg, *The Flowing Light of the Godhead,* trans. Frank Tobin (New York: Paulist, 1998), 61–62.

12. William Stacy Johnson, *A Time to Embrace: Same-Gender Relationships in Religion, Law, and Politics.* (Grand Rapids: Eerdmans, 2006), 150.

13. Ibid., 148.

14. John Gray, *Men Are from Mars, Women Are from Venus: The Classic Guide to Understanding the Opposite Sex* (New York: HarperCollins, 1992).

15. Margaret Farley, *Just Love: A Framework for Christian Sexual Ethics* (New York: Continuum, 2006), 151.

16. Judith Butler, *Gender Trouble: Feminism and the Subversion of Identity* (New York: Routledge, 1999), 22, 191.

17. Ibid., 179. Emphasis in original.

18. Ibid., 33.

19. Ibid., 43.

20. Verna Harrison, "Male and Female in Cappadocian Theology," *Journal of Theological Studies* 41, no. 2 (October 1990): 469.

21. Gregory of Nyssa, quoted in ibid., 469.

22. Augustine, *City of God*, trans. Henry Bettenson (New York: Penguin Books, 1984), 584.

23. See Sarah Coakley, "'Batter My Heart . . .?' On Sexuality, Spirituality, and the Christian Doctrine of the Trinity," in *The Papers of the Henry Luce III Fellows in Theology*, vol. 1, ed. Gary Gilbert (Atlanta: Scholars Press, 1996), 62.

24. Ibid., 65.

25. Jo Ind, *Memories of Bliss: God, Sex, and Us* (London: SCM, 2003), 142.

26. Farley, *Just Love*, 158.

27. John Calvin, *Institutes of the Christian Religion* 4.15.6; ed. John T. McNeill, trans. Ford Lewis Battles, LCC (Philadelphia: Westminster Press, 1960).

28. Johnson, *A Time to Embrace*, 147.

29. Elizabeth Stuart, "Sacramental Flesh," in *Queer Theology: Rethinking the Western Body*, ed. Gerard Loughlin (Malden, MA: Blackwell, 2007), 68.

30. Elizabeth Stuart, *Gay and Lesbian Theologies: Repetition with Critical Difference* (Burlington, VT: Ashgate, 2003), 107.

31. See Amy Laura Hall, *Conceiving Parenthood: American Protestantism and the Spirit of Reproduction* (Grand Rapids: Eerdmans, 2008), 213–89, for a horrifying and illuminating account of the American eugenics movement and the sometime allegiances of mainline Protestantism with its quest for the "ideal family" corresponding to idolatrous notions of beauty, race, and health.

32. Stuart, *Gay and Lesbian Theologies*, 2.

33. Stanley Grenz, *Sexual Ethics: An Evangelical Perspective* (Louisville, KY: Westminster John Knox, 1997), 26.

34. Margaret Kamitsuka, "Sex in Heaven? Eschatological Eros and the Resurrection of the Body," in *The Embrace of Eros: Bodies, Desires, and Sexuality in Christianity*, Margaret Kamitsuka, ed. (Minneapolis: Fortress, 2010), 274–75.

35. See Dorothy C. Bass, *Receiving the Day: Christian Practices for Opening the Gift of Time* (San Francisco: Jossey-Bass, 2000), 51.

36. Christine E. Gudorf, *Body, Sex, and Pleasure: Reconstructing Christian Sexual Ethics* (Cleveland: Pilgrim Press, 1994), 20. Statistic from Robert L. Crooks and Karla Baur, *Our Sexuality* (Belmont, CA: Wadsworth, 1984), 553.

37. Adrian Thatcher, *Liberating Sex: A Christian Sexual Theology* (London: SPCK, 1993), 3.

38. I have not specifically addressed masturbation in this book. In my view, any theological consideration of it ought to include the element of play. Like all other forms of sexual expression, masturbation can be used for good or for ill. In some cases, it can become compulsive and serve to cut persons off from fellowship with others. In others, it can allow us to pay closer attention to our specific pleasures so that we might be able to share them with our beloved, encouraging us to better attend to our beloved's pleasures as well.

39. Lisa Isherwood and Elizabeth Stuart, *Introducing Body Theology* (Cleveland: Pilgrim Press, 2000), 76. See also Mary D. Pellauer, "The Moral Significance of Female Orgasm: Toward Sexual Ethics That Celebrates Women's Sexuality," in *Sexuality and the Sacred: Sources for Theological Reflection,* ed. James B. Nelson and Sandra P. Longfellow (Louisville, KY: Westminster John Knox, 1994), 149–68 for a description of the *jouissance* not merely of orgasm, but of the touch, vulnerability, play and energy of lovemaking.

40. John Calvin, *Commentaries on the Four Last Books of Moses,* vol. 3, trans. Charles William Bingham (Grand Rapids: Eerdmans, 1950), 84.

41. Thatcher, *Liberating Sex,* 39.

Chapter 5: The Lord's Supper and Sex

1. Michael Hurt, "Sex Business Lives on Despite Crackdown," *Korea Herald* (May 27, 2005). S. Daley, "New Rights for Dutch Prostitutes, but no Gain," *New York Times* (August 12, 2001).

2. Jay Albanese, "A Criminal Network Approach to Understanding and Measuring Trafficking in Human Beings," in *Measuring Human Trafficking: Complexities and Pitfalls,* ed. Ernesto U. Savona and Sonia Stefanizzi (New York: Springer, 2007), 55-71.

3. Sheila Jeffreys, *The Industrial Vagina: The Political Economy of the Global Sex Trade* (New York: Routledge, 2009), 162. Statistics from Cathy Zimmerman, *The Health Risks and Consequences of Trafficking in Women and Adolescents: Findings from a European Study* (London: London School of Hygiene and Tropical Medicine, 2003).

4. Janice Raymond, et al., *A Comparative Study of Women Trafficked in the Migration Process* (Amherst, MA: Coalition Against Trafficking in Women, 2002), 112. Available online at http://action.web.ca/home/catw/attach/CATW%20 Comparative%20Study%202002.pdf, accessed November 29, 2012.

5. Unicef, *The State of the World's Children, 2002.* (New York: Unicef, 2002), 52.

6. Jeffreys, *Industrial Vagina,* 66. Statistics from Frederick A. Lane, *Obscene Profits: Entrepreneurs of Pornography in the Cyber Age* (New York: Routledge, 2001), xiv, and Top Ten Reviews, "Internet Pornography Statistics," www.toptenreviews .com/pornography, accessed November 29, 2012.

7. Robert Jensen, *Getting Off: Pornography and the End of Masculinity* (Cambridge, MA: South End Press, 2007), 80–81. Statistics from "State of the U.S. Adult Industry," *Adult Video News,* January 2006.

8. Jensen, *Getting Off,* 89–90. *Blow Bang #4,* DVD, directed by Derek Newblood (Los Angeles: Armageddon Entertainment, 2001).

9. Jeffreys, *Industrial Vagina,* 81.

10. Dave Montgomery, "Industry Trying to Take Its Image Upscale," *Fort Worth Star-Telegram,* October 3, 2005. Diane Sawyer and Bill Weir, "Undercover Stripper: Tyra Banks Spies on Different World," *Good Morning America,* aired March 1, 2006, ABC News Transcripts.

11. David Washburn and Jennifer Davies, "Shifting Fortunes: Long Targeted by Tough Zoning and Conduct Laws, S. D. Strip Club Industry Is Less Lucrative Today," *San Diego Union-Tribune,* October 19, 2004..

12. Kelly Holsopple, *Strip Club Testimony* (Minneapolis: The Freedom and Justice Center for Prostitution Resources, 1998).

13. Sebastian Horsley, quoted in Toni Bentley, "Meet, Pay, Love," review of *Hos, Hookers, Call Girls, and Rent Boys,* ed. David Henry Sterry and R. J. Martin Jr., *New York Times,* August 20, 2009, Sunday Book Review, http://www.nytimes .com/2009/08/23/books/review/Bentley-t.html?pagewanted=all&_r=0.

14. John Milbank and Catherine Pickstock, *Truth in Aquinas* (New York: Routledge and Kegan Paul, 2001), 71.

15. See Mark I. Wallace, "Early Christian Contempt for the Flesh and the Woman Who Loved Too Much in the Gospel of Luke," in *Embrace of Eros*, ed. Kamitsuka (Minneapolis: Fortress, 2010), 38–45, for further reflections on this passage.

16. In Luke, it is unclear whether Judas actually kisses Jesus, though he approaches Jesus to kiss him (22:47).

17. Paul F. Bradshaw, *Eucharistic Origins* (London: SPCK, 2004), 146.

18. Ibid., 74–75.

19. Robert F. Taft, SJ, *Through Their Own Eyes: Liturgy as the Byzantines Saw It* (Berkeley, CA: InterOrthodox Press, 2006), 88.

20. Ambrose, "Sermons on the Sacraments V, Symbols of the Eucharist," in Edward Yarnold, SJ, *The Awe-Inspiring Rites of Initiation: The Origins of the R.C.I.A.*, 2nd ed. (Collegeville, MN: Liturgical Press, 1994), 142.

21. Cyril of Jerusalem, "Sermon 5: The Eucharistic Rite," in ibid., 90–91.

22. Theodore of Mopsuestia, "Baptismal Homily IV," in ibid., 223.

23. Ibid., 222.

24. Ibid., 223.

25. Taft, *Through Their Own Eyes*, 90.

26. "Life of St. Matrona," quoted in ibid., 91.

27. Gerard Loughlin, "Introduction: The End of Sex," in *Queer Theology: Rethinking the Western Body*, ed. Gerard Loughlin (Malden, MA: Blackwell, 2007), 6–7. Robert Goss also reflects on the connections between the Lord's Supper and sex: "The distribution of communion becomes an act of sex as the communicants take Christ into their mouths." *Queering Christ: Beyond Jesus Acted Up* (Cleveland: Pilgrim Press, 2002), 44. Notice, however, in Goss's account that the Eucharist becomes reducible to an act of sex, whereas Loughlin points to the analogy between sex and the Eucharist. Loughlin's account is preferable because it is less totalizing—the Eucharist is analogous to sex, but cannot be reduced to it—and because it allows sex to be sex and the Eucharist to be the Eucharist. It maintains difference, while allowing for connection in much the same way that Thomas Aquinas's theory of analogy does. Goss reads the liturgy through sex; Loughlin reads sex through the liturgy.

28. Gerard Loughlin, *Alien Sex: The Body and Desire in Cinema and Theology* (Malden, MA: Blackwell, 2004), 10.

29. Hadewijch, *The Complete Works*, trans. Columba Hart (New York: Paulist, 1980), 280-81.

30. Gregory of Nyssa, "On Virginity," in *Nicene and Post-Nicene Fathers*, second series, vol. 5, ed. Philip Schaff and Henry Wace (Peabody, MA: Hendrickson, 2004), 366–67.

31. Augustine, "The Good of Marriage," in Eugene F. Rogers Jr. *Theology and Sexuality: Classic and Contemporary Readings* (Malden, MA: Blackwell, 2002), 82.

32. This section draws on previous research and writing. For a more detailed treatment of themes of scarcity, abundance, and gift, see David H. Jensen, *Responsive Labor: A Theology of Work* (Louisville, KY: Westminster John Knox, 2006, 75–96, 104–7).

33. See Jensen, *Responsive Labor*, 11–14, for further reflections on habits of consumption and habits of labor in the United States.

34. Charla Muller with Betsy Thorpe, *365 Nights: A Memoir of Intimacy* (New York: Berkeley, 2008). Douglas Brown, *Just Do It: How One Couple Turned Off the TV and Turned On Their Sex Lives for 101 Days (No Excuses!)* (New York: Three Rivers, 2008).

35. Teresa of Avila, *The Interior Castle,* trans. Kieran Kavanaugh and Otilio Rodriguez (Mahwah, NJ: Paulist, 1979), 131.

36. Thomas Briedenthal, "Sanctifying Nearness," in *Theology and Sexuality*, ed. Rogers, 348. For the parable of the Talents, see Matt. 25:14–30.

37. The phrase, "nuisances and nobodies" is from John Dominic Crossan, *Jesus: A Revolutionary Biography* (San Francisco: HarperCollins, 1994).

38. *Book of Common Worship* (Louisville, KY: Westminster/John Knox, 1993), 77.

39. Rodney Clapp, *Families at the Crossroads: Beyond Traditional and Modern Options* (Downers Grove, IL: InterVarsity, 1993), 138. Emphasis in original.

40. David M. McCarthy, "Procreation and the Development of Peoples," *Communio* 26 (Winter 1999): 710.

41. Elizabeth Stuart commenting on Kathy Rudy in Elizabeth Stuart, *Gay and Lesbian Theologies: Repetition with Critical Difference* (Burlington, VT: Ashgate, 2003), 95.

42. Kathy Rudy, in Lisa Isherwood and Elizabeth Stuart, *Introducing Body Theology* (Cleveland: Pilgrim Press, 2000), 112.

43. Patricia Beattie Jung, "Sexual Pleasure: A Roman Catholic Perspective on Women's Delight," *Theology and Sexuality* 12 (March 2000): 33.

44. Wendell Berry, *Sex, Economy, Freedom & Community* (New York: Pantheon Books, 1993), 133.

45. Elizabeth Stuart, "Sexuality: The View from the Font (the Body and the Ecclesial Self)," *Theology and Sexuality* 11 (1999): 18.

46. Berry, *Sex, Economy*, 137.

47. Robert W. Jenson, *Song of Songs*, Interpretation: A Bible Commentary for Teaching and Preaching (Louisville, KY: Westminster John Knox, 2005), 85.

Chapter 6: Vocation and Sex

1. See Dale B. Martin, *Sex and the Single Savior: Gender and Sexuality in Biblical Interpretation* (Louisville, KY: Westminster John Knox, 2006), 117; see also David G. Hunter, "Rereading the Jovinianist Controversy: Asceticism and Clerical Authority in Late Ancient Christianity," *Journal of Medieval and Early Modern Studies* 33 (2003): 453.

2. Toni Morrison, quoted in Joy R. Bostic, "Flesh That Dances": A Theology of Sexuality and the Spirit in Toni Morrison's *Beloved*," in *Embrace of Eros*, ed. Margaret Kamitsuka (Minneapolis: Fortress, 2000), 277.

3. Lee Butler, "The Spirit Is Willing and the Flesh Is Too: Living Whole and Holy Lives through Integrating Spirituality and Sexuality," in *Loving the Body: Black Religious Studies and the Erotic*, ed. Anthony B. Pinn and Dwight N. Hopkins (New York: Palgrave Macmillan, 2004), 117.

4. Simone Weil describes prayer as attentiveness. Prayer "is the orientation of all the attention of which the soul is capable toward God." *Waiting for God* (San Francisco: HarperCollins, 1973), 105.

5. Mark Jordan, *Blessing Same-Sex Unions: The Perils of Queer Romance and the Confusions of Christian Marriage* (Chicago: The University of Chicago Press, 2005), 18.

6. Dennis O'Brien, "Sex before God: The Body of Prayer," *Philosophy and Theology* 12, no. 1 (2000): 210–11.

7. Tertullian, "To His Wife," in *Marriage in the Early Church*, ed. David G. Hunter (Minneapolis: Fortress, 1992), 35.

8. He writes, "For by enjoining continence and restricting intercourse, the seedbed of the human race, he abolished that Increase and multiply. . . . In these last days, [God] has suppressed the seedbed and revoked his previous indulgence,"

suggesting that the command at creation to be fruitful and multiply is gradually being transformed in the new age heralded in Christ. Ibid., 40.

9. John Chrysostom, "Homily 20 on Ephesians," in ibid., 77.
10. Hunter, introduction, in ibid., 20.
11. "Two Nuptial Blessings," in ibid., 152.
12. *Verona Sacramentary*, in ibid., 151.
13. John Calvin, *Institutes of the Christian Religion*, ed. John T. McNeill, trans. Ford Lewis Battles, LCC (Philadelphia: Westminster Press, 1960), 405.
14. *The Constitution of the Presbyterian Church (U.S.A.)*, Part I, *Book of Confessions* (Louisville, KY: Office of the General Assembly, Presbyterian Church (U.S.A.), 1996), 152–53.
15. John Calvin, *Commentaries on the First Book of Moses Called Genesis* trans. John King (Grand Rapids: Eerdmans, 1948), 128.
16. Ibid., 130.
17. Ibid., 134.
18. *Book of Common Worship* (Louisville, KY: Westminster/John Knox, 1993), 842.
19. Ibid., 848.
20. Paul V. Marshall, "With My Body I Thee Worship," www.diobeth.org/Bishop/DLColumns/dlcolumn10.html, accessed February 1, 2010.
21. Lauren F. Winner, *Real Sex: The Naked Truth about Chastity* (Grand Rapids: Brazos, 2005), 119.
22. Robert W. Jenson, *Song of Songs*, Interpretation: A Bible Commentary for Teaching and Preaching (Louisville, KY: John Knox, 2005), 37.
23. John Calvin, *Commentary on the Epistles of Paul the Apostle to the Corinthians*, vol. 1, trans. John Pringle (Grand Rapids: Eerdmans, 1948), 229. Emphasis in original.
24. Sarah Coakley, "Pleasure Principles: Toward a Contemporary Theology of Desire," *Harvard Divinity Bulletin* (2005): 27.
25. Paul Lakeland, "Ecclesiology, Desire, and the Erotic," in *Embrace of Eros*, ed. Kamitsuka, 249.
26. Barth, *Church Dogmatics*, III/4, ed. G. W. Bromiley and T. F. Torrance, trans. G. W. Thomson (Edinburgh: T. & T. Clark, 1960), 225.
27. Janie Gustafson, "Celibate Passion," in *Sexuality and the Sacred: Sources for Theological Reflection*, ed. James B. Nelson and Sandra P. Longfellow (Louisville, KY: Westminster John Knox, 1994), 280.
28. Gregory of Nyssa, "On Virginity," in *Nicene and Post-Nicene Fathers,* second series, vol. 5, ed. Philip Schaff and Henry Wace (Peabody, MA: Hendrickson, 2004), 360.
29. See Coakley, "Pleasure Principles," 32.
30. See Winner, *Real Sex*, 145. See also Henri J. M. Nouwen, *Clowning in Rome: Reflections on Solitude, Celibacy, Prayer, and Contemplation* (Garden City, NY: Image Books, 1979), 45.
31. Elizabeth Stuart, "Sacramental Flesh," in Loughlin, ed., *Queer Theology,* 69.
32. Lisa Sowle Cahill, *Sex, Gender, and Christian Ethics* (New York: Cambridge University Press, 1996), 182.
33. Gustafson, "Celibate Passion," 278.
34. Sallie McFague, *Models of God: Theology for an Ecological, Nuclear Age* (Philadelphia: Fortress, 1987), 164.
35. Eugene Rogers, "Can God Use Sex for Our Sanctification," in *Frequently Asked Questions about Sexuality, the Bible, and the Church,* ed. Ted A. Smith (San Francisco: The Covenant Network of Presbyterians, 2006), 68.
36. Eugene Rogers, *Sexuality and the Christian Body: Their Way into the Triune God* (Malden, MA: Blackwell, 1999), 79.

37. Stuart, "Sacramental Flesh," 73.
38. See Allan Hugh Cole Jr., "Solitude and God: A Lonely Boy's Allies," in Robert C. Dykstra, Allan Hugh Cole Jr., and Donald Capps, *Losers, Loners and Rebels: The Spiritual Struggles of Boys* (Louisville, KY: Westminster John Knox, 2007), 99–127, for further reflections on the spiritual value of solitude.
39. The phrase is from Richard Lischer, *Open Secrets: A Memoir of Faith and Discovery* (New York: Random House, 2001), 67,
40. Stuart, "Sacramental Flesh," 70.
41. Jason King and Donna Freitas, "Sex, Time, and Meaning: A Theology of Dating," *Horizons*, vol. 30, no. 1 (2003): 38.

Chapter 7: Ethics and Sex

1. I have been helped in this interpretation of Aquinas by Timothy M. Renick, *Aquinas for Armchair Theologians* (Louisville, KY: Westminster John Knox, 2002), 77–93.
2. Thomas Aquinas, *Summa Theologica* II-II, Q. 153, A. 2. (New York: Benzinger Brothers, 1948).
3. One can see how this procreative norm has affected the abortion debate. Some have argued that the "right to life" should brook no exceptions, even in the case of rape. Aquinas's framework weighs heavily on those who argue in this manner, whether they are aware of this influence or not.
4. Martin Luther, "On Marriage Matters," in *Luther's Works*, vol. 46, ed. Robert C. Schultz (Philadelphia: Fortress, 1967), 291.
5. Ibid., 318.
6. Adrian Thatcher, *Living Together and Christian Ethics* (Cambridge, MA: Cambridge University Press, 2002), 228. The embedded quote is from André Guindon, "Case for a 'Consummated Bond before a 'Ratified' Marriage," *Église et Théologie* 8 (1977): 157.
7. Stanley Grenz, *Sexual Ethics: An Evangelical Perspective* (Louisville, KY: Westminster John Knox, 1999), 81.
8. Miguel De La Torre, *A Lily among the Thorns: Imagining a New Christian Sexuality* (San Francisco: Jossey-Bass, 2007), 125.
9. Anthony Kosnik, et al., *Human Sexuality* (New York: Paulist, 1977), 92–95.
10. Cahill, *Sex, Gender, and Christian Ethics*, 115.
11. Margaret Farley, *Just Love: A Framework for Christian Sexual Ethics* (New York: Continuum, 2006), 207.
12. Ibid., 231.
13. Guy Baldwin, *Ties That Bind* (Los Angeles: Daedalus, 1993), 187.
14. Karl Barth describes the being of God as the One who Loves in Freedom. See *Church Dogmatics* II/1, 257.
15. Laurie A. Jungling, "Creation as God's Call into Erotic Embodied Relationalilty," in *The Embrace of Eros*, ed. Kamitsuka (Minneapolis: Fortress, 2010), 220.
16. Ibid., 229.
17. Ibid., 230.
18. Cahill, *Sex, Gender, and Christian Ethics*, 10–11.
19. Stephanie Paulsell, *Honoring the Body: Meditations on a Christian Practice* (San Francisco: Jossey-Bass, 2002), 156.
20. Others have suggested that the churches need to encourage persons to marry at a younger age. See Mark Regnerus, "The Case for Early Marriage," *Christianity Today* (August 2009). www.christianitytoday.com/ct/2009/august/16.22.html, accessed October 25, 2012. These suggestions I find somewhat suspect since they

overlook significant educational and professional gains, especially for women, when marriage is delayed.

21. Barbara J. Blodgett, *Constructing the Erotic: Sexual Ethics and Adolescent Girls* (Cleveland: Pilgrim Press, 2002), 185.

22. Ibid., 184–85.

23. Ibid., 162.

24. Paulsell, *Honoring the Body*, 157.

25. Blodgett, *Constructing the Erotic*, 171.

26. Thatcher, *Living Together*, 217. Emphasis in original.

27. Ibid., 265.

28. See Dan Savage, "Why Monogamy Is Ridiculous," http://www.youtube.com/watch?v=w8SOQEitsJI, accessed November 29, 2012.

29. Marcella Althaus-Reid, *Indecent Theology: Theological Perversions in Sex, Gender and Politics* (New York: Routledge, 2000), 76.

30. Marcella Althaus-Reid, *The Queer God* (New York: Routledge, 2003), 58.

31. "The Holy Spirit is also understood, because He is the Spirit of the Father and Son, as the substantial and consubstantial love of both." See Augustine, "Lectures or Tractates on the Gospel according to St. John," in Philip Schaff, ed., *Nicene and Post-Nicene Fathers*, vol. 7 (Peabody, MA: Hendrickson, 2004), 396.

Index

abstinence, 20–21, 28, 48, 52
abundance, 8, 35, 87–88, 123
adultery, 5, 14, 120
agape, 7, 23, 26, 34, 104,
    144n43
Althaus-Reid, Marcella,
    133–34, 146n8
Ambrose, 82–83
androgyny, 63–65
atonement, 25
Augustine, 24, 58, 63–64,
    86, 133–34, 146n1,
    153n31

Baker-Fletcher, Karen, 24
baptism, xi, 60, 65–67, 82,
    117
Barth, Karl, 23–24, 26, 110
beauty, 30, 135
Berry, Wendell, 94–95
Bible, xi, 1–16
    books of
        Genesis, 2, 5–6, 8–9,
            28, 43, 53, 56–57,
            69, 74, 80, 132
        Exodus, 5–6, 9, 51
        Leviticus, 3, 10, 90
        Numbers, 9
        Deuteronomy, 9, 70
        Joshua, 74
        Psalms, 37, 79
        Proverbs, 81

Song of Songs, 12, 15,
    59, 79–80, 131, 136
Isaiah, 9–10, 63
Ezekiel, 79
Hosea, 6
Matthew, 2, 10, 33, 39,
    50–51, 73, 127
Mark, 2, 10, 49–50, 67,
    146n20
Luke, 11, 51, 61, 73,
    80–81, 149n16
John, 10, 49, 51,
    73–74, 88, 114
Romans, 4–5, 23, 46,
    57, 65, 91, 102
1 Corinthians, 3, 6, 13,
    47, 67, 86, 100–101,
    103
Galatians, 60, 65,
    141n3
Ephesians, 6
Philippians, 136
Colossians, 6
1 Thessalonians, 80,
    100
1 Timothy, 6, 63
2 Timothy, 5
1 Peter, 5
1 John, 24
Revelation, 6, 11,
    42–43, 59, 66, 74,
    79, 142n17

as guidebook for sexual
    behavior, 2–4, 14
and hermeneutic of suspi-
    cion, 5–7
as narrative of desire, 7–16
Blodgett, Barbara J., 58,
    129–30
body, 12, 16, 27, 35–37,
    43–47, 96, 101–2,
    107–11, 113, 145n10
Boer, Roland, 49
Bonaventure, 33
Bradshaw, Paul F., 82
Briedanthal, Thomas, 88
Brock, Rita Nakashima,
    25–26
Butler, Judith, 62
Butler, Lee, 102

Cahill, Lisa Sowle, 19, 113,
    123, 126
Calvin, John, 65, 70, 104,
    106, 108
Carmody, Denise, 21
Catholic theology, 56, 123,
    133
celibacy, xi, 13, 35–36, 56,
    86, 108, 111–15
children, 90–91, 105, 134–35
church, 53–54, 94–95, 116–
    17, 135, 139
Chrysostom, John, 104

Clapp, Rodney, 91
clitoris, 70
Coakley, Sarah, 34, 108
Communion, 10–11, 15,
    28–29, 34, 40–45,
    58–59, 61, 65–67, 71,
    88, 103, 110–11, 127
community, 132–35
consent, 124–26
consumerism, 16, 36, 70–71,
    100, 119, 123, 126,
    135–36
Countryman, L. William, 7
covenant, xi, 8–9, 14–15, 34,
    52–54, 60, 109–10,
    128–32, 134
Cranach, Lucas, 49
Cranmer, Thomas, 107
creation, 8, 21, 69
Crossan, John Dominic,
    150n37
crucifixion, 41–42
Cyril of Jerusalem, 83

dating, 117–18
De la Torre, Miguel A., 57,
    122–23
desire, ix–xi, 7–16, 71, 100,
    112–14, 120, 143n28,
    144nn36, 38
    and Christ, 48–54, 83–85
    and God, 17–37, 59,
    112–13, 139
difference, 39, 56–57, 61,
    66–67
discernment, 115–18
discipleship, 24, 28, 49, 113
discipline, 32

eros, 7, 22–28, 34, 36–37,
    104, 144n43
eschatology, xi, 31, 33, 35,
    37, 45–46, 48, 67–72,
    150–51n8
ethics, xi, 1–3, 7, 27–28, 46,
    119–37
extramarital affairs, 131, 133

faithfulness, 125
Farley, Margaret, 62, 64–65,
    123
Farley, Wendy, 24

freedom, 7, 37, 124–25
Freitas, Donna, 117
friendship, 18, 112, 114

Gagnon, Robert A. J., 3–4,
    141n3
gender complementarity, 4,
    52, 56, 60–61, 141n3
gender identity, 58–65
gifts, 86–89
Gilson, Anne Bathurst, 7
God
    as Creator, 8–9, 69, 125
    and desire, 13, 17–37, 110
    as goodness, 29–30
    and love, 136–37
    and promises, 118, 128–
    29, 132
Goss, Robert, 149n27
Gregory of Nyssa, 63–64,
    86, 112
Grenz, Stanley, 2, 28, 67–68,
    122
Gudorf, Christine, 26–28, 52
Gustafson, Janie, 112

Hadewijch, 85
Hall, Amy Laura, 147n31
Harrison, Verna, 63
heterosexuality, 7, 56–57, 62,
    113, 133, 146n8
Holsopple, Kelly, 77
Holy Spirit, 37, 47, 105,
    111–12, 115, 133–34,
    153n31
homosexuality, 3–4, 7, 12,
    14, 21–22, 53–54,
    56–58, 62, 95
Horsley, Sebastian, 78
hospitality, 53–54, 81, 86,
    89–92, 114–15, 117,
    135

idolatry, 4, 32, 37, 66, 113
incarnation, ix, xi, 10, 15–16,
    21, 27
Ind, Jo, 64
intimacy, 15, 31, 49–50,
    80–81, 107, 127, 132
Irenaeus, 48
Isherwood, Lisa, 70
Israelites, 28

Jantzen, Grace, 8
Jeffreys, Sheila, 77
Jenson, Robert W., 96, 107
Jesus Christ, 1–2, 10–11,
    15, 39–54, 64, 73–74,
    80–81, 89–90, 111,
    116, 127, 137, 145n17
Johnson, William Stacy, 60,
    65, 141n3
Jordan, Mark, 5, 102, 141n2,
    141n4
Jovinian, 13, 100
joy, 135–37
Jung, Patricia, 93
Jungling, Laurie, 125
Justin Martyr, 81–82

Kamitsuka, Margaret, 68
King, John, 117
kiss of peace, 81–85
kissing, 80–85, 149n16

Lakeland, Paul, 108
Lindbeck, George, 14
Long, Ronald, 21–22
Lord's Supper, xi, 3, 10–11,
    21–22, 27, 73–97, 127,
    149n27
Loughlin, Gerard, 85,
    149n27
love, 9–10, 13, 23–24, 31,
    91–92, 95, 125, 129,
    133–34, 142n14,
    143n34, 144nn36, 38
Luther, Martin, 121

Madges, William, 23
marriage, ix, 2–3, 6, 12–14,
    20–21, 32, 36, 43–44,
    52, 60, 66–68, 94–95,
    103–11, 120–21, 131,
    134, 152–53n20
    gay marriage, 12, 53–54,
    102, 109–11, 132
    as sacrament, 104
Marshall, Paul V., 107
Martin, Dale, 142n17
masturbation, 120–21,
    141n4, 147n38
McCarthy, David Matzko,
    91, 143n28
McFague, Sallie, 114

Mechthild of Magdeburg, 59
Men's Health magazine, 20, 22
Milbank, John, 80
monogamy, 133–34
Moore, Sebastian, 34–35
Morrison, Toni, 101
mutuality, 126–28
mysticism, 23–24, 28–34

natural law, 120–21
nearness, 45–46
Nelson, James B., 145n10
Nygren, Anders, 23–24

O'Brien, Dennis, 103
ordination, ix, 56, 66
orgasm, 34, 69–71, 101–2, 106, 127
Origen, 44–45

patriarchy, 5–6, 11–12, 14, 25–26, 51
Paulsell, Stephanie, 127
Pickstock, Catherine, 80
play, 69–72, 147n38
pleasure, 27–28, 53, 70–72, 89, 102, 120, 126–27, 135–36
porneia, 3, 14, 141n2
pornography, x, 19–20, 26, 41, 43, 70–71, 76–77, 144–45n6
possession, 8, 18, 35, 50–52, 87, 108, 127–28
prayer, 18, 101–3, 116
procreation, 50, 53, 56, 63, 90–92, 105, 120, 132–33, 150–51n8, 152n3
promiscuity, 18–22, 102, 133
prostitution, 75–76
Protestant theology, 23, 56, 78–79, 104–6, 109, 125
Pseudo-Dionysius, 29–30, 33

queer theory, 62

Rahner, Karl, 44, 53
rape, 124–25

Ratzinger, Joseph (Pope Benedict XVI), 56, 144n43
Regnerus, Mark, 152–53n20
regulation of sex, 94
reign of God, 7
relationships, 25–26, 30, 35, 125, 130
release, 51–52
resurrection, xi, 10–11, 39–54, 144n1, 146n20
Rogers, Eugene, 35–37, 50, 114
Rudy, Kathy, 92

Sabbath, 69
sacraments, 27
Savage, Dan, 133
scarcity, 86–87
Schneider, Laurel, 58
sensuality, 31, 73–74
sex
    and adolescents, 58, 123, 129
    and attentiveness, 16, 36, 95–96, 102, 131, 136, 147n38
    economic distortions of, 74–78, 93, 107
    and eschatology, 55–72
    and experience of God, 27–28
    and God, 34–37
    and Jesus Christ, 39–54, 80–81
    and Lord's Supper, 73–97
    and marriage, 107–9, 121–22, 131, 146n1
    mysticism and, 29–34
    as performance, 127–28
    popular attitudes toward, 18–22, 127–28, 132–33, 135, 145n15
    and prayer, 101–3
    premarital, 20–21, 115–18, 120, 122–23, 130–31
    and privacy, 93–97, 134
    and public good, 93–97, 134–35

and singleness, 115–18
and vocation, 99–118
and worship, 107–9
Sex and the City, 20, 51
sexual identity, xi, 55–65
sexual intercourse, 68, 105, 108, 121–22, 126–27
sexual union, 33, 71, 84, 88, 104–6
sin, 9, 26, 66
singleness, xi, 115–18
slavery, 6
social location, x
sociobiology, 19, 22
Spong, John Shelby, 57
St. Symeon, 43–44
strip clubs, 77–78
Stuart, Elizabeth, 66–67, 70, 94–95, 113, 116

Taft, Robert F., 82, 84
taste, 11–13, 78–86, 127
Teresa of Avila, 31–33, 88, 143n34, 144nn36, 38
Tertullian, 103–4, 150–51n8
Thatcher, Adrian, 6, 69, 71, 121–22, 130–31
Theodore of Mopsuestia, 83
Thomas Aquinas, 39, 113, 120–21, 132–33, 144n1
touch, 10, 12–13, 27–28, 37, 45, 51–52
Trinity, xi, 34–36, 114, 133–34
trust, 129–30

van Dyck, Leanne, 11
vice lists, 3, 14, 47, 141n2
violence, 7, 11, 25–26, 40–43
    sexual, x, 11, 40–41, 46, 75–78, 144–45n6
vocation, xi

Ward, Graham, 51
Weil, Simone, 150n4
Westminster Confession, 44, 104–5
Williams, Rowan, 36
Winner, Lauren F., 107

CPSIA information can be obtained at www.ICGtesting.com
Printed in the USA
LVOW061744050413

327860LV00006B/688/P